Psychoanalysis and the Time of Life

D0220118

Psychoanalysis and the Time of Life examines the relationship between therapy and the time of life, presenting an original and thought-provoking rereading of psychoanalysis in relation to questions of lived time.

Jan Campbell investigates the early work of Freud, Janet, Breuer and Ferenczi, linking their ideas to the philosophy of Bergson. The link between psychoanalysis and the question of time connects these early debates with current issues that are central to our global society. Questions considered include:

- Is the unconscious based on representation or affect?
- Is the Oedipal Complex hysterical?
- How is therapy related to the time of our life?
- What is the role of hypnosis, in relation to psychoanalytic theory and transference?
- Freud conceptualised the unconscious as timeless space, but what would it mean to think of the unconscious as the very essence of psychic bodily time?

This book draws on the fields of traditional psychoanalysis, philosophy, neuroscience and trauma studies, providing a valuable new perspective on familiar concepts such as identity and consciousness. It will be of interest to students across the humanities and social sciences, and practising psychoanalysts and psychoanalytic psychotherapists.

Jan Campbell is a Senior Lecturer in the Department of English at Birmingham University and a Psychoanalytic Psychotherapist in private practice. She has published widely on psychoanalysis, film studies and cultural theory.

Psychoanalysis and the Time of Life

Durations of the unconscious self

Jan Campbell

Routledge
Taylor & Francis Group

LONDON AND NEW YORK

First published 2006 by Routledge
27 Church Road, Hove, East Sussex BN3 2FA

Simultaneously published in the USA and Canada
by Routledge
270 Madison Avenue, New York, NY 10016

Routledge is an imprint of the Taylor & Francis Group, an informa business

Typeset in Times by Garfield Morgan, Mumbles, Swansea
Printed and bound in Great Britain by TJ International Ltd, Padstow,
Cornwall
Paperback cover design by Sandra Heath

This publication has been produced with paper manufactured to strict
environmental standards and with pulp derived from sustainable forests.

British Library Cataloguing in Publication Data
A catalogue record for this book is available from the British Library

Library of Congress Cataloging-in-Publication Data

Campbell, Jan, 1958–
    Psychoanalysis and the time of life : durations of the unconscious self / Jan
Campbell.– 1st ed.
        p. cm.
    Includes bibliographical references and index.
    ISBN 1-58391-177-4 (hbk : alk. paper) – ISBN 1-58391-178-2 (pbk : alk.
paper) 1. Psychoanalysis. 2. Psychoanalysis–Miscellanea. 3. Time–
Psychological aspects. 4. Time perception. I. Title.
    RC506.C285 2006
    616.89'17–dc22

                                                                    2005036567

ISBN13 978–1–58391–177–8 hbk
ISBN13 978–1–58391–178–5 pbk

ISBN10 1–58391–177–4 hbk
ISBN10 1–58391–178–2 pbk

For Jan Harbord

Contents

Foreword

Psychoanalysis is all about the individual's experience of time, of the time of his or her life. And yet Freud makes reference to the then famous French philosopher Henri Bergson, his vital contemporary, only in *Jokes and their Relation to the Unconscious*, and there, unsurprisingly, only to Bergson's work on humour *Le Rire*. Freud gave us a new language for the ways in which people involve each other and avert acknowledgement of their involvements. Freud's seeming lack of interest in Bergson's work, so germane to psychoanalysis, is perhaps of a piece with his phobic relationship to philosophers, his wariness of encroaching vocabularies (the indexers of the *Standard Edition* have gone along with Freud here; Bergson's name is not in the index). By referring to Bergson's work in so localised a context, and in relatively early work, Freud more or less forecloses Bergson's influence and distracts us from his effect on psychoanalysis; it is only in reading Proust that we see that Bergson and Freud so obviously overlap. Bergson is used by Freud, and then apparently dropped. There is no sense of Bergson being akin to Schopenhauer or Nietzsche for Freud; that is to say, being someone that Freud needs to fight shy of, to push out of the picture.

And yet Bergson, like Schopenhauer and Nietzsche in their quite different ways, was speaking up for something that was at the very heart of Freud's psychoanalysis, and of contemporary life: the powers of enchantment in a supposedly disenchanted modern world. What Freud couldn't help but notice, as the so-called psychoanalytic movement began to take off, was just how hypnotised some people were by psychoanalysis itself, and it was hypnosis itself that Freud had most famously needed to relinquish in his inventions of psychoanalysis. As Freud had begun to realise the power of trance states – the ubiquity of trance states in psychic life – he saw them as perhaps part of the problem rather than part of the solution (hypnosis, from this point of view, exchanges one trance for another, belief in the hypnotist replacing belief in the symptom). Psychoanalysis, as an analytic technique, entered the arena of competing turn-of-the-century therapies as a cure for the spell-bound, and as a description of how and why spells are binding, modern people being more spell-bound than contract-bound. Once

Freud had seen psychic life as a series of trance states, he began to wonder whether it was possible, what it might mean, for people to wake up (or out). Psychoanalysis became his enquiry into what, if any, alternatives there were to the hypnotic. It is not difficult to see Freud's virulent antipathy to religion, mysticism and the paranormal, and his insistent over-commitment to science as an anxious scepticism about the unentranced life. The trance of Reason was not what the so-called Enlightenment had in mind. Freud did not want psychoanalysis to be another superstition. The notion of transference was supposed to add something decisive to the conversation about hypnosis. This, in a sense, is where Jan Campbell's fascinating book starts. She wants us to see with hypnosis; she wants us to stop simply trying to see through it. She wants us to see what hypnosis and Bergson's writing have to say, and to add to the impoverished mêlée that is contemporary psychoanalysis.

It is abundantly clear in this book that hypnosis, and something of Bergson's writing, have continued to haunt psychoanalysis. It is part of the real interest of Campbell's work that she begins to link these things up without doing that; she is mindful of her debts and derivations in a way that lets her often understated originality shine through. There is here a usefully new account of how psychoanalysis might be, as both a theory and a practice, were it to take into account what has effectively become a lost legacy. What would psychoanalysis be were it to privilege experience over insight, aliveness over accountability, the dissociated over the repressed? These are Campbell's questions in this book. They are questions that threaten to refresh contemporary psychoanalysis.

Adam Phillips

Acknowledgements

I would like to thank the Arts and Humanities Research Council for their support in funding the research leave which enabled me to finish this project.

Special thanks and love go to my daughter Esmé for showing me the differences at stake in living the time of your life.

I also wish to especially thank Mike van Duuren for his friendship and love.

Thanks also go to my friends Pam Oliver, Erica Carter, Prue Green, Anita Rupprecht, Elena Gualtieri, Chris Blake, Karen Phillips, Heather Perera, Tricia Hynes, Fiona Mason, Steve Pile, Sarah Kember.

To Adam Phillips – for teaching me about the creative time at stake in being a therapist.

To Stella Maile and Jenella Ritchie for exploring the mysteries of hypnosis training.

To Alan and Penny Blight for sharing stories about my father.

Acknowledgements to colleagues present and past especially Stuart Hanson, Ann Gray, Helen Wood, Mark Erickson, Danielle Fuller, Marion Thain and Debbie Parsons.

To James Thompson for helping me to understand trauma.

I also want to acknowledge and thank the 7/7 Centre in London, not just for the support it offered me, but for the all the help and invaluable support I know it has provided for the many people affected by the bombings last summer.

Creative time is now, perhaps, rather a nostalgic ideal for the academic life, and it is perhaps all the more important when we come across the people with whom we can make that kind of time and space happen. So I wish finally to thank Jan Harbord for her intellectual companionship, her role as reader and editor, her friendship and humour, and for all our conversations over the years on psychoanalysis and the time of life. I dedicate this book to her.

Introduction

This book is about psychoanalysis and how we live time. Therapy is all about how we live time – how we live the time of our life and our bodies. The unconscious has always had a dual function in the history of psychoanalysis. It has been seen as both science and poetry, as a store-house of representation and as a body of affect. Enlightenment ideology positions the unconscious as a repository of knowledge and recollected meaning – desires which have once been conscious and are now repressed. But psychoanalysis has since Freud held onto the unconscious as another kind of memory, a memory that cannot be stored, or recollected, because it has never been known – this unconscious as an affectual psychic body unravels the master plot of Oedipus, revealing its defensive self-mastery.

This book explores several key questions, in relation to this dual narrative of psychoanalysis. If the Oedipal plot, as a master discourse of self-knowledge, is hysterical, a defence against a more lived time of the body, then what does this mean for the theory and practice of psychoanalysis? Indeed, what does this mean for a theory of the unconscious? Freud conceptualised the unconscious as a negative and timeless entity, but what if the unconscious can be seen as the very essence of creative time, a lived duration of the body?

We think of the hysteric, whether that is Freud's Dora or Shakespeare's Hamlet, as someone who is essentially unable to resolve their unconscious Oedipal conflicts. In this story, Dora's identification with the father is also her difficulty in transforming that form of being into active desire, whereas Hamlet's guilty secret is his sexual desire for his mother and murderous hate for his stepfather. Resolution of the Oedipal Complex in the form of Dora's desire for the father or Hamlet's paternal identification is the route out for the hysteric, into a more healthy psychic world of symbolic functioning and object relating. But what if the Oedipal Complex is a structure governed by castration anxiety, one which divides identification and desire, imaginary and symbolic, and is fundamentally hysterical?

For Winnicott, Hamlet's hysteria, his dilemma of 'to be or not to be', resides in a dissociation between being and doing, between identification

and desire. This of course makes us rethink the Oedipal Complex differently, not only as being governed by dissociation rather than repressed
desire, but also as having, as its central point or origin story, not one
difference, but many. If incest and its prohibition, or the question of
castration and sexual difference, are not the founding moments of the story
we call psychoanalysis, what can we use instead? I suggest that we follow
Winnicott in positing the relation between dreams and reality, or what
he called being and doing, as a simple but key way of thinking of the
unconscious and the production of culture and cultural beings.

For Winnicott, excessive doing is a 'masculine' false self and what he
calls the true self is an essential form of being or 'feminine' element, bound
up with identification with the good breast. When these male and female
elements become split off and dissociated, as Winnicott tells us they do for
Hamlet, then we descend into relations of sadomasochism. Quoting
Hamlet's famous soliloquy, Winnicott ponders on the mysterious question
that Hamlet can't work out, because he can't formulate an alternative
to being:

> 'To be . . . or . . .' and then he would pause, because in fact the
> character Hamlet does not know the alternative. At last he would come
> in with the rather banal alternative: '. . . or not to be'; and then he
> would be well away on a journey that can lead nowhere. 'whether 'tis
> nobler in the mind to suffer / The slings and arrows of outrageous
> fortune, / Or to take arms against a sea of troubles, / And by opposing
> end them?' (Act III, Scene I). Here Hamlet has gone over into the
> sadomasochistic alternative, and he has left aside the theme he started
> with.
>
> (Winnicott 1971b: 98)

Winnicott suggests that when Hamlet finds himself unable to formulate an
alternative 'to be', he is stating a dissociation between his female and male
elements, of being and doing. So, Hamlet's unsatisfactory alternative to
being is not being, when in fact the alternative to being, being's essential
double if you like, is active desire or doing. A consequence of Hamlet's poor
answer and his dissociation is that the rest of the play then stages this
splitting between being and doing, into repetitive sadomasochism. In this
tragedy the unwelcome male self threatens to take over Hamlet's personality
in the play – his false self. Meanwhile, his female element of true being is
rejected and projected onto Ophelia, which explains Hamlet's cruelty to her.
So, it would seem that Hamlet's alternative to being is that he cannot access
more than one self, more than one way of being in the world.

Winnicott's terms, the true and false self, are perhaps the most mis-
interpreted terms in the history of psychoanalytic literature. The false self
for Winnicott is a self that lives in the mind, in an intellectual register cut

off from the living body of psychosomatic process. As Hamlet's tale shows, this is an Oedipal or false self cut off from being and the psychic life of the unconscious. The opposite to the one false self is not a single true self, but just the sense of being alive and having multiple selves that are brought to life as imaginary and real worlds that can penetrate and transform each other.

In his essay 'Winnicott's Hamlet' Adam Phillips (2000) describes doing and being as two ways of relating to the object and suggests that we don't have to gender them. He then goes on to ask what, in psychoanalytic terms, would be the equivalent of Hamlet's search for an alternative being. This alternative, Phillips muses, might be something other than the instinct-driven self of Freud's Oedipal theory. He writes:

> What if say the Oedipal crisis – as described by Freud and Jones's Hamlet – killed off the possibility of being, made it impossible; that like the secular Fall it, irredeemably, put being and doing at odds with each other: 'contaminated' them, to use Winnicott's word. Perhaps, Winnicott is suggesting, the tragedy of the Oedipal Complex ineluctably dissociated being from doing.
>
> (Phillips 2000: 90)

If the tragedy of the Oedipal Complex is a fundamental dissociation between 'feminine' being and 'masculine' doing, then isn't the Oedipal Complex also irredeemably hysterical? Furthermore, doesn't this understanding of Hamlet – and Oedipus – make us realise the hysterical nature of gender, of masculinity and femininity? Winnicott talks about the problem with the false outer self which becomes too compliant and does not really exist, a self for example that lives in the mind, but is cut off from the vital forces of the psychic body. When ego and body are not integrated, depersonalisation occurs. This can happen when a person is in passive retreat from reality, the schizophrenic for example, who lives a more dream-like existence. But Winnicott also describes the illness that results when a person lives too much in objective reality and is cut off from their dreaming subjective self. Hysteria occurs when being and doing are dissociated and this is, as Hamlet shows us, the Oedipal arena of the false self, a 'masculine' self of certainty and self-made doing or desire. However, I want to suggest that the true self is not just being, in a passive sense, for that returns us to madness. The true self is, as Winnicott tells us, the alive self who I argue is continually translating being into doing and back again. This is a creative dissociation that moves to produce difference. It is an identification with the breast which links passive and active; a mimesis which repeats to produce creative difference between an immanent body and the world. The false self thus becomes the one self of certainty and doing, whereas the true self becomes multiple selves that continually retranslate our dream worlds in terms of reality. Winnicott calls this 'object usage' where the object is destroyed in fantasy, so it can be remade (along with the self) in reality. Phillips shows us how this re-creation of multiple selves and objects is at work in Winnicott's rereading of traditional psychoanalysis and Hamlet: 'The object-usage method entails destroying something in order to recreate it – as Winnicott does, silently, with Freud and Jones's reading of Hamlet' (Phillips 2000: 91).

Maybe the dead and alive self would be better terms for Winnicott's false and true personalities. Either, compliant existing where dreaming and reality, being and doing are hysterically split. Or, the re-creation of dreams in terms of reality, as each seeds and transforms the other in a continual, creative production of the self. Although we don't have to gender Winnicott's forces of being and doing, it is interesting to see how these dispositions as gender terms translate not just within psychoanalysis, but also within culture. If the compliant hysterical self, like Hamlet, is a dissociation between masculine and feminine, then the alive self would be one in which these dispositions become continually intertwined with each other, creating something different in time.

The conflict is well known between Freud the medical man who wanted to mark out psychoanalysis for empirical science and Freud the artist who tells us that 'because of my restricted material interests' he cannot follow a theoretical career. Indeed, nowadays this argument in psychoanalysis still rages between those who want to claim Freud for science and those who insist his creative genius lies in the art of psychoanalysis as literature or fiction – something we can continually redescribe and recreate.

This book is about how the science and poetry of psychoanalysis are inseparable but it also argues that the unconscious as multiple 'true' selves is – poetry. This is an unconscious as motion and instinctual flows that lie at the heart of our external, rational perceptions – continually remaking who we are in relation to the world. Freud's Enlightenment self, his Oedipal story of self-mastery – or the one that knows – is a false self. Necessary, in all the ways that Winnicott describes, as a caretaker and defender of our more secret instinctual selves, this is the external ego that Freud tells us must represent, repress and manage our needs and wishes in relation to the world. But it is an ego that is in constant danger, if too compliant, or too focused on doing, of becoming split off from the life and poetry of the unconscious id. Science or knowledge that can't recognise the imagination or the suggestive poetry that brings it into being is a dead truth, and so too is a psychoanalysis that can't acknowledge how its empirical 'truths' are founded on the unrepresentable life force that makes up the unconscious psychic body.

The false self of psychoanalysis and science is also the unequivocal religious believer or fundamentalist. Paradoxically, it is the false self that thinks it is the true self with all the certainty that One description prescribes. The false self is a self that splits off life from death. It is Oedipus or the analyst at his or her most knowledgeable and certain. It is also the quintessential hysteric and the war zone he or she inhabits between the imaginary and real. If the false self wins out over the true self, then, as Winnicott tells us, intellectual activity becomes dissociated from psycho-somatic existence. There is a lack of continuity of being as the psyche fails to live in the body, or as our psychic, unconscious durations fail to materialise and create real differences and objects. As a true self we are always multiple and other. Meanwhile, as the split-off, false self we are certain of the One – morality or identity, where we live the life of the cult at the expense of a more lived and ordinary time of life.

Today's global world is full of the dangers of false-self mentality. We have western leaders like George W. Bush and Tony Blair describing and prescribing their self-styled global democracy or neo-liberalism as a uni-versal. Answering them we have the suicide bomber, for whom justice and paradise equate with the literal murder of themselves and other people. Arguably, these are all fundamental narratives, where certainty of ourselves and the world strips being of its ordinary, core possibilities – its creative unknowability.

Conflict between reason and passion, argues Freud, is at the root of our discontented civilisation but there is a difference between a passion and reason that are split off, and in a stand-off with each other, when the war between what is imaginary and real in each of us becomes solidified into two dualistic opposing forces – the life and death drives. And on the other hand, a passion that constantly undoes reason, where death is a part of life, where we murder our mothers in fantasy, precisely because this leads us to imaginatively remake them and love them in reality.

The unconscious is not, as Freud thought in his more Enlightenment moments, a negative lump or substantialism underpinning conscious life. It is not some regressive death drive that leads back to inorganic existence. Fascism and the rise of fundamentalist beliefs in Nazi Germany were arguably a historic instance where life and death drives became set up against each other, where reason and passion, both real and imaginary, went to war with the most horrific results. Murdering of Jews went hand in hand with the murder of cultural life. Perhaps we also need to understand how for Freud, himself a Jew, this conflict came to seem an inescapable part of the human condition.

However, if we see this opposition between life and death as the work of the false self – a self, after all, whose self-mastery is a defence against death that has become split off – then we have to understand the true self as the creative time of an unconscious that is inseparable from our conscious external self. An unconscious that is, in health, constantly interspersed with real perception and activity. One that loves and hates, lives and dies, and moves with a force that constantly remakes the world and the object in relation to multiple differences within the self.

As analysts and therapists we have to be good-enough mothers in the sense that we have to meet and make sense of the fantasies of our clients in all their omnipotent force so that the unconscious durations and flows that make up their true selves can begin to live – the time of life. When we force our own meanings and Oedipal certainties onto our patients, then they become hysterical and compliant, and of course one result of this is that they never grow to live their imagined experience. As I shall discuss, this is one explanation of why Freud failed so badly with Dora.

Rather than splitting the mind and body in accordance with Freud's Enlightenment Oedipal narrative, we can agree with the philosopher Henri Bergson when he says that the body and the mind are found together:

> Between the plane of action – the plane in which our body has con- densed its past into motor habits, – and the plane of pure memory, where our mind retains in all its details the picture of our past life, we believe that we can discover thousands of different planes of conscious- ness, a thousand integral and yet diverse repetitions of the whole of experience through which we have lived.
>
> (Bergson 1912: 322)

This creation of different planes of time – between unconscious and con- scious – are the repetitions of difference that make up our multiple psychic and material selves. We don't have one true self, but we do have many creative memories or durations of self. Bergson understands lived duration as the constant seeding of virtual in relation to actual, and of imagination in terms of the body. Habit memory repeats and what he calls pure memory imagines, and yet the interaction of the two is necessary, not just for the functioning of memory but also for the psychic health of the individual. We only have to think of how hysterics are divided between intellectual activity and psychosomatic existence, how their bodily movements, repetitive and split off, are so disconnected from their mental imagination. How this in turn means that fantasy cannot be metabolised and remains dissociated from actualisation in reality.

Living for Bergson is time and the flow of duration. When this flux is externalised – cut up and represented in relation to linear clock time – it becomes space. Bergson sees the 'Self' as a spatial, external upper crust which is seemingly unified and stable. However, this is a projection onto the external world which allows the person to function, but it is an essentially dead entity that has ceased to move in time. In Winnicottian terms this upper crust would be the false compliant self that is defensive but enables us to interact in the world; whereas, the so-called true 'self' is the fluidity of durations that underpins this less mobile representative personality. Of course both these dispositions or characters are necessary and whether we think in terms of Freud's civilising ego defending against a more primitive id, or Lacan's unified and illusory ego masking the fragmentation of desire, we can see how in all these models the unconscious undoes any sense of a coherent, knowing subject. Bergson's ideas of multiple selves of duration underpinning a more public and reconstructed self is enabling because it allows us to see the importance of the unconscious as positive, deconstructive and creative forces. The ego gets recreated and embodied time and time again through the forces and durations that penetrate it. Like Freud's famous 'Mystic Writing Pad', these two dispositions – the perceptual ego and the durational unconscious selves that feed it – are linked by memory. Translation of creative durations and difference becomes the work of therapy and dynamic conflict is part of the vitality that can open up a way, or passage of being, between the familiar self or known performance and our multiple others or durations.

The imaginative unconscious is made up of immanent psychic durations which move between imaginary and real, so bringing the mind and body into being in relation to each other. One of the important things that Winnicott's thinking adds to Bergson's theory of time and immanence is the importance of the environment. Objects are central in helping to bring the true self or psychic immanence into being. The environmental mother or world helps or hinders durations of the creative unconscious self. The time of life, for us, is all about how our psychic durations meet objects in the world and materialise into connecting, or disconnecting minds and bodies. Now a psychoanalysis that becomes too much of an Enlightenment or false self wants to divide minds and bodies, whether that means reifying either Oedipal meaning or the biological body as the true origin story. Here, Oedipal psychoanalysis and neuroscience have arguably much in common.

The origins of neurophysiology and psychoanalysis lead us back to the late nineteenth century, and the clinical neurologist Jean-Martin Charcot. His famous hospital the Salpêtrière became a focal point to study hysteria, with Freud himself studying there in 1885 and 1886. Charcot understood hysteria as an organic, neurological disease caused by a traumatic wound to the central nervous system. Freud went on to revise this trauma theory, replacing it with his psychoanalytic account of unconscious Oedipal fantasy. Whereas Charcot saw hysteria as a unified organic disease, Freud was always interested in it as a psychological neurosis characterised by repression, conflicted sexuality and fantasy. Hippolyte Bernheim and Pierre Janet were contemporaries of Freud who influenced him and also believed in the psychological rather than the neurological aetiology of hysteria. So, we can see how the conflict between whether hysteria is organically or psychologically located has been a historical one, linked as Foucault has shown to disciplinary powers and the morality of the social order.

Initially, Freud was educated as a neurologist through the theoretical approach of the German school of medicine. Working with Charcot, Freud became increasingly persuaded by the French school, whose emphasis (exemplified by Charcot) relied on detailed clinical observation. At the time neuroscience saw organic disease related to localised lesions in the brain, diagnosed through autopsy. Charcot discovered, however, that unlike conditions such as epilepsy, hysteria revealed no localised lesions in post-mortem autopsy. This led Freud's German teachers to give up on neurosis: no lesion meant no disease, although this was not a problem for Charcot, who prioritised first and foremost the answers gained through the clinical picture, rather than explanations drawn from theories of anatomy and physiology. Through the tutelage of Charcot, Freud turned away from theories of a localised trauma or lesion to the brain and became convinced that hysterical paralysis was due to a disturbance of dynamic relationship between elements in the nervous system. Rather than psychology arising from a specific anatomical or physiological site, it was the result of a complex interplay within a *functional system* where the act of consciousness doubled as a bodily organ. Freud writes:

> We have several times heard from M. Charcot that it is a cortical lesion, but one that is purely dynamic or functional . . . the lesion in hysterical paralysis must be completely independent of the anatomy of the nervous system, since in its paralyses and other manifestations it behaves as though anatomy did not exist or as though it had no knowledge of it.
>
> (Freud 1893a: 168–169)

Freud now saw hysteria as a psychological disturbance, which was correlated with the physiological nervous system:

> The lesion in hysterical paralyses consists in nothing other than the inaccessibility of the (paralysed) organ or function concerned to the associations of the conscious ego; . . . (a) purely functional alteration.
>
> (Freud 1893b: 172)

Mark Solms describes how Freud's abandonment of neurophysiology, and his new focus solely on psychology, was because he understood that localised mental functions were an inadequate explanation. The dynamic mental process at stake could not, at the time, be explained in terms of neurophysiology. Freud's findings at that time were based on his research into the neurological condition of aphasia not hysteria: he was then working as a neurologist. Freud's break, therefore, was not with neurophysiology per se, but with a localisationist tradition. Because the dynamic interplay between consciousness and physiology could not be explained at the time, Freud abandoned neurophysiology for psychology. Still believing in the correlation between psychology and physiology as a complex dynamic system, an analogical relation between the psyche and the bodily organ, Freud rejected the localisationism of classical German neurology.

In 1895 Freud's project was to try and connect psychoanalysis with the neuroscience of the time. His early trauma theories of organic hysteria, following Charcot, were then abandoned in favour of a theory of psychological and Oedipal fantasy. Neuroscientists such as Mark Solms and Karen Kaplan-Solms have argued that there was simply a lack of scientific evidence in Freud's time; their work completes what Freud started and never finished, bringing together psychology, neurobiology and psychoanalysis. If neuroscience is not opposed to psychoanalysis, being on the contrary its constitutive ground, then the older critiques levelled against Freud of biological destiny and a biologically determined psyche have to be rethought. Mark and Karen Solms highlight the analogical relationship in Freud's thinking, between mind and body, and the dialectical process that exists between them (Kaplan-Solms and Solms 2000). Their work is strongly influenced by the research and writing of Antonio Damasio, a leading neuroscientist, who investigates the emotional effects of brain damage (Damasio 1994). Challenging Descartes' division between mind and body, reason and madness, Damasio contends that rationality is actually predicated on our experiences of embodiment and emotion. Consciousness is brought into being through the interrelationship between body and neurological images. When brain damage occurs, consciousness is impaired, but so is our ability to be reflective and knowing about our feelings. Having a feeling is not the same as knowing a feeling and this developmental pathway from expressing emotion, to experiencing a feeling and then to reflexivity of that feeling is a journey from emotion to feeling and then to consciousness. These three phenomena are all dependent on neural mapping and processes, which become increasingly sophisticated. However, emotion, feeling and consciousness are also body related; they all 'depend for their execution on representation of the organism. Their shared essence is the body' (Damasio 2000).

Current advances in neuroscience and psychoanalysis, influenced by thinkers such as Damasio and Solms, have argued for a dialectical relationship between brain and the regulation of affect. Just as the brain influences our affectual relationships with others, so our early affectual relationships structure our brain function. It is important to distinguish between a neuroscience that wants to establish identification of the mind with the brain or body and a neuro-psychoanalysis, where I suggest the very acceptance of the unconscious as a psychological or imaginative entity must refuse the more determining principles of neuroscience, or indeed the science method as one with which we can measure and empirically test psychoanalysis as some kind of true or, should we say, false self.

Neuro-psychoanalysis has shown that unconscious, non-verbal attachment between people, initially between mother and child, regulates the mind and the body. Non-verbal attunement and communication between people is the basis of social interaction and structures all verbal exchange. In her introduction to a collection of papers bringing attachment theory and neuroscience together, Vivien Green suggests that 'attachment theory with its roots in ethnology, more accurately belongs to a socio-biological category' (Green 2003: 3). Regina Pally in *The Mind–Brain Relationship* sets out how neuroscience takes as axiomatic how mental life develops from biological and neural circuits. Equating the mental with the biological is in her view a mistake as psychic life is derived from neurophysiology not identical with it (Pally 2000: 4).

This is an important point to consider. In a sense we can know our neuronal and physical circuits only in terms of the phenomenological affects that we experience, so how can they be said to be determining? And this in turn must make us question the scientific, rationalist framework that originally Freud, but more recently neuroscience, has translated psychoanalysis within. Although, as I will argue, the very debate between psychoanalysis and neuroscience is becoming one where the boundaries of what 'rational' means are being questioned. A lot of neuroscience has idealised the brain as somehow determining of consciousness. In this scientific materialism, ideas and what we think of as the mind become reduced to electro-chemical impulses and neurons firing off from the brain. And yet there is no hard evidence that the brain *produces* consciousness, although there is plenty of evidence to support the links between the mind and the brain, for example the fact that mental illness is accompanied with corresponding chemical imbalances or that mental symptoms can be alleviated by changing brain chemistry.

Arguing for an analogous relationship between mind and body, as Freud did, is not the same thing as reducing the mind to the brain, nor is it the same as proposing that our brain wiring simply causes consciousness and brings it into being. Most psychotherapists would totally disagree with the view that you could simply cure depression through drugs, so there has to be a more complicated explanation. Solms among others returns the neurophysiology of the affectual tie between mother and infant, ego and object, to a history of science and metaphysics; however, if we understand the unconscious in Bergsonian terms, then affects and mental representations are brought into being in the imaginary and actual flows of our lived durations. In this account it is not science that can explain the unconscious; rather, it is the hypnotic and creative trance that creates our rational and empirical world and then keeps on creating it anew. Solms links his arguments to Freud's meta-psychology or classical theory, rather than to Freud's earlier emphasis on trauma and dissociation (Kaplan-Solms and Solms 2000: 244). This is because Solms is a Freudian psychoanalyst and he uses neuroscience to prove Freud's hierarchical model of the mind. Alternatively, I will argue that Freud's early work on neurophysiology points to a model of the unconscious which emphasises dissociation rather than repression. This work was largely in agreement with the neurophysiology of Charcot and the more psychological theories of consciousness and dissociation associated with Joseph Breuer, William James and Pierre Janet.

What does it mean to understand the structure of the psyche in terms of dissociation rather than repression? One consequence of using dissociation as a dominant metaphor is that it enables us to see psychic life or the psychic body as a movement in time that is creative. It also enables us to see dissociation as a defensive trauma that stops the movement of time and the body. Henri Bergson's idea that dissociation brings the time of life into being is thus an important one to compare with psychoanalytic concepts of the unconscious. Bergson was a philosopher at the turn of nineteenth and twentieth centuries, a contemporary of Freud and Janet, whose ideas of time and duration are, I suggest, of the utmost importance in rethinking psychoanalysis. Bergson's metaphysical thinking on the correspondence of psycho-physiological processes centred, like Freud, on aphasia; and again in a similar vein Bergson was concerned that science was ultimately inadequate in understanding the duration of life and matter.

Bergson's philosophy is in contrast to the traditional Cartesian view that the mind is somehow separate from the body, or that the world has to be represented internally, to our consciousness. For Bergson no such separation exists; everything is movement and matter and consciousness is an extension of this. Deleuze (1988b), in his excellent book on Bergson, sums this up when he says, 'there cannot be a difference in kind but only a difference in degree between the faculty of the brain and the function of the core, between the perception of matter and matter itself' (Deleuze 1988b: 63). So a continuous and connected relation between the brain, matter and consciousness exists. Consciousness is merely a movement within a larger organism or continuum made up of the body, brain and our sensory systems. Antonio Damasio also sees the mind, body and brain to be connected as a continuous organism: they are all anchored in relation to each other. He writes, 'body, brain and mind are manifestations of a single organism' (Damasio 2004: 195). Damasio's work on feelings is a modern appraisal of the ideas of Bergson and William James when he says that feelings are perceptions and thoughts of body states (Damasio 2004: 89). As I will describe in Chapter 2, Bergson argues that feelings come into being in relation to perception: the actualisation of what we feel and think happens together and these processes are part of a larger bodily whole.

Bergson sees matter as composed of images. The brain for him is simply one image amongst many; he does not privilege it as an autonomous entity. He writes:

> To make of the brain the condition on which the whole image depends
> is, in truth, a contradiction in terms, since the brain is by hypothesis a

part of this image. Neither nerves nor nerve centres can, then, condition the image of the universe.

(Bergson 1912: 4)

For Bergson the mind and brain are not identical. Motor activity cannot be separated from the processes of perception and neither do sensory nerves generate our perceptions of the world. Rather, perceptions for example of hearing, sight and touch meet motor activity as complex relations. Because the duration of time and the body lies between real sensory action and virtual perception, then perception is part of things and our affects and emotions do not arise from an inner essence and extend: they are there, *as a relation between bodies*. What Bergson calls the duration of time and the unconscious psychic body always lies between people and things; it is not something that moves from inside to outside.

Intersubjective and attachment psychoanalysis is therefore an important reminder to a neuroscience that would want to idealise the brain by making a separation between perception and motor activity. Bergson's theory of duration provides an interesting context in which to examine the relation between psychoanalysis and neuroscience because for him the brain is not a container of ideas or creativity. Although everything seems to happen as though our perception is a result of the internal activity of the brain – 'issued . . . from the cortical centres' – in fact the brain cannot tell us how perception arises, only how it is limited (Bergson 1912: 35). The brain is like a kind of telephone exchange, receiving, organising and redeploying stimulus and response, perception and action. He writes: 'the brain is no more than a central telephone exchange; its office is to allow communication, or to delay it. It adds nothing to what it receives' (Bergson 1912: 19). For Bergson, then, the function of the brain is one of selection, organising movement received and executed. The brain thus chooses memories:

> The role of the brain was to choose at any moment, among memories, those which illuminate the action begun, and to exclude others. Those memories capable of being inserted into motor framework forever changing, but always prepared, emerged once more to consciousness; the rest remained unconscious.
>
> (Bergson 1946: 86)

The body, for Bergson, is like the conductor of an orchestra who reproduces as activity the life of the mind, accentuating motor movement as a conductor would do with a musical score. The brain does not think: its function is 'that of hindering thought from becoming lost in dream'. It is an 'organ of attention to life' (Bergson 1946: 87). Consciousness is part of the body and it is a selective process. If the brain is an image that exists in the material world amongst other images, then the nervous system cannot determine the external world. Because the brain is *part* of the material world, then what we call the world cannot be seen to arise solely from within this organ. For Bergson, this also means that if the images of the material world disappear from view, the brain is also eliminated. The brain is not separate from the images that it receives and the body is therefore not abstracted as representation – it is a living organ of action.

It is perhaps interesting to note here that Bergson's model of the brain, as an image amongst many and an instrument of selection, challenges Damasio's ideas of the brain actually producing mental images in its own right, although, to be fair to Damasio, he has recently acknowledged that 'there is a major gap in our current understanding of how neural patterns become mental images' (Damasio 2004: 198). Likening the brain to a conductor's baton, Bergson describes how it conducts the symphony of consciousness, extracting from mental life a particular play or movement. This means the life of the mind is not reducible to cerebral activity and that outside the current music that is playing lies a world of unconscious memories and objects.

Neuroscience can be criticised for an idealistic materialism that sees the brain as a distinct entity or organ, producing ideas and images of the world as though it were synonymous with the mind. Nevertheless, the increasingly complex relationship between neuroscience and psychoanalysis (particularly attachment theory) reveals how the function of the brain is actually influenced by the affectual relationships and images of people in the world, and here the brain is clearly being conceived as some kind of receiver of images.

If we accept that neuroscience can provide interesting biological evidence of psychological functioning without being deterministic, we can also envisage the brain as functioning in the way Bergson describes, as an organising centre that does not produce consciousness of the world but operates as a sort of telephone exchange or even route planner, receiving stimulus and rerouting it, selecting the particular musical score of consciousness that will be made to live in the world.

Bergson challenges both biology and mind as origin stories, he disturbs what we think of as science by putting hypnosis as its core and refuses the Cartesian division between mind and body which still provides psychoanalysis with its most conservative Oedipal story. We do not have to make psychoanalysis a scientific truth; the extreme danger of neuroscience is that we completely endorse the brain as mind – consciousness reduced to the right neural impulses. Even the neuroscience that negotiates with more environmental stories is in danger of providing psychoanalysis with empirical truths verified by the right quantitative methods. Pinning down the unconscious into something knowable makes it an abstract representation that lives only through the analyst's interpretation, or the meaning it delivers. But this deprives the unconscious precisely of its lived essence: the durations in time that make up our as yet unknowable true selves and future experiences.

If the durational, unconscious self refutes scientific definition, so too does it refuse the oppositional stance of retreating into a kind of dualistic philosophy, echoing Descartes, where the mind is seen as distinct and self-reflexive of the body. Bergson refuses materialist and idealist philosophies and for him the brain is one image amongst many. The brain is an image, as are the nerves, the body and the world. All we have is the difference between images. Images are all real and exist, but they occupy vitalities of virtual or actual, and so are not all perceived. The brain or nervous system cannot exist independently from the world or from the images of the world it receives. And so the body here is not something to be transcended, abstracted or reflected on by a Cartesian ego, but neither is it some material thing that can be distinguished from the world. Quite the opposite: the body is intimately connected with the world. The key to Bergson's thesis of life as movement is that we have these different planes of recollection, action and dreaming which interact, but these planes all occupy a particular place within virtual or actual modalities: they are either past or present.

Bergson has famously divided memory into two forms. First, a more superficial memory attached to the conscious will and bodily habits, a functional memory that makes use of the past. Second, Bergson outlines a more involuntary or spontaneous memory associated with a 'pure recollection' which arises from the subconscious and is not always retrievable. Bergson clearly privileges the latter spontaneous memory as being deeper and attached to a virtual past, which is distinct from the action-orientated present of sensation and perception. However, just as the virtual and actual always exist together, so too are these two forms necessary for the functioning of memory. Both habit memory and pure recollection are ultimately directed towards action although pure memory has to turn back to a virtual past in order to aid becoming in the present.

Interestingly, neuroscience has been recently able to find evidence, through functional imaging scans, that different parts of the brain are activated or stimulated by procedural (habit) and semantic memory. In brain damage, for example, these different memories break down independently. Whereas Bergson attributes habit memory to a world of action and a functional conscious will, Oliver Turnball and Mark Solms (2003) discuss how bodily or procedural memory is executed automatically and unconsciously. Turnball and Solms (2003) give the example of how, in sport, game playing improves without any increase in explicit or abstract knowledge. In fact explicit knowledge of how to play a shot results in a decrease in performance: Turnball and Solms (2003) flag up how experienced players often ask their opponents how they hold a racquet or play a shot, as this is a well-known strategy to ruin the competitor's game. Sports people play at their best when they become immersed in automatic and unconscious activity, but such procedural memory is also associated with semantic and episodic memory.

This seems to suggest that sports players don't just utilise motor memory, but that their bodily memory is also connected to an imagination or virtual world which is subconscious rather than consciously reflective. Perhaps this is why hypnotism is so effective in improving athletes' performance? Through Bergson's work we understand that conscious perception is active, not a passive contemplation. The present is the body and perception; it is sensory and motor, whereas the pure past of recollection is the virtual place of dream we start from, stepping gradually through different planes of consciousness until memory become materialised into perception. So, we don't regress from present to past – we move from past to present. This is of course contrary to one of the main ideas of psychoanalysis that we start from conscious repressions and open up a regressed container of unconscious desires. Nevertheless, the idea that the unconscious is a stream of time, moving forwards, gives it a creative immanence that is lacking in Freud's understanding of it as an ultimately regressive, negative and non-organic entity.

Turnball and Solms (2003) argue that experiences are encoded differently as habits, abstract knowledge and lived episodes. Now, this is also Bergson's argument, that we occupy different planes of representation, action or dreaming that interact. For Bergson, conscious perception is always a reliving of the past as something new – a continual translation of virtual and actual, or the movement between unconscious and conscious. This duration of lived time, or what Bergson calls an 'attention to life', are moments of being where we relive and feel memory as we remember it.

Turnball and Solms (2003) see lived or what they call episodic memory as very close in meaning to Damasio's notion of core consciousness and the 'autobiographical self' (Damasio 2000). Here, episodic memory is the conscious activation of stored brain patterns representing past perceptual events. Now, the difference between this neuroscience argument and Bergson's is that in Bergson's view memory is not stored in some container like the brain. We don't relive unconscious memory that has been actually stored, we move between virtual and actual. Such movement or duration involves unconscious representations entering lived time, becoming a memory we can feel; however, the emphasis is on the movement of memory not on the conscious representation of the unconscious. Turnball and Solms equate representation with the living of time. They say that it is 'questionable' whether a state of self can be 'represented' without necessarily being 'reactivated' (Turnball and Solms 2003: 68). For them conscious representation equals lived experience, whereas for Bergson, memory is not a house of representation but something which is continually produced. In terms of therapy, what is at stake is not so much the making conscious of what has been repressed or unconscious but the bringing to life of a traffic in images, which move between virtual and actual worlds.

Living a creative time of the unconscious is not about ego or self-knowledge or finding the right meaningful story, but about being enriched and in tune with a very real energy of sensations, impulses, feelings and being, in a moment-to-moment way. These moments of being do not add up into an intelligible whole, they are disconnected, sometimes fleeting and although they have to be actualised – we have to absorb them in a bodily sense. They can't be described as an identity; rather they are flows of being that make constant connections and disconnections between our conscious and dream worlds.

As I will discuss in Chapter 2, Bergson's view of the unconscious differs from Freud's in that for him unconscious representations are not stored away in the mind as another separate psychological reality. Instead they exist as virtual, unperceived memories that are subconscious. Bergson asks why recollections that are invisible need a container. Nonetheless, he accepts, 'in a purely metaphorical sense the idea of a container in which recollections are lodged' (Bergson 1920: 55). Consciousness does not have to go outside itself to access this metaphorical container of the mind; it has to 'withdraw a veil'. The brain is this vehicle of selection that seeds the mind into reality. Madness is nothing more than the absence of this insertion into reality, a dream-like state which is non-active and disembodied.

Schizophrenia, for Bergson, entails a lack of attention to life and a mind that is disengaged and disembodied from reality. Historically psychoanalysis has regarded psychosis as a sort of regression to the primary process of the bodily id, a kind of return to a childhood state of primitive affects where ego boundaries are weak and ineffective. Louis A. Sass (1994) has rightly challenged this definition, arguing that schizophrenia is not a Dionysian disease of unruly, uncontained desire, but an Apollonian illness of hyper-reflexivity and solipsism, what he calls 'the mind's perverse triumph over the body, the emotions and the external world' (Sass 1994: 117). Henri Bergson's duration of time is a useful framework with which to understand mental illness, because he understands psychosis as the mind's retreat from reality, a dream-like existence which is also overly intellectual and split off from the body and the emotions. Lived memory is the movement between dream and reality, but this is not a duration which is dependent on representation and knowledge, any more than it relies on the occupancy of some unconscious body which is free of images.

In therapy we are always listening for the story or the feeling that is not being articulated or represented but this, I suggest, is not about dragging dark unconscious events and thoughts into the light of representation and consciousness. Therapy is about the production and elaboration of reality and dreams so that we can move between them in a creative way. Too much consciousness, as we can see in the case of the hysteric and the schizophrenic, is not at odds with too much dreaming. In fact, as Sass (1994) has brilliantly shown in the solipsistic and hyper-reflective world of the schizophrenic, we are at our most mad when we think too much and are psychically disembodied.

Representation and knowledge make up the Enlightenment narrative implicit in Freud's Oedipal narrative. Here, the unconscious body is necessarily repressed and brought to meaningful conscious representation within the therapy session. This, as Adam Phillips reminds us, makes the psychoanalyst into an expert, but the unconscious is always undoing this knowledge, just as it continually thwarts and unravels the authority of the Oedipal Complex. Phillips writes:

> For the Enlightenment Freud, paradoxically, the Oedipus Complex makes the unconscious intelligible; it gives it a discernible function, and a master-plot to keep the story going, the story of our forbidden life.
>
> (Phillips 1995: 10)

Phillips suggests that Freud made Oedipus into the tragic hero of psychoanalysis instead of, say, a dream or a screen memory, because this gave an absolute truth and credence to his role as detective or doctor. If this is so, then we have to question what it means to make this particular incest story the origin story of the unconscious. Forbidden knowledge or wishes and their transgression were perhaps in Freud's day a more obvious phenomenon, although Foucault would disagree that repression of sexuality was the core issue. But surely nowadays the repression or transgression of forbidden desires is not the central dilemma. If anything people are far too full of wants and consumption: our society endlessly reproduces our needs and satiates them. Perhaps what the Oedipal Complex gives psychoanalysis is the parent as a desired ideal – this is Lacan's argument of the symbolic phallus, a figure of desire that we can never have, but can aspire to be.

One of the problems with just seeing wants, as a desire to have, is that being certain of our wants, however transgressive, turns us into perpetual perverts. If capitalism really worked, then we would all be happy perverts and no one would come to therapy. It is not surprising that this endless and certain wanting doesn't work and people turn up in therapy feeling empty and paralysed by the seeming impossibility of their desires and identities. The unconscious and our dream worlds are always undoing our certainties, our wants – and therefore make a mockery of their prohibited status. Dreaming allows us to constantly remake what we want, without suffering the tyranny of always having our needs met. Children want to be their parents and they need them, not just as real objects to discover, but as virtual objects and fantasies that they can make up, over and over again. The Oedipal Complex as the incest taboo works because the child has to learn to defer their desires, but if we simply see these desires as sexual wishes that have to be deferred until adulthood, we are left with a story of either sacrifice or gratification.

Phillips says that once Freud makes the Oedipal Complex take precedence over the dream or screen memory, then he knows and becomes an expert about what he is doing. But what if the Oedipal Complex, like so-called pre-Oedipal sexuality, is just the real and imagined objects and fantasies – the dreams and screen memories that we have to constantly remake and move between, in order to feel alive and at home in the world? The unconscious constantly undoes the certainty and knowledge of our Oedipal relations, and there is something necessary about this unknowability. Milton Erickson (1980) is famous for showing how the unconscious can heal us, not by being transformed into consciousness, but by being left to its own devices. We need to be active in our desire but there is a difference between an ongoing conscious will and a desire which is always changing and making itself unknowable through its ability to appear and disappear between real and imaginary worlds.

Children, just like adults, get disappointed with getting what they want and this, amongst other things, makes us question the nature of desire. If we always get what we want, as perverts or happy capitalists, then there must also come a time when we simply stop wanting what we desire; and this, especially if we are too certain or reliant on knowing, brings on a crisis because our desire does not lead anywhere else.

The psychoanalysts who know that the unconscious is always a foil to self-knowledge are called post-Freudians by Phillips; but all too often contemporary analysts set themselves up as interpreters of meaning, rather than elaborators of something more suggestive. We are concerned with what cannot be remembered and represented, as therapists, because quite simply, it is not making something conscious or finding the right meaningful story that heals. What heals is the bringing to life of our emotions, affects, our dreams and our reality. Therapy entails putting us back into a creative motion or dissociation between these different planes or intensities. Now dissociation is both creative and defensive, it is implicit in the structural movement or stagnation of our psychic world. And this is also why hypnosis both mirrors the souls of the sick as well as being integral to the restorative process. The difference between hypnosis and Oedipus, between suggestion and knowledge, has not always seemed as great as it does now. Freud did his utmost to keep these two things separate, by calling them Oedipal and pre-Oedipal orders and ascribing to them different qualities – masculine and feminine, active and passive, language and the body. One aim of this book is to undo this hysterical division.

In discussing the relationship between psychoanalysis and lived time, Chapter 1 returns to the famous case of Dora and rereads her story in relation to questions of time, life and the unconscious. Dora's symptoms have been read in terms of a repressed Oedipal Complex, or as some pre-

Oedipal retreat into a pure maternal order. My reading refuses the split between Oedipal representation and the so-called pre-Oedipal body and explores how Dora's dilemma is her inability to live the time of her life. Chapter 2 explores the relationship between time, affect and the unconscious. Putting psychoanalysis in dialogue with the work of Henri Bergson, I consider whether the unconscious is based on representation or affect. Freud always insisted it was both, but if this is true, then how can we understand it, not as some negative binary opposition to conscious reality but as a positive and creative immanence?

Chapter 3 explores the historical legacy in psychoanalysis between hysteria and hypnosis, comparing the early therapists who explored hysteria and the methods of hypnosis, such as Freud, Breuer, Janet and Ferenczi, with more contemporary analysts and thinkers such as François Roustang and Mikkel Borch-Jacobsen. I discuss and critique Borch-Jacobsen's (1996) argument in *Remembering Anna O: A Century of Mystification*, where he defines hypnosis as conscious simulation and thereby dismisses the Freudian unconscious. Is hypnosis the ability to move in a creative dissociation between different intensities or planes of dream and reality? Or is it simply hysteria's double – the defensive dissociation integral to the melodramatic monologue of the hysteric, where only one self, albeit massively split, comes out to play? If hysteria is how we get stuck between our representations and our affects, then what is the role of hypnosis in allowing these different vitalities to move again? What are the implications for the analytical transference in seeing hypnosis as both hysterical and healing – as the movement with which we reconnect with lived time? Chapter 4 returns to the hysteric double in relation to questions of death, life and the Oedipal Complex. Connecting Freud's early, Oedipal and late texts on hysteria and anxiety to an immanent model of desire, I argue for hysteria as an Oedipal mimesis or doubling that defends against death. However, the Oedipal Complex is not simply a hysterical defence against death, manifesting itself through self-knowledge and mastery. It is also creative immanence and fantasy; a mimetic doubling that puts us back into the motion of different durations.

Chapter 5 focuses on the question of trauma in relation to recent debates between trauma studies and psychoanalysis. Within an immanent model the hysteric can be seen as a character split between conscious perception and a virtual world of fantasy. Does this character sketch also fit the trauma victim? Trauma theorists argue that it is dissociation, rather than repression, which constitutes the main psychic defence at work in trauma, and in this I agree with them. However, Cathy Caruth (1995, 1996) and van der Kolk, in different ways, argue that trauma is a kind of literal event or blank wound carried and stored in the mind which cannot be represented and is subsequently, belatedly repeated and performed. This literal trauma manifests in the victim as a regression from representation and language to bodily perception. Bergson would of course dispute that traumas, literal or otherwise, can be actually stored in the mind. Instead of suggesting that the flashbacks of trauma victims can be attributed to the literal event, repeating as a form of possession, I argue that these images can be seen as repetitive fixed ideas and fantasies that have become strangulated in relation to affect. These symptoms, in other words, are a fixed dissociation or splitting between actual and virtual flows of time.

Finally, Chapter 6 considers how my argument in relation to psychoanalysis and lived time can be applied to our current global age. How is the immanent desire I have discussed in this book linked to therapy and life in contemporary society? Comparing Anthony Giddens's story of the reflexive self and Michael Rustin's Enlightenment 'child' of reason, this chapter explores how both of these accounts in different ways privilege representation and reason at the expense of the bodily movement of lived time – between fantasy and reality. Transformation of the self in society and therapeutic cure cannot take place without a reimagination of the cultural clearing in which we live. Neither a lifestyle politics of reflexivity nor a rational grasp of reason and knowledge will enable us to live time as immanent beings in the world. If reason and knowledge are brought into being by suggestion, and hypnosis is not simply a mirror of our alienated hysterical identities, but the clue to how we move again, in terms of the time of our lives and bodies, then what does this mean for the academy, psychoanalysis and therapy?

Each chapter in this book finishes with a story or case history which illustrates the relevant themes of time, dissociation, hysteria, death, the double and trauma. The final chapter ends with my own story of hysteria, my dilemma as Hamlet, in an encounter with a potential suicide bomber in July 2005. My lucky escape from this extraordinary event has enabled this book's movement, from virtual to actual production, into its time of life.

Chapter 1

Dora

Dora is Freud's famous case history of hysteria. Entitled 'Fragment of an Analysis of a Case of Hysteria', this clinical case study is also a late Victorian melodrama dramatising all the politics and power relationships of the heterosexual romance implicit in the family, feminism, medicine and science. *Studies in Hysteria* is the acknowledged origins of psychoanalysis. It is a study of the hysterical symptoms and romantic longings of Victorian women, whom Freud originally thought were suffering from real sexual traumas. He then replaced this seduction theory with his famous discovery of infantile fantasy and the unconscious Oedipal Complex.

But how removed are the romantic fantasies of the hysteric from the Oedipal Complex? In Freud's Oedipal theory hysteria becomes the generational love and hostility for the mother and father. Incestuous love must be demolished through the law of the father. The hysteric fails to repress desire for the mother, 'she' fails, therefore, to internalise the prohibition on paternal incest. In Freud's famous case history of Dora, he analyses her hysteria as essentially identification with her father. Dora becomes her father in order to be successful in her love – with the woman her father loves. Freud's Oedipal explanation frames hysteria as the conversion into bodily symptoms of a repressed fantasy or wish. Dora or Ida Bauer (her real name) was understood to negatively refuse her heterosexuality or love for Herr K, her father and Freud. She was unable consciously to accept this Oedipal love and in common psychoanalytic parlance this refusal of paternal law and prohibition, this refusal of the place of the father, is also a refusal of castration, sexual difference and a mature acknowledgement of genital love. Such a refusal marks the idealised romance of the hysteric who wishes to live an ideal transcendental union of mother and babe, and who cannot integrate violence with love. 'She' cannot accept the break-up of the infantile dyad. In other words she cannot accept maternal desire or her own, as this desire is what will travel beyond both mother and child to become symbolised in the paternal phallus.

This of course raises interesting questions as to the nature of desire. For Freud it is, first, the trauma caused by real heterosexual child abuse, and second, unconscious heterosexual fantasies of the child, for the real father. For Lacan, desire is not so much sexual passion for the literal father but a symbolic desire for what lies beyond the mother–child dyad, i.e. language, subjectivity and culture.

But what if desire for the father, whether that desire is literal, a fantasy or symbolic, is just as hysterical as the child's desire for the mother? Christopher Bollas's (2000) fascinating book *Hysteria* still adheres to the Freudian framework where the father's position is to negotiate the child's passage to the outside world. Oedipal sexuality and love for the father (for the girl), or identification with him (for the boy) is then the route to the social, whereas the mother holds sway over the child's narcissistic, primary needs of being and being nurtured.

Bollas agrees with the criticism put forward by French psychoanalysis against psychoanalysis elsewhere, that current emphasis on hysteria, within an object relations framework, desexualises psychoanalysis. In this latter framework, hysteria is compared with borderline disorders which emphasise an ultimately narcissistic aetiology. Definitions of hysteria become inescapably merged with pre-Oedipal preoccupations and thus the crucial arena of sexuality as a route out of childhood innocence, towards maturity and negotiation of a more adult world is missed. The problem of course with this essentially Oedipal reading of hysteria is that it posits heterosexuality as somehow more mature. We can move beyond this, as some Lacanian feminists have done, offering the paternal place as something not attributed to the literal father, and indeed this is Bollas's position too. The symbolic father, then, becomes a third term potentially open to lesbian mothers, or to a paternal function operant within the single mother. However, there still remains a problem with the whole Oedipal and pre-Oedipal binary, where the Oedipal represents language, culture, sexuality and complex, mental identity. The pre-Oedipal, on the other hand, remains the arena of primary needs and narcissistic being associated with the maternal body.

This binary between being and sex, mother and father, supports a dualism that in many ways Bollas's book on hysteria rejects. Hysterical characters in this work walk on in every guise and under every diagnostic definition. They are, however, essentially pre-Oedipal entities, locked in self-idealisation: the innocent solution and defence against complex sexuality and object love for the other. Hysteria is where we become narcissistically stuck in the ego ideal as a perfect reflection of the self.

> The child who will become a hysteric will sustain a rigidly pure ideal that specifically targets its sexual life as degrading, and will seek to transcend such contamination by continually asserting the presence of an ideal self through testimonial good behaviour or ascetic removal from all relation.
>
> (Bollas 2000: 21)

Hysteria begins for Bollas with the lack of maternal sexual desire for the child. It begins with a mother who cannot celebrate her child's genital sexuality and who transmits to the child a horror of sexuality, confining the hysteric to an auto-erotic sexuality, a sacrificial love and identification with the virgin mother. This is a pure love untrammelled by the necessary sexuality, needed to break up and separate the hysteric from the mother, and set him or her on a journey towards future destiny.

Bollas then rereads Dora's case, pointing out how her flight from sexuality and the father is to reassert a desexualised self. Let us remind ourselves of this story. Dora, an intelligent and attractive 18-year-old girl, is referred to Freud by her father, on finding her suicide note. In analysis Dora reveals the cause of her distress, the sexual advances of a middle-aged man Herr K – a friend of her father. This man, who kissed her when she was 14 and attempted a more serious seduction beside a lake when she was 16, is married to Frau K, her father's lover and Dora's one-time mentor. Dora is furious at being exchanged in sexual barter for her father's mistress, and this pain is intensified on learning that her father's insensitivity and his abandonment of her have been initiated by the very woman whom Dora has unconsciously loved. The woman with whom Dora could identify and feel an ideal love was different from her own disappointing mother, who suffered from 'housewives' psychosis'.

Freud's interpretation of Dora's case arises from his new Oedipal theory of fantasy elicited through dream interpretation. He analyses Dora's unconscious desire for the father and Herr K through her loss of voice, fainting fits and nervous cough. Only later on, through the failure of the analysis and Dora's departure, does Freud rewrite this heterosexual narrative in a series of famous footnotes, acknowledging Dora's even deeper unconscious homosexual desire for Frau K.

In the first dream Dora is woken by her father and finds the house on fire. Although her mother wants to save her jewel case, her father says, 'I refuse to let myself and my two children be burnt for the sake of your jewel case' (Freud 1905: 64). Dora's associations with the dream are jewellery bought for her mother, by her father, and her mother's distress at being bought a bracelet, instead of the pearl earrings she wants. Furious at the money spent on something she did not want, Dora's mother tells her husband he might as well give it to someone else. Dora also remembers being given jewellery she does not want from Herr K. Freud points out that the jewel case refers to Dora's genitals and that her father is saving her from masturbatory activity, signified by her continual bedwetting as a child. The dream reveals unconscious desires for her father, Herr K and Freud himself. When Dora refuses these interpretations Freud replies there is no smoke without fire, and then links the fire in the dream to the three men she supposedly desires, who are all smokers.

For Bollas this is only half the story and misses the significance of how Dora wants to retreat from her sexuality in an assertion of her mother's innocence and virginity. He points to the significance of Dora's second dream. Here, Dora finds herself wandering in unknown streets. Finding where she lives, she comes across a note from her mother telling her that as Dora had left home without parental knowledge, she does not know her father has been ill, but now she was writing to say that he is dead and Dora could return home if she wished. Dora sets out for the station and asks a hundred times, where is the station? The answer is always five minutes, but on entering a thick wood she meets and asks a male stranger, who tells her it will take two and a half hours. He offers to accompany her but she refuses and carries on alone. She sees the station in front of her but cannot reach it and has the anxiety of a dream that cannot move forward. On arriving home she is told that her mother and the others are already at the cemetery.

Freud urges Dora to associate in relation to the strange man and she remembers refusing the company of a male cousin on a visit to a Dresden art gallery. Going alone, she becomes rapt before Raphael's *Sistine Madonna*. Freud's interpretation of this is that the young man signifies the threat of defloration and Dora's anxiety becomes soothed by the picture of the Madonna. Bollas spells out what is hinted at by Freud, that Dora takes refuge in the Virgin Mother as a retreat from her sexuality and the father who embodies it.

In these readings Dora's dilemma is either an unconscious sexual and Oedipal wish for the father, or a retreat from that sexuality into a pre-Oedipal narcissism of innocent transcendence with the mother. Although Bollas's reading is persuasive, like Freud it puts the emphasis on sexuality – either too much or too little. As many feminists have pointed out, this reading makes a pathology of Dora and ignores the ideological constraints of her context in a Victorian, patriarchal society. Therapy has to take seriously the issue of immanent desire or the lack of it in relation to the client, but it also has to focus on the context. I want to suggest that one of the ignored themes of the Dora case is time. Dora's family is in many ways simply dysfunctional. She has a loved father infected by syphilis who embarks on an adulterous relationship with the woman whom Dora has set up as the ideal replacement for her own destroyed and collapsed mother. Moreover, her father barters Dora in exchange for Frau K, with the repulsive Herr K. Repulsive to Dora because his need for sex seems identical to the polluting sexuality that has deprived Dora of a protective father and an ideal mother.

The father's gift of jewellery to the mother is unwanted. His unwanted bracelet that might as well be given to someone else – Frau K – is matched by the mother's preferred jewels, the pearl ear drops that signify her complete lack of desire. Likewise, Dora does not want anything to do with the sexuality or expensive jewels that Herr K proffers. Sexuality is not just polluting in this family drama because it threatens the ideal mother–child bond in the shape of the father. It contaminates the family because it is a real signifier of the family's dysfunction and because it represents the inability of both parents to provide Dora with the desire and the context necessary to leave them behind. The gift of jewellery by the father is one which is rejected by the mother and accepted by his mistress Frau K. These jewels figuring sexual desire also signify Dora's betrayal by her father and his lover. Dora admires Frau K's jewels and is given some identical ones by her father, but eventually realises in sorrow that they have been purchased by Frau K. Dora feels humiliated and ignored as she recognises how she is being managed and used by the two people she loves. The father's syphilitic unfaithfulness, rendering him literally impotent, is matched by Dora's mother, a figure of psychic destruction, suffering from 'housewives' psychosis'. Sexuality for Dora's parents is either too much or too little, figuring their own hysterical escapes, his philandering and her obsession with housework.

Dora's father is the seductive, if needy, parent whose constant illnesses and affairs (one is the excuse for the other) take him away from her. This disappointment is made unbearable for Dora because it also takes away from her Frau K, who embodied for Dora the ideal mother and model of womanhood she wanted to be. Frau K is a route out to the world for Dora, away from her family and the conflict of sexuality between her parents, represented by the unwanted jewels her father wants to give and the jewels her mother insists on keeping for herself.

Freud's line of interpretation puts Dora back into repressed Oedipal desires for her father and it is not surprising that she is furious with him in suggesting that she carries the same repellent sexual desires that have been the source of her parent's dysfunctional relationship. Dora finds herself incapable of leaving her family because her parents' unresolvable conflict renders her unable to use creatively any of the Oedipal identifications available to her: fantasies which would enable her to move forward in time.

The father, in the first dream, who wants to save her from the fire, and the conflict of the jewel case, is the ideal father Dora wants, one who will protect her and not abandon her to the advances of Herr K. Likewise, in the second dream in her walk through the woods, the man who offers to accompany Dora in her search for the station is obviously Freud. The second dream represents the issue of time. Dora asks a hundred times where the station is and is told five minutes. When she comes across the thick wood she is told it will take her two and half hours, by the man and therapist, who represents the route towards the station and out of the family romance. Whereas Freud insists on associating the station with a box and then the female genitals, I suggest that the station is symbolic of a place in time, one which will either return her to her family or set her on a road to her future. Dora refuses the man's offer because this offer is flawed. Freud does not recognise Dora's need to leave the Oedipal romance in relation to her father and mother behind.

The associated story of Dora's rapt immersion in the picture of the Madonna is not simply a retreat into pure pre-Oedipal transcendence with the mother. Bollas emphasises the Madonna as the hysteric's pathology, contrasting it with his 'ideal' of the Oedipal moment where narcissism is swapped for object choice. If the Oedipal phallus is symbolically ideal, why not the pre-Oedipal mother? What about the creative possibilities of the Madonna?[1]

In Dora's rapt admiration of the Madonna she finds what has been removed by her father's affair. The Madonna is the ego ideal, previously symbolised by Frau K. As such she is more than a retreat into pre-Oedipal fantasy, and figures as a route out for Dora in imagining herself as the longed-for adult woman. The Madonna is the ultimate cipher and projection, she is anything we want her to be, and for Dora she represents a creative future self as well as an idealised past one. This reading does not cancel out either Freud's Oedipal, or Bollas's more pre-Oedipal, interpretation of the Dora case. Repression of Oedipal desire for the father or an idealised bond with the mother are valid readings of the case, but they both take Dora back into an infantile romance from which there is no escape. No escape, because the hysteria of both Dora's father and her mother prevent her from finding a route out from the family to the outside world. We are told repeatedly in psychoanalysis that the father represents the route out to society, and in Bollas's account this route is one where the child can internalise sexual desire and separation. But in Dora's case the father is as hysterical in his sexuality as the mother is hysterical in her sacrificial role. He is the one who retreats into illness and health resorts and has to make his sexuality into a sordid dirty secret; one that, like his syphilis, renders impotent a more life-affirming father who can be sexual and protective, both seductive and ideal. Dora's second dream is all about her need to kill off her father in fantasy so she can remake her relation with him and leave him for her future.

But this of course also begs an interesting question of what is Oedipal sexuality and fantasy. I suggest that the Oedipal romance is symbolic *and* imaginary. It is fixed as a representation or myth, but it is also imaginary and as such is synonymous with so-called pre-Oedipal fantasy. These infantile fantasies are regressive, the fantasies of our past that we flee into, but they are also all the possible creative desires and identifications of whom we can be. Oedipal and pre-Oedipal fantasies are our escape within therapy, dreams and everyday life, but they are also the fantasies that we select, to consciously embody and remake in our movement towards future possibilities and selves. Too much fantasy, like too much sexuality, can be as bad for us as not having enough. We all flee into the family romance of fantasy whether that is personified by the ideal mother or the sexual father, but we can only move forward in time when we select the fantasies we choose to embody and make creatively real in terms of future identities.

The Oedipal Complex, as Freud realised in later years, is simply a repeat of the relation to the early mother. The sexual father and the ideal mother are fantasies and fictions; they are the myths of psychoanalysis. Recognising psychoanalysis as myth does nothing to diminish its power.

Bollas talks interestingly of how the hysteric wants to retreat into a pure transcendent world of maternal/child innocence, and such hysterics, quite often female ones, are indeed recognised characters in clinical therapy. But hysterics also turn up as characters who seem too lost in enacting a powerful sexuality; a melodrama, where ordinary everyday matters seem dull and dead by comparison. Perhaps one of the hallmarks of hysteria is that it splits the body from language, the carnal from the transcendental and identification with the father from identification with the mother. Of course in this reckoning nothing is more hysterical than the Oedipal Complex, or Dora's family romance, where the mother is the pre-Oedipal body and the father is the symbolic marker of language and desire (Freud and Lacan). Or where the mother is ideal transcendence and the father is the embodied seat of complex sexuality (Bollas). These two readings are not exclusive, as Bollas (2000) demonstrates. For him, the father represents sexuality and a desiring identification with the outside world. And Bollas is acute enough to recognise that in order to leave the ideal mother we also have to acknowledge her sexually desiring body.

However, as feminist theory has made clear, acknowledging the mother's sexually desiring body is a contradiction within Oedipal psychoanalysis where the phallus is ideal. Phallic psychoanalysis separates the mother from the father and the transcendental from the carnal. As Luce Irigaray (1991a) has shown us, the Oedipal Complex privileges a masculine transcendental or symbolic realm and leaves the realm of the maternal to the realm of the abject, unmediated body. She calls it the 'one-way mirror'. Irigaray challenges Oedipal theory and practice as a system of representation, accusing it of projecting violence and castration onto the body of the woman. For her the imaginary and symbolic value of the phallus becomes all-powerful precisely because in Lacan's account there is no sexual relation in the real. She asks 'whether the real might not be some very repressed-censored-forgotten "thing" to do with the body' and suggests 'there is no question of underestimating the real if we interpret its effects' (Irigaray 1991a: 86). Irigaray is suggesting here that we must not cut off or castrate the relation to the maternal 'pre-Oedipal body', because we need that relation to the body in order to move and create. She suggests that an exclusively analytic/representational perspective on the transference destroys the potential to imagine and create. Whereas writing and language seek to contain and repress bodily identity, a more figurative imagination linked to the senses can express it. Transference, in other words, cannot be resolved simply by deconstructing the analysand in relation to knowledge and language. Whereas, within a system of Oedipal representation, the hysteric occupies a mental imaginary that is at war with the real as death drive, a more creative imaginary can provide analysis with imaginative power to paint the senses and recreate the self.

Irigaray's solution to the mental fragmentation of the hysteric is to encourage her to paint her senses in relation to images and dreams within the therapeutic encounter. Now, for Irigaray, this painting will equalise space-time perception because it 'will spatialize perception and make time simultaneous', so building bridges between past, present and future (Irigaray 1993: 155). I will argue in Chapter 2 for a perspective where space and time are made to move in relation to each other through a lived time or duration.

Let us consider for one last time Dora's dilemma and the professed need in her dreams to move forward in time, her yearning for a protective father and a mother who is also a subject. Parents in other words who don't split off either their sexual needs or their adult responsibilities and can thus allow Dora ideal desires and depressive compromises, so she can move forward to future, possible identities. For Bollas, Dora's rapture in front of the Madonna is her hysterical refusal of the sexual paternal order where Oedipal exchange seduces the child away from auto-eroticism. In this account successful Oedipal exchange enables the child to replace narcissism with object love and joins sexual passion with romantic love. Such union allows deferral and sacrifice of gratification until the arrival of adolescence. The non-hysteric thus moves into a sexual future, whereas the hysteric like Dora remains stuck in auto-erotic fantasies which idealise the parents as asexual figures. This argument depends on a division between, on one hand, a primary maternal order of being and non-verbal reception and on the other, an active Oedipal paternal order associated with language, the law and sexuality. According to Bollas, mothers and fathers inhabit both orders and help or hinder the child in their necessary struggle to move from pre-Oedipal narcissism to the sexual seductions of Oedipal exchange.

We could argue that Bollas substitutes the ideal asexual hysteric with the equally ideal and romantic sexual couple. For why make such a distinction between these two orders? In Oedipal theory these two orders are the necessary result of repression, where limits to narcissism are brought by the prohibition and law of the paternal order. However, if pre-Oedipal and Oedipal orders are only fantasies or fictions, which I argue they must be, and again I repeat it does nothing to reduce the power of psychoanalysis to acknowledge these founding concepts are myths, then, to give only Oedipal fantasy the role of reality-bringing and symbolic functioning in terms of the world seems a contradiction in terms. The symbolic is the imaginary made law. Only our imaginary Oedipal relationships not separated from the real of the 'pre-Oedipal' body can cast the seeds of a more lived duration and future.

If idealism is giving power to one fantasy over others (for Dora it is the Madonna whereas for psychoanalysis it is the Oedipal Complex), then we can see idealism and hysteria going together as a necessary splitting of the psyche in terms of fantasy and reality. However, problems arise (for Dora and, we could also argue, for psychoanalysis) when that hysterical splitting becomes institutionalised in terms of society. Dora's ideal rapture in front of the Madonna can be seen in two ways. It can be seen creatively as a fantasy of who Dora wants to become, a fantasy I would argue that replaces Frau K in its ability to be a cipher to Dora's future, one which, if selected and embodied, can lead Dora away from her family. Or, it can remain a haunting fantasy, a narcissistic split world of asexual mothers and sexually needy fathers. Dora's case is the essential Oedipal plot because it reveals the hysteria implicit in Oedipal rivalry, where fantasy is always doubled and split between the carnal and transcendental. The Oedipal complex is both hysterical fantasy which we nostalgically flee into to escape reality, and it is also a creative complex of possible identifications which we can regress with, in therapy, dreams and imaginative life, in order to select new selves and futures.

Of course this suggests another way of thinking about the unconscious, not as some dynamically repressed meta-psychology, but in a phenomenological sense as something immanent to us in terms of desire and time. In the gendered two orders that Bollas discusses, the unconscious is divided up between first, a phenomenological, primary maternal order of affectual being, and second, a more developed introspective order of mental representation and reflection, taking place after the event. I want to refuse this hysterical division, especially as it seems to privilege the secondary paternal order as the route out to the social, and consider the unconscious in an immanent phenomenological sense.

W. R. D. Fairbairn, the object relations analyst, pointed out in the 1940s that Freud's work on repression concerned itself mainly with the contents of repression and ignored the repressive agency. He said it was regrettable that Freud 'did not pursue his study of the agency of repression within the same field as his study of the repressed and thus did not make the phenomena of hysteria the basis of his theory of the mental apparatus' (Fairbairn 1952: 168–169). If Freud had done so, Fairbairn suggests, his conception of repression would have been nearer to Melanie Klein's schizoid position and would have to acknowledge that repression implies a splitting of the ego. Of course, this would have taken Freud back to his original work on hysteria as splitting and dissociation that he had so famously abandoned.

Freud's Oedipal theory is at odds with his original seduction or 'trauma' theory that was indebted to the famous Charcot and Joseph Breuer. However, we can also see Freud's early theory as one that emphasises phenomenological affect over Oedipal representation. For Charcot, traumatic shock was comparable to hypnosis since both were emotional moments where the will became paralysed and the trauma fixated as auto-suggestion.

Whereas shock or trauma in normal circumstances is expressed or abreacted, in cases of hysteria the trauma and affect become blocked. The cathartic method in Freud and Breuer's initial *Studies on Hysteria* (1895) was to abreact or discharge this blocked affect. Both Freud and Breuer followed Charcot in seeing hysteria as a result of a dissociation and a profound splitting of consciousness. Observing the hysterical twilight states of his and Breuer's patients, Freud realised that 'hysterics suffered mainly from reminiscences'.

It is interesting to consider what Freud meant by this. Hysterical reminiscences were the repetition of pathogenic thoughts, or memory pictures, which could not be remembered by the hysteric and became converted into bodily symptoms. Like Pierre Janet's subconscious fixed ideas, these reminiscences belong to a virtual unconscious world of being and memory. Freud faced a dilemma, however, because his patients often could not remember having these ideas, even when they accepted having them. He writes:

> Are we to suppose that we are really dealing with thoughts which never came about, which merely had a *possibility* of existing, so that the treatment would lie in the accomplishment of a psychical act which did not take place at the time?
>
> (Freud 1895a: 387, original emphasis)

Now this scenario makes sense only if we see Freud's repressed memories as part of an unconscious where the hysteric is immersed in virtual, repetitive memories and fantasies which haunt him or her as a double somnolent state. The work of therapy is to make conscious these fantasies and to embody them psychologically, but as Freud speculates, it is not a question of the patient remembering a conscious past event that has somehow been repressed. Instead these memories are possibilities that are made concrete through their actualisation within the therapy.

Reminiscences are then virtual hallucinations that act as a block to the emotional selection of memory and they prevent actualisation, or we could also say discharge of the affect. For Charcot (1991), traumatic shock was comparable to hypnosis since both were emotional moments where the will became paralysed and the trauma fixated as auto-suggestion. For Janet (1965), trauma caused fixed ideas, which accompanied a repetitive unconscious memory. Unblocking of these fixed ideas went hand in hand with the patient's ability to embody these fantasy memories through a more active perception. As we shall see presently, this also entailed the important ability for the hysteric to forget or push away those virtual memories that were not actionable in a conscious and bodily way. As I shall argue throughout this book, the reminiscences of the hysteric are both fixed representations that have been once conscious and are now repressed, but they are also virtual fantasies that have never been conscious as such.

Freud gradually abandoned the idea of unconscious auto-suggestion caused by trauma, focusing on a more sophisticated psychological explanation. But this movement away from his early trauma theory, in favour of the Oedipal Complex, ended up focusing on infantile repressed memories, which had supposedly been repressed because they were prohibited by the incest taboo. If we read Freud's trauma theory through a more immanent lens, we can perhaps see the Oedipal Complex as simply a range of possible identifications and virtual fantasies that the child has to move away from, by learning to selectively embody the particular identification which allows him or her to actualise lived time and move into the future. In this sense, then, the Oedipal Complex is hysterical in adults because it is composed of virtual fantasies, fixed ideas and romantic longings. Like Pierre Janet's fixed ideas or Freud's reminiscences, this retreat into unconscious fantasy is an escape from embodiment within lived time and reality.

Freud's Oedipal theory singled out his work as unique, whereas an emphasis on splitting and dissociation rendered his ideas far too close to those of his former colleagues. Jung's work on early explorations of the unconscious and hysteria not only made connections with Freud's ideas of the unconscious and hysteria but also marked sharp differences. He writes in relation to Freud:

> As you know, by 'repression' we mean the mechanism by which a conscious content is displaced into a sphere outside consciousness. We call this sphere the unconscious, and we define it as a psychic element of which we are not conscious.
>
> (Jung 1913: 92)

In Jung's view, however, repression was primarily dissociation (tracked through association tests) where feeling toned and painful complexes were forgotten. Hysteria is not a suffering of reminiscences that lead back to the past, but a staged performance in the present, that is in flight from present reality and takes refuge in neurotic infantile complexes. Jung says:

> The fright and the apparently traumatic effect of the childhood experience are merely staged, but staged in the peculiar way characteristic of hysteria, so that the *mise-en-scène* appears almost exactly like a reality. We know from hundreds of experiences that hysterical pains are staged in order to reap certain advantages from the environment. Nevertheless these pains are entirely real. The patients do not merely think they have pains; from the psychological point of view the pains are just as real as those due to organic causes, and yet they are stage managed.
>
> (Jung 1913: 161–162)

Hysteria is then a staging of affectual emotion – a *mise-en-scène* rooted in a dissociation and splitting from reality. Repression, here, is not an internal, hierarchical and intra-psychic split between the body and language, but fundamentally speaks to the phenomenological (intersubjective) relation (and splitting) between the self and the world. For Jung, it is not a return of the repressed from the past, but a regression of the libido to infantile states in the present. Jung did not privilege infantile sexuality. In his view there is no distinction between hunger and sexuality for the infant, and so-called 'sexuality' in the infant is in fact a dynamic unity of embodied and psychic energy. Jung writes: 'the libido concept puts in the place of a divided sexuality split into many roots a dynamic unity, lacking which these once-significant components remain nothing but potential activities'. He goes on to say, 'This conceptual development is of the greatest importance; it accomplishes for psychology the same advance that the concept of energy introduced into physics' (Jung 1913: 112).

The Oedipal Complex for the boy, and what Jung termed the Electra Complex for the girl, is therefore a neurotic, heterosexual and infantile jealousy, which in optimum conditions is moved away from, as the child and young adult develops social objects outside the family. However, when things go wrong, when conflict arises, say a conflict between staying at home or going into the world, then the Oedipal Complex (hitherto unconscious and inoperative) becomes reactivated, and libido is directed towards this complex – producing extreme feelings and fantasies. What is striking in Jung's account is that sexual difference is not the primary guarantor of loss; rather it becomes a retroactive defence against loss, a defence against leaving the family and entering a more social world. The Oedipal conflict for Jung, like Lacan, is also symbolic, and not defined as literal incestuous wishes of children. Whereas Lacan makes sexual difference a requisite of the symbolic, for Jung it is an imaginary complex that can be transformed into more intergenerational and historical symbols, through mediation of the archetypal image. Jung's sees fantasies of incest clearly related not to infantile sexual wishes but to a symbolic and internal image of parental union (see Samuels 1993). Jung studied under Janet, using his concept of fixed ideas to form a theory of unconscious archetypal complexes. Like fixed ideas, the Oedipal Complex, in Jung's view, was a regression to precisely the kind of repetitive virtual world that produced Freud's earlier notion of the hysterical memory picture, or reminiscences.

Jung's archetypal theory is problematic because its rooting in some biological universal leads back, as Franz Fanon (1986) insists, not to history as difference, but to an essentialist account of white European colonialism. Nevertheless, for Jung, the route out of the Oedipal Complex is not premised on the difficulty of resolving sexual difference; rather it is based on the generational need to leave the family of sexual difference behind and replace it with a more historical (social and spiritual) mediation of the psyche.

Jung's description of the libido is rather vague; he argues for a dynamic psyche and a mobile embodied energy. When infantile complexes are provoked, then the energy of the libido becomes unbalanced, with more libido becoming directed into the complex, depleting somewhere else: 'From this point of view psychoanalysis is a method which helps us to discover those places or functions over-invested with libido' (Jung 1913: 113). Jung makes a distinction between what seems to be intense activation of the libido in neurotic cases such as hysteria and obsessions and, conversely, the virtual disappearance of the libido in the psychotic or schizophrenic, where adaptation to reality becomes non-existent. Giving the example of Freud's famous analysis of the Schreber case, a man suffering from schizophrenia or dementia praecox, Jung describes how fantasy takes the place of the external world. As the patient withdraws more and more, there is a 'progressive increase in the production of fantasies' (Jung 1913: 113). We can see, here, how psychosis entails a regression to a virtual world of fantasy where conscious perception of reality is weakened as the subject loses a sense of bodily affect and the ability to act.

Although Jung agreed with Freud initially that neurotic displacements of libido were sexual in nature, he argued that, in psychosis, sexuality disappeared along with any adaptation to reality. This led Jung to question what sexuality in infants really meant, and instead of conferring what he saw as an adult concept of genital sexuality on the child, he proposed a more sensual and embodied libido that moves from nutrition to sexuality. Infantile sexuality was situated in what Jung called a 'caterpillar stage' containing all the physical and psychological aspects of mature sexual attitudes, but remaining at a more diffuse and primitive stage. But, whereas developmental readings of Freud posit the pre-Oedipal arena as a ruthless, primitive sexuality and aggression that must be moved away from and repressed, Jung saw regression as destructive only if it becomes our final destination. Regression was also positive for Jung, a necessary stage of teleological value where we find 'the first beginnings of spiritualization, the first groping attempts to find new ways of adapting' (Jung 1913: 180). Neurotic regression then, as not only the destructive family house of pathological fantasy, but also a birthplace of new and creative fantasy.

This view is close to Janet's and Bergson's notion that consciousness can be expanded through a regression to unconscious being, but those virtual fantasies also need to be transformed in a more conscious selection of reality. It is in this Bergsonian sense that Jung shows how regression to the supposed real past is actually a flight to the virtual past in the present. It is a fantasy of the past that substitutes for lived reality.

Freud's early lecture on hysteria seems to agree with Jung's phenomenological description when he describes hysterical symptoms as mnemic symbols of past traumatic experiences. Freud links hysterical symptoms to the mnemic symbols of the past that adorn large cities such as London, such as the Monument of the Fire of London. The melancholic Londoners, who stop and weep at the past destruction of London by fire, fail to acknowledge its present, rebuilt glory. In similar vein the hysterics behave like these melodramatic and 'unpractical Londoners', in weeping over past traumas (Freud 1977: 40). What is striking about Freud's account, here, is that he attributes hysteria to a double consciousness and a melancholic dwelling in the past, a melancholia that is an escape or flight from the present. This model of hysteria accords with Jung's early thinking and is quite different from the subsequent moves Freud makes in formulating an Oedipal meta-psychology.

Hysteria in these early accounts of Freud and Jung is a flight from the present. It is in a phenomenological sense a flight from inhabiting lived time. As I have discussed, in *Studies in Hysteria* it is not Oedipal repression but a doubling or splitting of consciousness that Freud and Breuer discover: the hypnoid or twilight states that are accompanied by the conversion, or displacement, of an earlier traumatic event into bodily or somatic symptoms. Jung was critical of Freud's early trauma theory of hysterical memory, arguing that the twilight states of the hysteric were in fact a retreat into infantile and regressed fantasies or complexes. Such fantasies enabled the hysteric to escape from the conflicts of reality. In two case histories written at the time, by Freud and Jung, we can compare their different interpretations of the hysterical dilemma. Freud's more famous case of Elizabeth Von R is a story of a young woman whose hysteria and somatic conversions are finally traced back by Freud to the repressed trauma as erotic desire, not for her father, but for her sister's husband. In Jung's more anonymous case history, the young woman is in love with her best friend's husband. On leaving a farewell party for her friend/rival who is off to a health resort, the young woman in question suffers from a hysterical attack. This attack is brought on by the sound of galloping horses behind her, horses which remind the patient of an earlier trauma witnessing bolting horses as a child.

Now, Jung is unconvinced by this hysteric's reminiscences and argues against Freud's trauma theory. Jung describes how the young woman's hysterical attacks are not due to repressed traumatic memories. On the contrary, the fright with horses is 'stage managed', with the result of the young woman being taken back to her friend's house with the now alone husband – her unconscious object of desire. This is not a conscious desire, nevertheless, it is a peculiar staging of hysteria, 'so that the *mise-en-scène* appears almost exactly like a reality' (Jung 1913: 161–162). Hysterical pains are, according to Jung from a psychological point of view, organically real yet they are stage managed.

This melodramatic staging which is both real and a fantasy accords with Bergson's virtual and affectual unconsciousness. Jung describes the same splitting and staging of fantasy as the patient's refusal to consciously embody her relation to present reality and life. But if we follow my more phenomenological reading of Freud's trauma theory, then Freud is also right. Bound up and lost in traumatic memories, the hysteric is not remembering a repressed, once conscious event. Instead, she is lost in a boundless world of creative memory and fantasy. Recovery for the hysteric is dependent on a selective conscious embodiment of the past. Actualising what is needed for engagement with the present and future, forgetting what is superfluous, enables the hysteric to move into lived time. This phenomenological reading of Freud's early seduction or trauma theory admittedly rewrites it, but as Breuer's own account testifies, the links between Freud's thinking on hysteria and Janet's is far closer than Freud ever acknowledged. And of course the same thing can be said of Freud and Jung.

In the more traditional reading of Freud's early trauma or seduction theory, he theorised neurosis and hysteria as symptoms resulting from repression of a traumatic event: child sexual abuse. Freud's subsequent abandonment of the seduction theory developed from his increasing realisation that he could not distinguish between the truth and fiction of his patients' memories. Through his famous case history of *The Wolf Man* Freud (1918) argued that the traumatic, historical event was a delayed experience or deferred action (*Nachträglichkeit*). Freud hypothesises that the Wolf Man's trauma was located primarily at the age of 18 months, witnessing a primal scene of parental sex. This scene became traumatic only later through his sister's seduction and is experienced by the patient only in terms of his dream of wolves. In other words the primary traumatic event is not remembered at the time, and it is only through its recall in a later therapy session that the wound is felt. Memory is not simply factual recall but also a fantasy or fiction, a story that is recreated or constructed to incorporate lost, traumatic events.

Trauma theory, which is becoming increasingly popular within psychiatry and cultural movements, emphasises the real event rather than fantasy. Its core belief is that a traumatic event, too painful to be assimilated, is walled off. False memory syndrome or 'recovered memory syndrome' is where patients remember previously forgotten sexual abuse (often through therapy). The central idea here is of a damaging traumatic event which cannot be assimilated. Because in a sense the event is not consciously experienced, it is never represented and becomes incorporated. The literal event then repetitively possesses the person, a repeating of the trauma, without the possibility of conscious knowledge and representation.

We must, however, take issue with the reading of trauma perpetuated by Judith Herman (1992), Cathy Caruth (1996) and others who describe victims of trauma as victims of history because the real event (in the Lacanian literal sense) has invaded them. This seems to miss the fact that trauma victims, like hysterics, retreat into a virtual world of repetitive memory and fantasy. Juliet Mitchell (2000) argues correctly that, for trauma victims and hysterics, perception and memory become incompatible. But this is not simply, as she suggests, because the victim or patient has regressed to bodily perception and is incapable of narrative memory and representation (Mitchell 2000: 281). Rather, the hysteric or trauma sufferer has become split between perceptual consciousness and virtual memory. Memories of the event repeat for the trauma victim because he or she can neither lose nor transform the fixed representations or virtual memories.

Janet actually called this repetition of fixed ideas and virtual fantasy 'traumatic memory', where conscious perception and attention to reality are weakened. In this traumatic memory the patient loses the ability to be separate from the event and so cannot condense or change it. Janet gives the famous example of his patient Irène, who relived her mother's death as hallucination and an actual reproduction of the event – minute by minute. She could not synthesise or substitute the event through her own narrative elaboration.

Judith Herman (1992) uses Pierre Janet's (1919) distinction between traumatic memory as unconscious repetition, and a narrative memory that narrates the past, as past, to understand how victims of post-traumatic stress disorder need to transform their trauma by reconstructing the veracity of it through their story or narrative.

Ruth Leys (2000) points out that this attention to narrative memory in Janet's work misses the importance he attributed to his patient's forgetting. Narrated recollection is not sufficient for cure because recovery for the victim also depends on a certain liquidation of memory. Leys notes how Janet's narrative memory does not really signify truthfulness so much as the connection of the event to the present which Janet termed 'presentification' (Leys 2000: 112). This 'presentification' is not primarily about the ability of the patient to verbalise what has happened, it is about the *flexibility* of memory. Plasticity between the virtual and the real entails the capacity to locate the event temporally and to move between self-abstraction (or representation) and an immersion in the relived action.

I suggest that in this 'presentification' it is not the act of representation as such, because trauma victims suffer not from an inability to represent the event, but from the inability to feel it was real and the incapacity to elaborate the representation in relation to other temporal orders and events. Such dissociation can lead in some people to the repeat of a literal acting out, as in Irène's case, or a fixed representation where the victim feels as if they are looking down on themselves. Often rigidity and fixed ideas go together with a repetitive acting out. This splitting between experience and self-representation is also a profound dissociation between fantasy and reality.

Telling the story of the trauma to another can enable movement between fantasy and reality; only when such movement in time is re-established can the present be created in relation to the past and distinguished from it. This duration in time connects us with the present as an attention to life, at the same time allowing virtual fantasies of the past to die away. Once the past loses its possession of us, we can move again in the rhythm or time of life.

This involves, in therapy, the necessity of choosing the fantasies to consciously embody and move forward with in reality, and forgetting the ones that do not elaborate one's future destiny. We don't always consciously choose, and this is important. Often the materialisation of important fantasies comes about by our being open to unconscious contingency, the images we stumble across in dreams or everyday life. Dora's second dream was a warning to Freud that his interpretations of her sexual desire in terms of the father were unhelpful. Freud did not recognise in the second dream Dora's refusal of him as a therapist, or her intention to find her way out of the woods on her own. His interpretation of her refusal, as the threat of male penetration, led her to take refuge, as Bollas (2000) suggests, in the ideal Madonna figure. But rather than seeing this as merely the hysteric's asexual refusal of Oedipal exchange, I want to suggest that the Madonna was the only fantasy that Dora had to cling on to and as such it was a vital fantasy to elaborate on within the therapy, not as a retreat into some pure maternal order, but as an identification with her present life and future.

If we return to Freud's case of Elizabeth Von R, we can elaborate on Freud's interpretation of her repressed erotic desire in a more phenomenological way. This hysterical woman who suffered from mental and physical pains had been confined within her family, first nursing her sick father, then his widow. Turning away from a desired prospective suitor whilst nursing her father, Elizabeth settled for a life nursing sick parents, too immersed in guilt to lead her own life. Her older sister becomes the first daughter to escape family bonds by marrying a man who has no interest in his wife's ailing mother, moving his family as far as possible away from her. Elizabeth is very angry with this brother-in-law but becomes unconsciously attracted to the younger sister's husband. This recognition of her desire, and the guilt attached to it, comes about only after her younger sister's death, brought to light by Freud's interpretations.

This is one of Freud's successful case histories. Elizabeth subsequently rebels against her mother and eventually becomes betrothed to another man. Freud sees her some time later at a dance, whirling past him happily in the arms of a man. So we don't have to see this girl's hysteria as just focused on a repressed erotic desire, but a desire in a more phenomenological sense to leave home and become a woman, like her sisters, who can participate in the world.

Dora's and Elizabeth's hysteria is a flight into hysterical fantasy which becomes traumatic because those pre-Oedipal or Oedipal fantasies cannot be activated within conscious perception. These women have to forget and remember: forget their hysterical or invalid parents, on whom they have modelled themselves; remember and elaborate on the right creative fantasies, the Madonna for Dora and the brother-in-law for Elizabeth, so they can be made real. Dora walked out of her analysis with Freud and, from the later clinical information we have of her, we know that she never recovered from her hysteria. She never managed to creatively remake her Oedipal relationships and leave her old ones behind. Felix Deutsch (1957) relates the story of his analysis of Dora some twenty-four years after her encounter with Freud and describes how she has become her mother, a woman who hates and rejects men and who is compulsively obsessed with being clean. The only difference for Dora is that she obsessively cleans her body, rather than her house.

Bollas is absolutely right to state that Dora's issues were located in her inability to access a complex sexuality, where her desire can locate 'a continuously new erotic other' (Bollas 2000: 38). However, interpreting her desire, or identification with the father, is not going to solve the problem or lack of maternal desire. Maybe the real missed opportunity with Dora was that Freud resisted making associations with the desiring identification that Dora could make – with the Madonna. To read this back as simply a return to a cleanly maternal order is to miss the point that hysterical fantasy is any pre-Oedipal or Oedipal fantasy that we escape into in order not to face our present and future lives.

Elaborating on the fantasy of the Madonna would not be about making her into an ideal symbolic representation; it would be a destruction of that fixed fantasy or idea and the re-creation of a more immanent desire, which could release and paint senses. Sexuality, or the lack of it, is not the primary issue for the hysteric; what is at stake is the ability to lose representations that alienate the creative psychic body. The key to therapy is not whether we elaborate so-called pre-Oedipal or Oedipal fantasy, but that we encourage our patients to choose, and this paradoxically means encouraging them to be open to contingent accidents, the fantasies that will enable them to move into their future. Choice, accidental discovery and movement of our destiny fantasies into conscious perception, destroy the past Oedipal romance and put in its place a new identification which can be realised within the vital forces of present life.

If we understand Freud's trauma theory in an immanent sense, then the traumatic event would be stored as a fixed consciousness and as part of our virtual past. It is not so much a question of whether this event is inside or outside representation, but whether or not it can be activated to move again between virtual fantasy and an embodied conscious perception. Hysteria and trauma mirror each other because in each there is a flight back into an unconscious and virtual world. However, there is also a fixation within a consciousness that repeats because it cannot access the imaginative psychic body. Division between conscious and unconscious worlds, as Jung tells us, keeps the patient flying back into the arms of infantile complexes.

Jung's theory of hysteria is phenomenological: he sees the hysteric's melodrama as a stage-managing of the past in order to evade the present. In

Freud's early 'Five Lectures', he is in agreement with Jung: hysteria is a melodrama that defends against time by rooting everything in a causal past. In *Studies of Hysteria*, Freud moves his emphasis to memories, but, as this argument has made clear, these memories are tied to the movement of the affectual psychic body; it is not primarily the question of representation which is at stake.

When this woman first came to see me, she told me that she was not sure whether I would be able to help; her pain was mainly physical. But as seeing me was cheap and convenient (I had agreed to a low cost fee, and she lived nearby) then she thought that maybe therapy would not take up too many resources.

Her current trauma was her myalgic encephalomyelitis (ME), which prevented her from working, or socialising very much. She talked about her physical pain as something I might not be able to understand, which would be difficult for her. On the other hand, if I understood too much that would also be bad.

I asked her why it would be so bad for me to understood her. She told me that her last body therapist and her mother also suffered from ME: 'It's vital you know how I feel, but if you do, then you are no use to me because you are also ill.'

I replied, 'Maybe I need to listen some more to how you feel, because that will give me some idea, even though I won't know exactly how it feels for you, I can try and understand some of it.'

She agreed but pointed out that she did not want me to jump to any conclusions. She was quite afraid that being a psychotherapist I might be prejudiced against lesbians and this was quite a worry.

Over the weeks this woman told me traumatic stories about abusive men in her life and about her ideal fantasies of relationship with women. Her mother suffered repeated psychotic breakdowns when she was a child, and she remembered either being alone or subject to her volatile tantrums. Hospitalisation, due to psychotic collapse, occurred when the woman's younger brother was born and the woman, then aged 3, was subsequently separated from her mother for some time. Mother and daughter made friends as the woman approached late adolescence and adulthood, and had both attended the same postgraduate course on feminism. The woman told me that whilst she and her mother were very close, she did not really like seeing her mother — it made her feel ill. She was only really happy with talking to her on the telephone. Her father, meanwhile, was a big disappointment. Loving her as a little girl, he had become a remote figure as she grew up, leaving her and her mother eventually for a new wife whom my client particularly disliked.

One of the things I quickly realised in listening to the woman was that any interpretations I offered that conflicted with her account of the facts was rejected in a summary fashion. Once I suggested that she felt very abandoned by her mother and she immediately grew furious with me. Another time when she was venting her anger on another aggressive patriarch, one of the managers of her part-time job, I suggested that maybe there was something about the aggressive power of these men that she wanted and identified with: 'Maybe there is something of these men in you?'

'You don't understand do you!' she replied. 'These men are repellent to me, they just want to objectify women – I want nothing to do with them!'

Although angry with men, she was much happier talking about her negative feelings about them and her anger with her father, than talking of her relationship with her mother, who was both a protected and phobic object. Mutuality summed up this mother–daughter relationship and from my perspective it was often hard to disentangle child from adult. This woman had non-sexual romances with feminine 'boys', romantic crushes on unavailable women and occasional sexually abusive encounters with adult men. In many ways the woman can be seen as a current version of Dora. Her refusal of adult sexual relationships was contrasted with her desire to live in an auto-erotic maternal world of transcendental innocence. Like Bollas's (2000) Dora, the woman refused the sexuality and separation that would break up her idealised bond with the mother; idealised, because in reality this bond with the mother had failed to exist.

We can see this woman's hysteria as a refusal of the paternal incest law and a consequent bisexual identification and rivalry with both parents. Or we can see it in Juliet Mitchell's (2000) account of sibling rivalry as the woman's displacement early on by the birth of her brother. The first classical account privileges heterosexuality and splits desire from identification, giving pathology to this woman's desire for other women. The second account of Mitchell's leaves symbolic Oedipal theory intact by attributing lateral rivalry to siblings. It thus ignores the principle of desire as mimetic identification, which, as Borch-Jacobsen (1988) has shown us, resides at the heart of the Oedipal Complex. Children desire their parents not primarily in a situation of triangular rivalry, but within an intense dyadic bond of competitive envy.

Freud, in his later texts, realised that the father was seen as dangerous because identification with him simply replicated the earlier bond with the primal mother. If the Oedipal Complex gives us an account of how children desire their parents and, in a phenomenological sense, want to become them, then identification with them can be passive, narcissistic, hysterical – in thrall to a virulent super-ego. Or identification can be active and embodied. Here, identifications move and recreate, transforming those virtual fantasies of the other into actual, actionable and affectual experiences in terms of the present and future. Envious displacement in terms of parents or siblings is not first and foremost about a desire to get the third party out of the way, be that the father or sibling. Desiring and wanting to be your parent inevitably brings in a conflict of love and hate with that mimetic figure because of the implicit rivalry in that dyadic relationship.

In *Hystories*, Elaine Showalter (1997) describes hysteria as a response to an impossible, traumatic situation: the powerless response by the Victorian hysteric, the war soldier, or the working-class male to his situation. For Mitchell (2000), this emphasis on powerlessness does not explain the physical symptoms of the hysteric – signifying unconscious conflicting wishes. But if we see hysteria as a mimetic identification – and the Oedipal Complex as hysterical mimesis – then physical symptoms are a result of passive identifications locked into a virtual world of past fantasy where affect is blocked. Because fantasy has retreated into past Oedipal romances, it is unable to connect with present reality. Affect becomes fixed and transmuted into physical symptoms because it cannot be mobilised in a present psychological relationship with reality. Hysterics perform the body, but remain psychologically disembodied. Their affectual relationships are stopped from moving forward in time.

Lacan understands that Freud's analysis of Dora misses her homosexual transference onto Frau K and he sees too that Frau K represents the mimetic, ideal other for Dora, the key to her sexuality. Dora has, in Lacan's words, to 'take on the assumption of her own body' or else fall back into the fragmentation of the imaginary mirror stage. Now for Lacan this is achieved through a sort of Hegelian dialectics where the analyst's symbolic function allows the patient integration within a universal discourse of the subject. Lacan writes: 'transference does not arrive from any mysterious property of affectivity' (Lacan 1985: 102). But what if it does? What if Dora's hysteria is precisely her inability to actively embody her sexual identification with Frau K: to transform her identifications into affectual desires in terms of a future becoming? Lacan criticises Freud for his paternal prejudice, one that 'falsifies' the Oedipal Complex, making it seem natural, rather than normative. But then Lacan goes right ahead and says that Dora's fundamental problem is the same for all women, namely 'accepting herself as an object of desire for the man' (Lacan 1985: 99). This is, according to Lacan, what motivates Dora's idolatry of Frau K and translates into her solution of identifying with the Madonna as a divine and transcendental object of desire.

What Freud and Lacan both miss in different ways is that Dora's problem is her mimetic desire in relation to her mother. As Mitchell (2000) discusses, Dora's mother constitutes a sexual problem for Dora because she suffers from gonorrhoea. Moreover, there is a danger that the mother has contracted her husband's syphilis. This would make Dora's mother not just sick but potentially mad. Mitchell notes that this was a standard revolving door between sexuality and sickness in the bourgeois, Victorian age and it raises dangerous identifications for Dora in relation to her mother. For Mitchell, the hysteric is noted for the lability of her desire. Non-resolution of her Oedipal Complex means that Dora is filled with bisexual desires and wants, for the mother and father. However, this emphasis on the lability of hysterical desire seems to miss the point that Bollas (2000) makes so eloquently, that the hysteric can't really desire because she has not been seduced into her future by the mother. The mother has to desire her daughter in order to lure her away from auto-erotic narcissism and into the eventual recognition of both parents as objects of sexual choice.

What Mitchell (2000) calls the lability of the hysteric's so-called desire is, I suggest, the hysteric's immersion in auto-erotic fantasies. The hysteric has to choose and select from these differing fantasies in order to move into a more actualised and embodied perception of reality. This movement is described by Henri Bergson (1912) as the creative flux of time and affectual being which flows from virtual memory to actual perception and life. Such active actualisation of fantasy is difficult for the hysteric who is stuck in a passive identification with the other – the mother. Hysterics can't access necessary active identification and desire if their mother does not actively desire them.

Now, Bollas (2000) makes the Oedipal era the moment of exchange where the hysteric exchanges narcissism for object love. But if we understand the Oedipal Complex as mimetic identification, then object love and narcissism (ego and object) are not distinct. And this makes the Oedipal Complex not primarily symbolic, but an arena of imaginary fantasy. The problem for hysterics is that they cannot actualise any of these fantasies. Hysterics live in a retreat, where fantasies abound, but none of them is creative because fantasies cannot be transformed into actual experience. In this sense the Oedipal Complex is hysterical. It cannot be resolved, but it can be recreated and left behind. To place the Oedipal Complex as a symbolic discourse or moment of exchange from ego to object love is to fix it in some kind of identity, heterosexual, normative. Alternatively, to see the Oedipal Complex as a bedrock of possible mimetic fantasy in relation to mother, father and siblings is to understand how we can regress to these familial fantasies again and again and then transform them into who we want to be. To call the mother pre-Oedipal and the father Oedipal is to symbolise a hierarchical notion of gender relations which might have been prevalent in Freud's time, but is becoming far less certain as the norm these days. To argue, on the other hand, for the Oedipal Complex as an imaginary matrix, which we can return to again and again, as a mimetic gallery of identificatory loves for each parent, allows us to be mobile in our object choices. Not in the negative sense that Mitchell (2000) attributes to the hysteric's labile bisexuality, but in the sense of our desires as plural and changeable over time. The importance of Dora's meditation and ideal fantasies of the Madonna is that the Madonna represents a safe fantasy of who Dora can become, uncontaminated by sexual disease and madness. True, this fantasy is an auto-erotic, narcissistic fantasy of a transcendental pure relation to the mother. But if Freud had worked with it, acknowledging his role as mother as well as father in the transference, then maybe this ideal fantasy would have taken on a more embodied and affectual life within the therapy. Maybe it would have been transformed into a more real experience for Dora, moving her towards a future destiny.

The woman in therapy with me had experienced a mad mother and like Dora the terror of identifying with her mother and becoming her sexual other was a very real fear of going mad. Her Oedipal fantasies around her father when she was young were ideal, and yet they simply seemed a repeat of the ideal fantasies with which she chose to represent her mother. There was nothing symbolic about this woman's Oedipal relationship with her father: he was an escape from her mad mothering when she was little and became, as the older detached man she remembered, a safe repository for all the hatred she could not feel about her mother. The fantasy/memories of the mother consisted of vague impressions of a frightening, volatile woman. She had been too unsafe to identify with. I was interested in what fantasy meant for this woman in a phenomenological sense, where it put her in relation to time, and what it said about her symbolic sense of sexuality. What identities, in other words, it helped her to create.

Fantasy for this woman in the beginning was either threatening – what men did to objectify and dehumanise women – or it was a kind of nightmare world she often inhabited instead of sleep where fantasies seemed too present, more like hallucinations, and she would look on at herself as if she was on screen or stage. Fantasy was hard and hard to talk about for this woman because she could not envisage it belonging to her. My sense was that she inhabited an imaginary, split world at these times, where consciousness was absent, and fantasy subsequently became persecutory as there was no active perception with which to make it real or embodied.

Naming sexual fantasies – sharing them with me in the therapy space and free-associating – was very difficult for this woman. I wondered with her at one point whether she was frightened of acknowledging these sexual fantasies to me. She replied:

> I don't really know what fantasy is. At least what a fantasy would be like for me – a nice fantasy. Fantasy for me is being aggressively objectified by men. It's about what men do and want to do with my body. I have no idea what a sexual fantasy, that I could want, would be.

The woman brought an image or memory which had haunted her throughout her life.

> I remember my teddy bear which I absolutely loved and then when I was about 3 or 4, it got put in the washing machine and shredded. I told my parents later on how upset I had been. But they just got cross and accused me of making it up. They said I had asked them to throw the teddy bear away and to buy me a new one.

'Maybe it's important for children to create the world, rather than just discover it,' I said.

'What do you mean?'

'Well, your fantasy of your teddy bear and what you felt about it, got ruled out by your parents' tell the truth stance.'

This woman's sexuality was very much a performance put on to show and seduce, but underneath she was still the innocent child who shied away from adult sexual relationships. Her close male relationships were either with men, who in her words were 'sexually abusive' and 'bullies', or with quite young seeming brother figures, feminised and forever boys, like the boys who don't grow up in Peter Pan. These boyfriends were the closest relationships this woman seemed to have, they were easygoing and fluid and reflected the close bond she still felt for her younger brother, who was always known as 'Bro'. But as we talked about her closer relationships with her boyfriends as brothers, the woman became confused, because it blurred her ideal women/bad men split.

Maybe this woman's hysteria was (as Mitchell (2000) tells us) initiated by sibling rivalry and the cruel displacement of a younger brother's birth, although for this woman the relationship with her brother seemed to be her only experience of shared intimacy as she grew up. The feminine boys this woman went out with were not proper sexual relationships: normally they just cuddled; the abusive men she seemed to find were a projection of her dangerous hatred towards her mother.

At one point the woman started to talk about her bisexuality and her ambivalence about being heterosexual. She was kind of sorry her new 'girly' boyfriend Paul was a 'boy' because she had been kind of hoping to go out with a girl. Paul was a particularly ideal partner because he turned up for a nice time and then disappeared back to Cambridge. She called him her 'holiday romance'.

Vivid fantasies that appeared when this woman started to own them for herself were of ideal women, present-day Madonna figures who were mimetic identifications of this woman's auto-erotic narcissism. These ideal women represented the spiritual sacrifice of the body. Bollas (2000) describes this as the passionate and painful soul of the hysteric. The woman's pleasure within these transcendental fantasies was her masochistic eradication of the other's carnality. In other words she hysterically attached to an ideal maternal picture, an ideal which operated as a defence against the experience of her mother as dead and unavailable.

The fantasies or reminiscences this woman brought were romances around women whom she met in her female spirituality group, the unemployed centre, and the peace centre in which she worked. In the spirituality group she became attracted to an older woman, River-Dance, whom she associated with American-Indian mythology. Pagan religion and white witchcraft were central to this woman's beliefs and as we discussed these fantasies, the woman began to talk about her fear of sexuality in relation to her own body. Sex was fine in the sense of making this woman feel close to her partner but the physicality of genital sex was both repulsive and frightening. Where the body was eradicated in fantasies around sex, it became more forcefully present in the woman's sick body and she would come to sessions bent double from the pain of her ME, a pain she assured me I was powerless to help:

'I don't know why I come to therapy. My ME has nothing to do with my mind. It's purely in my body.'

Luce Irigaray (1985, 1991b) critiques Lacan's (1977) tripartite structure of the symbolic, imaginary and real by arguing that he Oedipally separates the orders of the symbolic and imaginary, making them oppositional. Consequently, he splits off language and symbolic identity from the real of the maternal body. In Irigaray's view therapy must open up the hysterical woman's imaginary to a creative real of the maternal and psychic body.

As the therapy progressed, this woman carried around these three registers of the symbolic, imaginary and real as three separate, dissociated states: a spiritual idea of the Madonna; the pain of her real sick body and an imaginary world of unacknowledged aggression and fear towards her mad mother. Of course Lacan would criticise this assessment. He defined Dora's idolatry in front of the Madonna as Christianity, a pre-Oedipal and therefore imaginary, transcendental solution. But, as Irigaray's critique of the Lacanian phallus makes so clear, for the woman in society, or the female hysteric in therapy, there is no difference between pre-Oedipal and Oedipal registers for the woman. In both she is divided between abject maternal madness and the sacrificial transcendent, Madonna. The phallic Oedipal economy that Lacan espouses is nothing other than a male imaginary made law. Irigaray's solution is a mimetic, two-way mirror that will enable the woman and the hysteric to connect transcendental and carnal polarities.

The Madonna figures that my female client imagined were imaginary, but they also became fantasies in the sessions that became increasingly bound up with the pain of her ME and a growing desire to explore her sexuality in a more bodily way. The woman started to become very interested in the physical side of lesbian sex. She sent off for lesbian pornography, and started to fantasise about opening a women's sex shop. She decided to have a symbolic fertility symbol tattooed just above her pubic bone. Great preparation went into having this done, and the woman designed the symbol and the colours, bringing them to therapy in eager anticipation.

'This tattoo is about grounding my sexuality in my body. It's a "sexual initiation",' she said. It seemed very apt that this ritual should involve painful suffering and the woman described the ceremony, which one female friend attended, in rich detail. It seemed important that I did not disapprove of the tattoo or find it repulsive. At one point I said:

'Perhaps you fear I find it repulsive like your mother would. Her disgust makes it impossible for you to embody your sexuality.'

The woman responded by discussing how her mother's illness was due in part to a bullying grandmother, now dead, whom the woman had feared and hated. I wondered what connection she thought this had to her interest in seeking a female genealogy with her spirituality group. She replied that she felt severed from her female line or genealogy, because of the destructive relationship between her mother and grandmother. The spirituality group helped her to recreate this female line.

The hysteric's sexuality and seduction is an eroticisation of the dead, unavailable mother or parent. Because the hysteric cannot properly hate or mourn the mother, she keeps turning up as new lovers. Sexual relationships for this woman were either short-lived abusive relationships with men, or romantic dalliances with feminine boys. The woman would move very quickly from feeling exuberant and full of power to feeling extremely empty and depleted.

Eventually she entered into a sexual relationship with an older woman. This relationship characteristically did not last long. The new girlfriend was a 40-year-old single parent to several children from different fathers, who lost interest as soon as the children left babyhood. At this time the girlfriend had a new baby whom she played with constantly, oblivious to the chaos of her surroundings and the older children, who were left to fend for themselves. My client entered the scene as a lover, but soon began to feel like the jealous, displaced daughter. Eventually, she got angry and made a decision to leave the relationship.

After this there was a significant change in the therapy. The woman managed to get really angry with her mother and the therapy became not just an altar to bring the pain of her ME, but a more shared place to cry for what she had missed. One day she said: 'I have been having fantasies about having a child, a girl. I've also been having fantasies about my mum dying. I don't think I really want a baby, but I like having the fantasy.'

'Maybe it's a fantasy about who you are going to become?'

'Yes, the thought of having a child makes me able to imagine my mother's death, and that makes me feel more hopeful about the future.'

The therapist's function is not, as Lacan and Freud seemed to think, a disembodied, phallic law. If analysts set themselves up as this implacable law, then they become all-powerful and are just as likely to carry on producing the hysteric in her masochism, rather than move towards a cure. An implicit function of my role as therapist with the woman described was not to collude with being the all-knowing father or the ideal mother in the transference. Neither was my role as an absent so-called symbolic phallic function. The most important thing was to be interested, have desire, in my client's ideals, whilst never losing sight of their hidden aggression. For sure, the Madonna fantasies were a defence, but they were also the beginnings of a more embodied desire that carried this woman's future.

Chapter 2

Time, affect and the unconscious

What does it mean to understand psychoanalysis and the unconscious in terms of different ideas of temporality? How can we think of the unconscious in terms of a positive and creative attention to life, rather than in Freud's more positivist moments as a negation?

Phenomenology and immanence

Phenomenology and psychoanalysis have historically occupied very different territories, with sociological methods of interpreting reality, indebted to the transcendental phenomenology of Husserl (1964), set in opposition to psychoanalytic interpretations, of an unconscious, empirically unverifiable psychic world. However, psychoanalysis and phenomenology have historically been brought together under existential phenomenology, a psychology influenced principally by Husserl's assistant Martin Heidegger (1967). R. D. Laing (1960) is probably the most famous psychoanalytic thinker who based his work on the existential phenomenology of Sartre (1958) and Merleau Ponty (1962). The early work of Ludwig Binswanger (1963) takes up Heidegger's notion of *Dasein* to argue for the unconscious as part of our thrownness or existential being in the world. In a similar vein Sartre criticises the Freudian unconscious for bad faith. By splitting the psyche into ego and id, Freud produces the idea of a lie without a liar. Psychoanalysis replaces 'the duality of the deceiver and the deceived, the essential condition of the lie, by that of the "id" and the "ego"' (Sartre 1958: 74). This infinite splitting of the subject posits an unconscious self that determines consciousness but is inaccessible to it.

Much of the history of traditional phenomenology is then devoted to understanding the intentional and hermeneutic ways we are conscious of our being. Heidegger's (1967) concept of *Dasein* or dwelling is equally important for understanding our consciousness as a lived being in the world, a consciousness that is interpersonal and contextualises the lived body within place and community. R. D. Laing is perhaps the most famous psychoanalyst to utilise phenomenological ideas. Laing (1961) was very critical of Freudian meta-psychology that divided the internal mind from external physical reality. Laing states reasonably that individuals might experience themselves as split, as having a mind with internal contents, and a body that is outside the mind, but that belief should not be taken as the grounding conceptual basis of psychoanalytical theory (Laing 1961: 24). Phenomenology is an important philosophy with which to contextualise psychoanalysis. It reminds us that the unconscious exists between people and foregrounds the importance of the intersubjective relationship between people and between the person and his or her world.

However, we can also understand psychoanalysis in terms of a radical immanence of living affect. This immanence of the body can be traced in an alternative philosophical tradition that runs through Spinoza, Nietzsche, Bergson and William James. Whereas traditional phenomenology emphasises the intentional consciousness of the subject and the directness of experience towards the world, the more alternative tradition focuses on the affectual vitality of the body as multiplicities and forces. This tradition, also known as vitalist philosophy, has then often been understood as a critique of traditional phenomenology and its delineation of subject and object. Deleuze (1988b), who traces this tradition of difference and affect back to David Hume, calls it a transcendental empiricism because, instead of emphasising experience as integral to a human being or subject, transcendental experience is an immanence that extends beyond what we can as individuals know.

Bergson's idea of the movement of time is essential to this understanding. Rather than the conscious relation of the subject to the world of object, Bergson argues for being as time, which is a constant flux of creativity, difference and becoming. Instead of the conscious subject are the virtual tendencies of being, body and memory captured by the image. Perception subtracts from this immanent whole of matter, selecting what is needed for action. Memory, as Bergson says, is like a constant mirror image in the background and we subtract from it, actualising the real through perception. This subtractive attention is an attention to life and demands a tension, which when missing leads to hysteria, mental illness and false recognition. Here, Bergson's ideas are very close to those of Pierre Janet. Janet (1920) describes how the hysteric's lack of psychological energy or tension leads to a narrowing or lessening of consciousness. We can also see how Nietzsche's (1967b) idea – that we are an amalgamation of powerful life forces and affects – fits with Bergson's (1912) notion of virtual tendencies.

So, the difference between Bergson's radical or transcendental empiricism and phenomenology is that philosophers of the latter, like Sartre, see subjectivity as always belonging to us: consciousness is intentional and constructs time in relation to the object or world. For Bergson, however, time is not ours, it is always other. Subjectivity is, therefore, virtual. We can understand this by seeing matter as an aggregate of images. In perception we subtract from these images to get consciousness. But this means that psychologically existence cannot be reduced to consciousness. What exists also lies outside consciousness and therefore unconscious psychical states are images which exist but are inactive. This is then a non-psychological unconscious, the virtual is ontological not psychological. In his first book *Time and Free Will* (1889) Bergson conceptualises duration as a subjective or psychological multiplicity; external reality is simply space. But in *Matter and Memory* (1912) and his later works, Bergson argues that duration is extended to external things and is indeed immanent to the universe. So there is not an internal and external for Bergson, because we always leap from the subjective to the ontological: all we have is the difference between images. Duration belongs to things as much as to subjective consciousness and so we might think we are the subjective centre, and that all objects are simply projections, but according to Bergson external matter endures. Time and life is not our subjective centre, it is always other – objects as images have a life of their own.

Now we might think that this move away from the psychological in Bergson's thinking makes it irrelevant for psychoanalysis. After all, what is psychoanalysis if it is not our subjective and psychological lives determined by family personal relationships and Oedipus? To say we are always other is, as Deleuze and Guattari (1984) note, to make desire transpersonal; we move from subjective consciousness to the notion that we are so many objects and images amongst many. This is their idea of being in the world as a machine, which is precisely the schizophrenic dilemma. However, as I will argue in Chapter 6, the schizophrenic is actually cut off from flows of lived time because he or she is unable to move between a subjective real sense of perception and a fantasy world of virtual others. We get our psychic sense of being real from actualising our relationship with others. We take away from a world landscape of possibility and cut out from that who we want to become. So, movement between real and imaginary worlds is not some ultimate variety of being 'virtually' anything, which is actually a psychotic dilemma, but the ability to choose and select from the virtual universe, our creative differences between self and other.

Henri Bergson

I will argue that Bergson's philosophy can add to psychoanalysis precisely because it gives us an understanding of our psychic world as a creative multiplicity of duration. To say that we are always other means that we are always in motion between our real and imaginary flows of being. The other is always self, and self is always other. The other is, therefore, always another self we can be and as such it is potentially real, whether that is the unconscious others we have yet to meet within ourselves, or the images and objects that exist externally to us and have yet to come into view.

Psychoanalysis, I would argue, is not a purely personal or familial narrative. Children don't just discover their parents as they grow up, they also learn to become who they are in relation to social and physical objects in the world. Schizophrenics, as Laing (1961) notes, can neither exist within the family nor leave, and it is perhaps the understanding of how we need to belong in families and leave them that links psychoanalysis to Bergson's notion that time endures within ourselves and beyond ourselves – in the world of objects.

Bergson sees the world as dualistic, made up of two opposing tendencies, the life force or *élan vital* and the resistance of the world against that force. People know matter through their intellect, with which they measure the world. They formulate scientific laws where things are abstracted and distinguished as separate units within space. Intuition is opposite to intellect and derives from animal instinct; it is derivative of the life force that structures all becoming. Intuition, therefore, perceives time as duration, a time directed towards life rather than being divided and measured. Duration is memory but it is the movement of virtual memory into actual perception that marks this duration as a constant becoming. So, although there is dualism between matter and memory, perception and recollection, past and present, these are experienced only as a moment before they reform the monism or whole. In other words, pure memory is a virtual past that is continually being translated and actualised within the present. The virtual is real but can exist, or live, only through transformation into the perception image.

Experience is then determined by a composite of the two tendencies of memory and perception and these tendencies are heterogeneous – they coexist. So this is not a representational model: we don't arrive at the past from a present extension or representation. Instead we jump into the virtual past and, as we focus on it, the virtual memory pushes up the memory until we can actualise it through perception. Memory has to be actualised and transformed for us to experience it; however, we don't really ever leave the past, rather the past, as duration and time, is continuously translated as movement into the present. This coexistence of memory and perception is understood by Bergson to mean that matter is an aggregate of images. There is continuity between consciousness, matter and time and all these things are indistinguishable from the image. Matter is perceived as an image and so is the mind or brain.

The image is halfway between being a representation and a thing and this means we experience the world and the object in a pictorial way. We approach the creative duration of time through an intuition that can embrace the heterogeneous movement of memory and perception, rather than intelligence that focuses on an abstract extension within space. Actual perception is then always arrived at from memory or the virtual. Experience is a constant re-creation of the present in terms of the past. In Bergson's work the unconscious is not the negative of consciousness and being. Rather, it is the seat of affectual being and creative life, what Bergson calls the *élan vital*. Traditional phenomenology privileges consciousness; the unconscious is peripheral to our senses. But for Bergson, it is the unconscious that takes precedence, as an immanent body of memory and the flow of time. Intuition is then Bergson's method of experiencing this duration or flow of time and it can help us to enlarge our consciousness of the unconscious.

For Nietzsche, the unconscious is also positive. Nietzsche's philosophy, a forerunner to so much of psychoanalysis, imagines life as immanent and as a power or force that is forgetful of itself. This immanence that characterises the unconscious is self-enclosed and therefore rejects the reflective movement of thought and representation. We can see this immanent world as a world where suffering and joy, life and death are merely parts of the whole: of our living being. Forgetting, then, is in Michel Henry's words,

> the 'preserve of psychic order'; that is, the thing that edifices from within, delimiting and conserving psyche's essence, the dimension of origin incompatible with all consciousness, where being becomes essentially life.
>
> (Henry 1993: 212)

Rejecting a morality based on a universal, observable world, Nietzsche (1966, 1967a) argued for a morality in which human beings impose their own moral values: individuals who have the power and courage to accept the meaninglessness of the world, to manipulate and overcome it. So, for Nietzsche the masters of the world are the ones who can see the illusion of morality, its contingency, but can also seek to impose their own morality or world meaning through power. Nietzsche's morality is then in a sense the freedom to choose based on an awareness of one's power of life and desire. Thus, it is not so very different from Sartre's (1958) notion of bad faith in the sense that both men propose the freedom of the individual. Existential phenomenology, however, proposes a conscious being in the world that has to differentiate and relate to others, a being which has to interpret and represent the world. Nietzsche would argue that the pinnacle of freedom is the assertion of your affective power. For Nietzsche, like Bergson, actualisation of history means becoming aware of the transformative power of time. Now, in Nietzsche's view, actualisation of life means a radical forgetting, but we can see also for Bergson that there has to be a forgetting in the changing attention we direct, when switching between virtual memory and perception. So, another way to think this forgetting is to understand it as dissociation. In Bergson's duration of time, the movement and becoming of multiplicity is dependent on dissociation and reassociation. In other words we move from perception to virtual memory and back again in actualising our life force. We forget or disassociate in order to move in time. A living corporeal memory is dependent on this creative movement.

This understanding of dissociation as a way of switching between different multiple states of duration is also why hypnosis works as part of the therapeutic cure. Hypnosis enables us to move between different durations or tendencies when they have become fixed, as in the case of hysteria. If, as Bergson suggests, our psyche is made up of multiple durations in movement between virtual and actual, then in the hysteric we can see how the movement between different temporalities has become blocked. In the late 19th century the notion of a double or secondary consciousness was theorised by Pierre Janet (1919) to account for how the hysteric would occupy different split-off 'selves'. He demonstrated the split consciousness of his subject Lucie through an experiment using hypnotism. Under hypnosis Janet spoke to Lucie's subconscious self, suggesting she could see certain things. Accordingly, her 'normal' self went blind. Janet's cure was then suggesting to the subconscious Lucie that she give up her sight so that it could be restored to her normal senses. This experiment showed not only how hypnosis heals but also how hysterics occupy a narrow field of attention. Whilst Lucie was engrossed talking to a third party, Janet would come up behind her and give her suggestions to move her hand, etc., which she would obey but be totally unaware of. Discussing this case history, William James (1901) suggests that we can see evidence of how consciousness is selective in less extreme circumstances. He gives examples of the mother who sleeps through everything but awakens to her baby's cries, or our ability to wake at a chosen hour in the morning without an alarm (James 1901: 131).

Misrecognition and the double

Bergson's understanding of the hysteric's dilemma is summed up in an important essay, 'Memory of the Present and False Recognition' (1908). False recognition is a weakened attention to life and it manifests itself in varying degrees between the healthy and mentally ill. In false recognition the conscious will (which in health pushes the person to an actualisation of his or her virtual memory) is slackened. The person becomes too self-aware of two temporalities which are split between memory and perception. Bergson understands this by saying that we all have a dream state that is a substratum of our conscious mind. But our dream world is nothing fantastic and is in a sense easier to explain than consciousness. In our dream world we remember and we perceive, without as Bergson says 'any recourse to life' (Bergson 1908b: 143). These two streams of remembering and perception are distinct: perception points towards the future and memory towards the past. For Bergson, memory gets created along with perception. Unconscious memory can suggest a sensation but it is perception that by springing forward into reality will actualise this sensation and bring it into a forceful being. False recognition is when we turn away from our will, our conscious perception and its selective attention to life, in such a manner as to reveal these two streams of temporality.

Bergson describes the relation between memory and perception as a kind of moving mirror stage. He writes: 'memory seems to be to the perception what the image reflected in the mirror is to the object in front of it' (Bergson 1908b: 147). The object is our actual duration within time but it is continually followed around by its double of virtual memory. Every moment of life is split between actual perception and virtual memory, but this moment of life is not simply captured by perception projected forward. This projection would be an abstraction were it not for the 'moving mirror which continually reflects perception as memory' (Bergson 1908b: 147). In health we are not aware of this uncanny double, although we might catch it at rare moments.

Describing this temporal double in relation to the watching of a play, Bergson discusses how in normal recognition we might see a play we have seen before and because we are sitting in a different seat or with different people it is familiar but distinct. Of course for Bergson, the past is only captured through present perception and so in normal recognition we have an awareness of having been in this situation before, but we are concentrated on the present and the past seems dim and shadowy in comparison. However, in false recognition we are too self-reflexive; we are aware of the present situation and our virtual mirror image of being. So we are split between being the person on stage and watching ourselves act. This double reality is an uncanny memory of the present. As Bergson says,

> It would appear as memory, since memory bears a distinctive mark, different from that of perception; but it could not be carried back to any past experience, because each of us knows indeed that we do not live twice through one and the same moment of our history.
>
> (Bergson 1908b: 151–152)

Normally, our double temporality is concealed. In conscious health there is an intermingling of states which coincide, so we are unaware of their differences. We select from virtual memory what we need to project through perception into reality. In mental illness and hysteria this will or penetration into life is missing; the person is haunted by a sense of being split and doubled. Bergson suggests that in this doubling the one watching, the spectator, is free, whereas the self being watched is an automaton and is felt to be lifeless and playing a part.

False recognition is thus a self-reflective awareness of our two temporalities, memory and perception, which in health intermingle and consequently we are unaware of their separate status. Self-reflection, here, is like a withdrawal into a dream state. In dreams we have an uncanny experience of being both the player who experiences the dream and the one that stages it and watches. We can see how this false recognition of dream-like self-reflexivity is heightened in psychotic illness. Although false recognition is a 'defect in will' and an inattention to life, for Bergson it can happen in a benign way where the inattention is momentary or in more prolonged severe states where mental illness is manifest. For him the more benign form of false recognition, as a momentary flight from reality, can protect us from the severe and prolonged absence manifest in mental illness. Bergson does not call false recognition 'dissociation', because for him dissociation is healthy; it is the way we subtract from the whole and move between our different temporal streams of fantasy and reality. But I suggest that we can call false recognition a defensive dissociated state where the force of one's conscious will and desire is paralysed. In this uncanny, virtual state we represent our reality rather than live it, and these representations that are fixated flows of time and affect become solidified as symptoms. So, as Bergson says, we live the haunted life of the double.

We also become fixated within our perceptual consciousness. This is not something that Bergson actually notes in relation to false recognition, which appears only when consciousness disappears. However, if the multiplicity and duration of time is dependent on memory and perception intermingling, then in hysteria we can say that we regress to an unconscious absence, but we also inhabit a hyper-conscious reflexivity where certain representations become rigid and solidified. The hysteric is thus lost in dissociative fantasy and rigidly fixed within certain conscious representations. In this split world fantasy and reality cannot transform each other or enter into lived time.

The unconscious as representation or affect?

Freud's thinking can be divided into two psychoanalytic models. In the first Cartesian model, the unconscious is repressed recollection and meaning. In the second the unconscious is a memory that has never been conscious; it cannot be remembered, only repeated. It is this second model that concurs with Bergson's idea of memory as a lived psychic time of the body. This is a virtual or unconscious memory that brings perception and sensation into being through suggestion. Alongside every perception there is a memory that accompanies and doubles it. The paradox that occurs in false recognition is that this awareness of the double acts as a brake to the suggestive power of the unconscious. Instead of a flow between virtual and actual where the real is constantly being brought into being, through the suggestive power of imaginative fantasy, we have two lifeless poles. On the one hand a fantasy world which substitutes for a dreaming, real life, and on the other neurotic representations where the flows of time and affect have become cut off from psychic existence and become solidified in consciousness as symptoms.

Bergson sees the unconscious as a reservoir of potential and creative tendencies whose virtual reality is psychologically embodied through a much smaller and selective consciousness. In health our psychic life of temporal flows moves in a multiplicity where the real is always becoming, suggested by a virtual double. This double ego was in fact the first model of the mind associated with hypnotism in early psychiatry. Bergson experimented extensively with hypnotism, and came to see the artistic world as something that is suggested to us. Of course, it was not just art that works suggestively on us. We can see from Bergson's account how the whole of our conscious and unconscious worlds operate in a suggestive manner.

Gilles Deleuze (1988a) describes how Bergson's concept of the unconscious is different from Freud's. Whereas for Freud the unconscious contains a psychological reality outside consciousness, Bergson means 'a non-psychological reality – being as it is in itself. Strictly speaking, the psychological is the present. Only the present is "psychological"; but the past is pure ontology; pure recollection has only ontological significance' (Deleuze 1988a: 56). However, if we take Freud's second meaning of the unconscious, as a body of memories and forces which have not yet become conscious, then the unconscious in relation to both Freud and Bergson becomes an immanent force.[1]

In Bergson's thinking the unconscious loses its position as a binary negativity and opposition to the conscious world, a negativity that Freud in his meta-psychological framework insisted on. For Bergson we take a leap into ontological being, which is our virtual past, or we could call it being in itself; in doing so we leave the realm of psychology and the present altogether. Only when this jump into being has been made, will recollection or memory take on a psychological significance as we pass from virtual to actual states. The paradox of Bergsonian time is that the past is contemporary with the present it has been. As Deleuze points out, the image retains something of the virtual memory where we have searched for it, but it does not 'actualise this recollection without adapting it to the requirements of the present' (Deleuze 1988a: 58). We are used to thinking of emotion as being dependent on a representation, but in Bergson's model emotion is like music. It is an essence that precedes objects and representation, generating new ideas. Emotion, like music, transcends the individual and we are introduced to it as it is created and suggested. William James (1901) sums up emotion when he discusses how it is never remembered; it is something searched for in memory and then with the image comes an actualisation of that emotion, as it is produced, always new and always in difference – Bergson's *élan vital*.

Bergson's ideas on the unconscious connect with those of Nietzsche and James but they are also very close to those of Pierre Janet. Janet was a close colleague of Bergson's and their respective psychological and philosophical theories of the unconscious were each very influenced by the other's. Both men experimented with hypnotism and theorised the unconscious as a mimetic simulation. They also both saw dissociation of the personality arising from a disturbance in the sensori-motor system, a disturbance that weakened psychological tension and destroyed the psyche's equilibrium. Hysteria, for both men, but especially for Janet, was seen in terms of the lessening of psychological tension, or attention to life. Janet was a pupil of Charcot and worked in Paris at the Salpêtrière. He conceptualised hysteria as an illness of fixed ideas and his thinking greatly influenced Carl Jung. Hysteria was psychological in Janet's view; it was a disturbance of consciousness, rather than an abnormality of reflexes, but Janet still adhered to Charcot's neurophysiology by arguing that sufferers were most likely to be individuals with an accompanying degeneracy of the nervous system.

In 1907 Janet published his lectures on hysteria and listed the major symptoms as somnambulism, multiple personalities, fugues, convulsions, paralyses, disturbances of vision, speech and difficulties with digestion and respiration (Janet 1920). Janet and Bergson saw reality as stemming from an awareness of the body movements in response to stimuli. When the correspondence between sensation and movement became weakened or tangled then the sense of reality also began to disappear. Mimesis, dissociation and suggestion were then fundamental to this hypnotic and creative unconscious that was both physiological or affectual and psychological. When split off from an attention to life, this unconscious resurrected itself in the double personalities so reminiscent of the hysteric. In contrast to Freud, Bergson's notion of the unconscious was positive. Dissociation and hysterical doubling occur when conscious perception of the world is weakened and a dwelling in a past virtual world of fantasy diminishes an attention to life. Affects in this double mimesis are not psychologically embodied or actualised as the *élan vital*. They cannot therefore be accessible for action in the world.

What does this mean for an affect not to be embodied? In Bergson's (1912) thinking affects and sensations emerge as part of perception and lived experience. Memory and sensation are different not in degree but in kind. Sensations occupy the body, but memory 'interests no part of my body' until 'it begets sensations as it materialises' (Bergson 1912: 179). Affects for Bergson are part of our active present, whereas the virtual world of being or the unconscious is within experience but inactive psychically or what Bergson calls 'ineffective': a world of unperceived objects. In his 1915 paper on the unconscious Freud talks about the impossibility of affects being repressed. We might make the mistake in therapy of talking about unconscious love and hate etc., but it is actually only ideas or representations that can be repressed. It might be, Freud reflects, that we perceive an emotion that has been misconstrued because its proper representation has become repressed and it therefore attaches itself to another idea. In other words, affects become dissociated. Freud writes:

> Although the affect was never unconscious its ideational presentation had undergone repression . . . there are no unconscious affects in the sense in which there are unconscious ideas. But there may very well be in the system Ucs affect-formations which, like others, come into consciousness. The whole difference arises from the fact that ideas are cathexes – ultimately of memory traces – whilst affects and emotions correspond with processes of discharge, the final expression of which is perceived as feeling.
>
> (Freud 1915b: 110–111)

We can see here that Freud's analysis concurs with Bergson's notion that whereas memory can be unconscious, affects and sensations either exist or they don't. However, in an essay in the same year, on repression, Freud (1915a) does suggest that there is a transformation of the affect into anxiety. If for example there is a libidinal wish and hatred of the father, then this conflict can be repressed and the father is substituted for by the image of an animal. Freud gives the example of the phobia of a wolf, reminiscent of his famous case history on the Wolf Man. But repression can also lead to the anxiety neurosis in conversion-hysteria. Freud writes:

> Here the salient point is that it is possible to bring about a total disappearance of the charge of the affect. The patient then displays towards his symptoms what Charcot called 'la belle indifférence des hystériques'.
>
> (Freud 1915a: 94)

At other times this suppression is not so completely successful; a part of the sensations of distress 'attach to the symptoms themselves' (Freud 1915a: 94). Freud goes on to say that the fate of affect is far more important than ideational content when it comes to repression, because the aim of repression is an 'avoidance of pain' (Freud 1915a: 94). If the modification and expression of affect is indeed the most important thing to address in relation to repression, remembering that affects are never repressed and can only be split off or dissociated, then how are we to understand the nature of the unconscious?

What does it mean to understand the unconscious in terms of phenomenological affect rather than in terms of representation? Michel Henry (1993) has read the genealogy of psychoanalysis as one of radical phenomenology and affect. Tracing Freudian thought back through the philosophy of Schopenhauer and Nietzsche, Henry argues that the psychical unconscious was taught in varying schools in the nineteenth century a long time before Freud and Bergson discovered it in their respective work. Freudian thought, in his view, belongs neither to the body of science nor the metaphysics of representation to which it has historically been attached (Henry 1993: 8). If we look at Freud's understanding of neurobiology, we see it underpins the representative drives; an energy that is apparent in his early scientific project of 1895 and his late papers on anxiety and the life and death drives.

What does it mean, though, to split the meaning of the unconscious into biological energy or its manifest representation? Henry emphasises the physical energy of the unconscious, an energy that can only be known qualitatively as affects and our experience of them. The roots of our subjective being and our unconscious are found not in representation but in affectual being and life forces. To follow such an unconscious back simply to the history of human individuality and childhood is therefore erroneous. Explaining love in adult life, through love of the mother is, Henry points out, to explain love by love. It does not tell us anything about this particular ontological or affectual being in the world. Henry writes:

> The father makes the idea of god clear only to those who have not understood that in these two figures the same ontological structure represents itself, *precisely life's essence, since it never ceases to feel itself and thus to experience itself as that whose foundation never is.* The situation of the birth trauma explains anxiety only from a being originally constituted as affective and susceptible of being affectively determined.
>
> (Henry 1993: 8, original emphasis)

To explain our affectual relation to the world and to others cannot be done by simple reference to the past: we have to understand the nature of our affectual being as it repeats in our past and present; not as some mythology or metaphysics of representation, but as the 'secret ground that we are, which is life' (Henry 1993: 9). This is true, although I think there is a problem with defining the unconscious as simply affect, as opposed to representation, because this prevents us from considering the unconscious status of ideas and images. And perhaps this is also where we have to differentiate the unconscious from the subconscious mind. Henry and Bergson both agree that affects repeat in the present. For Bergson, the unconscious is virtual being or matter – the arena of unperceived objects or things. It is the actualisation of the virtual or of memory that defines the becoming of life. Like Bergson, Henry also sees the unconscious as some virtual zero point; there is no such thing as the unconscious as such. All we have is a radical self-immanence of the body and life. I suggest that this is also true of Freud, for whom the unconscious is really only a limit; it is not knowable as such. So really when Freud talks about unconscious representations he is talking about the subconscious mind. Affects exist or they don't, although they can become displaced. Representations or ideas are a world that is visible, but can easily become invisible.

We have to accept the paradox, as Freud seemed to, that the unconscious refers to the world of representation and the world of affect. We can do this if we understand the unconscious to be a virtual limit that is not knowable. This means we can talk about the unconscious world, bearing in mind that it is virtual. There are conscious and subconscious representations, but there is no absolute dualism or negativity between conscious and unconscious. Henry argues that the forces and powers of affectual life are a different system from representation and are not capable of being repressed or represented. Repressed libido in Henry's view is 'libido whose self-experiencing has been taken to an extreme, to the point of being insupportable, to the degree of suffering at which, no longer able to support itself, it tries to flee and escape itself'. Quoting Freud, Henry suggests that repression is simply the 'damming up of libido over any great length of time' (Henry 1993: 313). Suffering and death are not the opposite of pleasure; they are not beyond the pleasure principle. Instead, they are exactly what constitutes and lies at the heart of life. What is most unbearable leads us back to what is most delightful.

As Freud points out, when libido is unemployed, it becomes anxiety. In Henry's terms this anxiety is the self's impossibility of being able to escape itself and its own self-immanence. Therapy is not a matter of recollecting or finding the repressed meanings, or ideations that have been buried, from consciousness; it is not a question of reflective intellect. François Roustang (1993) explains in relation to Henry's work how the key to psychoanalytic therapy is to confront the affectual forces that lie between patient and analyst. Abreaction of affect is therefore central to recovery, the uncovering of the deep passions in the transference so they can be modified. Language, Roustang tells us, is significant only in that it conveys the necessary affect; it is the vehicle through which affect travels. The aim in therapy, through the transference, is to uncover the 'primitive or animal speech' of the client and this is done through the analyst being not real but an object of transference. To begin with, in analysis, the analyst must simply be in the place of this transferential other, allowing the client to abreact and work through the repetitive affects. But there comes a point, according to Roustang, when the therapist must refuse to keep on taking this position that has been given him. He must confront the transference or the passions of the analysand with his own affective force and demand that the patient change also. Roustang writes:

> But there comes a time when the relationship is sufficiently strong for the analyst to play upon it and to change position; that is to say to refuse to carry the repetition any further. He will do this via a strategy

of ruse, of detour, and of paradox, going as far as to threaten breaking off relations, which can be understood as presenting the following dilemma; either you change or you leave. Like love, but unlike passion, the transference can in no way be unconditional.

(Roustang 1993: xxviii)

Thus Roustang underlines Henry's (1993) position, arguing that abreaction of affect is central to the therapeutic cure. However, I don't think that abreaction on its own makes people well. Implicit in what Roustang is saying is that the therapeutic endeavour entails a confrontation of forces between two, and so this meeting or exchange cannot simply be made up of affects, it also denotes a psychological relation. Not only does this meeting of forces question Henry's emphasis on self-immanence, but also it makes us understand how cure is dependent on an affectual and interrelational psychology. So, although Henry and Roustang are right to point out that the therapeutic cure is dependent on returning the client to a more affectual being within the world, we still need to understand how this occurs within a psychological relationship between two. Bergson can help us here because, like Henry, Bergson advocates an immanent ontology rather than a representational economy. His idea of psychic duration moving between perceptual and virtual allows us a model of psychic immanence; whereas Henry enables us to see Bergson's psychological multiplicities, all the tensions between virtual and the actual as streams of force.

Hysteria as splitting between affect and representation

Our psychical life is, in Bergson's view, an infinite number of states that all reside between the extremes of, on the one hand a pure virtual imaginary, and on the other sensori-motor action, or the real. Now these different psychic dispositions, or memories, are all in different states of tension between imaginary dream and the real of action. Dissociation and association govern our movement between different memories or multiple psychic states. This movement or duration contracts as we anticipate action and widens again to encompass a more personal dream world. The flow between our imaginary and real selves is a fluid and nuanced affair determined by the needs of life. But when the flow of tensions between these multiplicities becomes forced, artificially connected or disconnected, then we are in the realms of pathology.

In normal mental health we situate ourselves within these tensions, between dream and actual worlds, but when the translation or flow between virtual and actual becomes stuck we suffer mental illness. I suggest that the hysteric is someone who is unable to negotiate or place him- or herself within these different intensities and flows, and is consequently stuck in a dream-like world which cannot penetrate reality. The hysteric's memories get lost or stuck in unshakeable representations. Thus, the hysteric also occupies a kind of world of intellectual ideas and representations which are divorced from bodily action. Such an overly intellectual disposition results in fixed ideas detaching themselves, and it is these fixed representations that Janet (1920) so vividly described in his case histories. If these ideas become too elaborated they give rise to actual multiple identities. Bergson notes how the hysteric's intellectual fixity is accompanied by a display of 'scissions of sensibility and of motor activity' (Bergson 1912: 230). Therapists often notice that hysterics are lost in a kind of intense intellectual thinking, accompanied by a sort of split-off literal performance of the body. The body speaks because it is unconnected with the mental imagination. The mad split-off body movements and paralysis of the nineteenth-century hysterics is one example of this, although nowadays the bodily symptoms of the hysteric are more often associated with psychosomatic disorders. Emotions for the hysteric are also split off – hysterics will often seem to display melodramatic or labile emotions that don't really touch them.

Now this is interesting. If hysterics lose memories because they suffer from an over-intellectual vitality, this also means that they are denied access to their body and their present, what Bergson calls the sensori-motor realm of the real and action. In order for an idea to live 'it must touch present reality on some side; that is to say, it must be able, from step to step, and by progressive diminutions or contractions of itself, to be more or less acted by the body at the same time it is thought by the mind' (Bergson 1912: 226). The body fixes the mind, 'giving it ballast and poise', and without this interweaving with the body, mental states lose necessary tension or become unbalanced. In this scenario, attention detaches itself from life, 'dreams and insanity appear to be little else than this' (Bergson 1912: 227).

This is the dilemma of the hysteric, where memories are not destroyed but they lose their necessary penetration into the real. To live our relation to an object or a dream is to embody that imaginary relationship. Life is a constant translation of virtual into actual, a becoming of differences which is inseparable from the becoming of affect. Henry argues for a radical difference between affect and representation, privileging the former. Bergson also makes the body something lived, the action of the world, not something that is abstracted through representation. Because life or matter is an aggregate of images, something less than a representation but more than a thing, then the image is not something purely mental, it is also matter. This is similar to Nietzsche's view. So for Bergson, affect arises out of the image. Pure perception is only in theory and all perception is mixed with affects, but these affects swell, as perception turns from virtual into real action. Another way of describing this is to say that as perception increases its action on our body so it becomes affection. Bergson uses the example of a pricked finger:

Thus we pass insensibly from the contact with a pin to its prick.
Inversely the decreasing pain coincides with the lessening perception of
its cause, and exteriorizes itself, so to speak, into a representation.

(Bergson 1912: 53)

Perception is then the possible action of an object upon us, and our power
to effect the object. This is virtual possibility that becomes transformed into
real action as the distance between the object and our body decreases.
When the distance between the object and our body is at zero, then we have
affection.

We can think of this in slightly less abstract terms in relation to Freud's
(1900–1901) concept of dream-work and Winnicott's (1971d) notion of
object usage. Whether we are translating the day's residues in our nightly
dreams, or discovering our objects through our own fantasised destruction
and re-creation of them, we are translating the world into our own image.
Bergson (1912) would say that in order to exist, and to feel we exist, we
have to connect with objects in reality, translating them in relation to
differing psychical states. Our experience of memory in time and objects in
space occurs together in differing degrees, they are not distinct entities,
unless we split them off from each other through our intellect. And this is
also how Bergson arrives at a definition of the unconscious by saying that
we are quite happy to attribute an unconscious to objects that we know
exist, but cannot perceive. But when it comes to subjective ideas we find the
unconscious more difficult to understand. Our existence, according to
Bergson, is made up of memories and objects, only a small part of which
are consciously perceived. The unconscious is real and virtual; it comprises
of a world of unperceived objects and memories. He writes: 'the idea of an
unconscious representation is clear' (Bergson 1912: 183).

Thus Bergson is in accordance with Freud when he asserts the real
existence of unconscious representations, although, unlike Freud, Bergson
insists on their virtual status; they have no psychological reality, because
everything psychological is part of the present. More accurately, Bergson
designates the unconscious as unperceived life which is figured through the
image. So the image has the status of being subconscious; it is able to move
between conscious and unconscious worlds. This is then different from
Henry's (1993) assertion that the unconscious is life and affects as given.

For Bergson matter or life is given as virtual. Affects are produced,
brought to life and made actual through the image. The therapeutic cure, in
Bergson's terms, would not be strictly an exchange of a representational
world for one filled with affect, although the imaginative world arrived at
would be one of affection and action. Therapeutic cure would not simply be
a turning away from the world of representation towards self-immanence of
affect, although, immanence of affect would be integral to a becoming of
time and difference, as affects become separated from old representations,

and augmented again within new creative productions of the image. Perhaps there is not so much difference between Henry's affectual life and Bergson's creative imagination and duration. Both thinkers posit the unconscious as a psychic immanence or becoming that moves from virtual being – to affectual life.

Therapeutic cure in Bergsonian terms is holistic, the ability to make connections between mind and matter, body and spirit. Or, to enable the embodied flow of memory, as a translation and necessary tension between past and present, actualising memories and objects into the production of differences. The hysteric reveals how memory is carried in the body, or more accurately reveals how his or her memory is stopped from flowing in an embodied way. Because hysterics are stuck (to quote Bergson) in an overly intellectual tension or disposition, they make a division between past and present, between their ideas and their objects, between their memories and their sensori-motor world. This distinction that puts the imaginary at war with the real also makes a cut between the so-called pre-Oedipal body and the mental representation of the Oedipal Complex. Far from being too immersed in their pre-Oedipal affects and a bodily identification with the mother, hysterics would seem to suffer from representations or intellectual ideas that are cut off from the affectual body. Roustang (1996) seems to agree with this when he says that the hysteric suffers from representation, the hysteric suffers because,

> Affects become pathological, that is they turn into anxiety and symptoms, to the extent that they seek to be represented, and to the extent that rather than becoming affected themselves through concentration and non-intentionality, they become alienated through representation.
> (Roustang 1996: 77)

What is the dilemma of the hysteric then, if it is not simply Oedipal ambivalence and the conflict generated by an unsuccessful attempt to sublimate the body through words?

Michel Henry (1993) describes this hysterical anxiety as a damming up of libido because bodily affects try to escape their own self-immanence and can't. But there is no returning to the source of life and the body as biological or animalistic origin. As Freud knew so well, there is no possibility of returning to innocence and a primordial bliss, so we also have to understand how the body is translated into culture, how it is continually remade. Bergson and Henry both show how Oedipal sublimation of the body through language and representation is an inadequate theory on which to base psychoanalytic practice. Freud was always contradictory on the nature of the Oedipal Complex, eventually arguing in his *New Introductory Lectures* for its complete dissolution in most normal cases (Freud 1933). Freud, nevertheless, understood the dissolution of the Oedipal

Complex to be its desexualisation or sublimation. Confrontation with castration and the horrors of the biological maternal body enables sexual differentiation and freedom from bodily dependence on the mother.

Freud also says in 'The Ego and the Id', that in order for the unconscious to become conscious it 'transforms itself into an external perception' (Freud 1923: 358). This happens according to Freud when the unconscious becomes 'connected with the word-presentations corresponding to it'. Word presentations are for Freud the residues of memories or 'time perceptions'. In other words talking and language cure, because language is the route through which fantasies or dreams translate. But as Ferenczi and Rank (1925) pointed out with their famous active technique, remembering and representation through interpretative meaning does not work. Cure happens through repetitive acting out in the transference, a repetition of affect enabled by hypnosis. Surely, this means that the unconscious, or the infantile body, is not a conscious sexuality that has been repressed and stored away. Instead the id-like body, inseparable from the ego, is present as fantasy and dream which in health transforms reality through an external perception, based on affectual emotion in relation to objects.

The body, here, is not *sublimated* through the Oedipal Complex or culture; rather it is endlessly produced as reality and objects are created through the transformations of our dream world. Bergson and Henry in different ways show how the immanence of the body within culture is crucial to how we can understand the psychoanalytic treatment. Translation of affects and suffering into representation is, as Roustang (1996) points out, the hysterical dilemma; it may be Oedipal sublimation, but it is certainly not a cure. However, through Bergson we can understand how fantasy and dreams are transferred into a creation of our reality and objects.

The problem of course with the transference in the consulting room is that when we transfer our neurotic Oedipal relations onto the analyst, all our dreams of the other, we repeat the same, rather than anything new. Freud always acknowledged that recovery of memory on its own was not enough to constitute change in therapy, that a living connection to the blocked representation had to be established. Roustang and Bergson can enable us to see that memories are not simply recovered, but created anew, as old representations are lost and new ones accompanied by feeling tones are brought into being. So transference of our same old Oedipal representations onto the analyst can be forgotten as new creative differences – ideas and affects – move us into the future.

The unconscious in Bergson's view is not some underlying substratum of psychological reality that exists negatively beneath consciousness. In a letter to William James, Bergson explains the unconscious as a non-conscious psychological state or unperceived matter that is always in the process of becoming conscious: something that is not distinct from conscious life but intermingled with it. He writes:

> This existence of some reality outside of all actual consciousness is no doubt not the existence in itself spoken of by the old substantialism; and yet it is not part of what is actually presented to a consciousness; it is something between the two, always mingled with conscious life, interwoven with it, and not underlying it.
>
> (Bergson 1980a: 359)

It is the intermingling of imaginary and real, and of memory and perception, that allows us to move in time, remaking our past into our future. As far as the transference is concerned, we are dealing not only with old Oedipal memories and desires, but also with new desires and differences that are experienced in relation to the therapist as the client enters into a more lived duration.

Lived time and psychoanalysis

Marcel Proust revised Bergson's notion of selective memory and introduced another term of involuntary memory or *mémoire involontaire*. Involuntary memory is not called up by will but is encountered through accident or contingency. Proust uses the example of the smell of a Madeleine cake dunked in his tea, bringing to the fore a flow of memory of his past, growing up in Combray. The unconscious, here, is not something apprehended at first mentally. Rather it is found on stumbling across a material object found by chance. Walter Benjamin (1973) reads Freud's *Beyond the Pleasure Principle* (1920) and compares Freud with Bergson and Proust. Benjamin draws attention to Freud's claim that memory traces are most enduring when 'the process that left them behind was one which never entered consciousness' (Benjamin 1973: 114). So, Benjamin links Freud and Proust, making a distinction between unconscious memory and conscious remembrance as a critique of Bergson's willed consciousness. For Benjamin, involuntary memory is not willed but is encountered through shock or surprise. This underlines the unconscious nature of memory and shows that there is always an unconscious at work, unofficially so to speak. Again, I think this supposition of involuntary memory is implicit in Bergson's thinking as the duration of lived time which is immanent and therefore unconscious. Remember that duration is distinct, for Bergson, from a conscious memory of a representation. As Deleuze (1988b) points out, what really separates Bergson from Proust is that for Proust the past can be experienced, whereas for Bergson the pure past cannot be lived.

We can say that memory, for Bergson, Proust and Benjamin, is involuntary and affective. Bergson states that feelings live by their duration; it is only when we set out and represent these feelings in space that they become lifeless (Bergson 1960: 133). In other words, in order to access the duration of their lived feelings, hysterics have to access their involuntary affectual memories and thus leave the scene of representation. If the dilemma for hysterics is how they enter lived, affectual time and duration, then the issue is not how they sublimate their Oedipal conflict, but how they recreate it through immanent desire. Freud's thinking that desexualisation of the Oedipal Complex achieves this is erroneous. The problem is not how hysterics leave their body to enter language and meaning, but how they can leave representation and live the time of their body.

We can perceive the Oedipal Complex in terms of a fixed representation. In this case it is hysterical, the fixed ideas, conscious and subconscious, which we have to leave behind. Or we can perceive the Oedipal Complex as having a more immanent relation with the psychic time of the body. Here, translation of fantasies are part of our ongoing re-creation of objects and the real. So rather than seeing sublimation and the confrontation with castration as the key to lived identity, we should understand the need for the child and adult to relive their Oedipal fantasies and dreams as an ongoing creation of the world. This means a constant remaking of relations with the family, through fantasy and the body, as differences; not a remembrance of past experience, but the re-creation of unconscious memory and affects into new objects and realities.

This re-creation of future selves has to incorporate an affectual immanence; it has to be alive with our desire. And such desire has to move from virtual to actual. However, I would also like to argue that the attention to life or *élan vital* that Bergson describes also implies our phenomenological being and belonging in the world. Therapy needs to hold on to a sense of affectual life *and* phenomenological belonging. Quite simply we need to negotiate our desire in relation to others within our society and community. Freud was pessimistic about such negotiation but the fact remains that in therapy, as in life, we need to actualise desire and the affectual immanence of the body, and learn to contextualise this desire within our social and physical world.

Take for example a woman in therapy who is in a masochistic relation to her partner, male or female. The therapy can explore all the different ways of understanding this masochism in terms of immanent desire: as a refusal to actualise her own aggression, therefore relegating it to the partner, or as a symbiosis or merged form of relating where conscious will is lost in a regressive retreat towards the other and away from the world. We can even understand it in terms of a passion with a purchase price. You love someone enough to accept their abusive behaviour.

But the therapist also needs to understand this masochism in a context. Within late-nineteenth-century England such masochism was expected from women in their role as 'The Angel in the House'. Nowadays, it may be part of the cultural context for women in relation to their religious community, or simply the brute reality for the battered wives who lack economic means and independence. Understanding the immanent force of the body and our phenomenological contextual being in the world means claiming a philosophy of a more positive unconscious. One of the problems with Freud's Oedipal theory is that symbolic representation is seen as split off from a more affectual relation to the body. Being in the world and immanence of the body simply don't meet up in Freudian meta-psychology. Attention to life as a creative immanence that also connects to our being in the world cannot take place in this Freudian mythology because the latter case is predicated on repressing the body through representation. Sublimated Oedipus does not transform the body of the unconscious into a creative and psychological embodiment in terms of the world. Affects, in this Freudian story, are negative and unclean; something that, as *Civilisation and its Discontents* tells us, must be buried and pushed out of the way (Freud 1930).

In Freud's Oedipal narrative the unconscious is a repressed idea or wish that finds expression within dreams, everyday life and of course in the transference. Here, it is free association within language that is the key to representing the prohibited and forgotten desire, except that free association in the clinical session has very little to do with linguistic meaning. When we ask clients to free-associate we are really asking them to access unconscious affective memory with all the images and fantasies this entails. Roustang (1996) calls it primitive or animal speech, the kind of affective communication that a child understands when an adult says one thing, but betrays through their emotional manner something completely other. This is not conscious representation but the mnemic memory traces, the involuntary affectual memories that underline conscious thought. Language has been seen in classical Freudian and Lacanian thought as the key component in representing and sublimating unacceptable desires. Nevertheless, I want to argue in this book that there is a narrative of time and affectual immanence inherent to psychoanalysis which has been obscured by the historical emphasis on a Freudian, Oedipal meta-psychology. Against this hierarchical model of the mind is a more immanent and radical phenomenological understanding of the psyche where the transference is about how affects and fantasy can access a lived duration in creating new forms of existence and identity.

Repression or dissociation

Dissociation is, I would argue, a more useful term to think through the unconscious than intra-psychic repression. This is because in Bergsonian terms we start from dissociation; he writes:

> association, then, is not the primary fact: dissociation is what we begin with, and the tendency of every memory to gather to itself others must be explained by the natural return of the mind to the undivided unity of perception.

(Bergson 1912: 215)

We dissociate and subtract from the real, from the whole – consciousness is selective. Dissociation is the fundamental movement with which we move in time between dream and real worlds; like hypnosis it is an attention on one thing and distraction from another. Traditionally, the therapy relationship has been seen as a lifting of repression, expansion of memory and subsequent lifting of intra-psychic conflict. As Phillip Bromberg says, this 'at best underestimates and at worst ignores the dissociative structure of the human mind' (Bromberg 1998: 8). In Bromberg's view, personality development and growth is dependent on elements of dissociation, where interpersonal work in therapy can open us to the range of perceptual realities. Healthy operation of the dissociative mind makes way for intra-psychic conflict. What Bromberg describes as a healthy dissociation is the ability of a person to have multiple self-states, of both dream and reality, which also in a trance-like way link intersubjectively with objects. In health then, the ability to occupy a trance of reality and dreaming is also an ability to allow the surprise and penetration of other objects and worlds in relation to ours. In the schizoid state, dissociation becomes a defence against such surprise or trauma from the other, whether that other is another object or self-state. So the schizoid personality is rigidly enclosed; it is a safe environment that keeps itself 'from being rearranged by the outside' (Bromberg 1998: 9). In this safe and more rigid enclosure, dissociation becomes the defence against being retraumatised, whether that is by other people or other more threatening self-states.

Breuer and Freud originally saw this defensive dissociation as the hypnoid states that hysterics such as Anna O retreated into. However, there is a danger in seeing dissociation as merely a defence, when it is also the essence of creative generation. Bromberg describes how the work of therapy is to move the patient from defensive dissociation to an acceptance of multiple psychic realities, where conflict can be acknowledged. But he also underlines how dissociation is a healthy basic process allowing

> Individual self states to function optimally (not simply defensively) when full immersion in a single reality, a single strong affect, and a suspension of one's self-reflective capacity is exactly what is called for or wished for.
>
> (Bromberg 1998: 273)

He goes on to ask why dissociation, and the division of psychic experience into different parts, is the means through which we achieve integrity of the ego. His answer is that we originally develop in these unlinked self-states and that our mentally integrated ego is an adaptation. This is of course a plea for the decentred self which Lacan's thinking has done so much to elaborate. Nevertheless, this explanation still privileges mental representation as the main adaptive end to therapy, when the object can be conceived and rep-resented as mentally whole.

Such a privilege on mental representation, repression and intra-psychic conflict returns us to an Enlightenment ideology that Freud subscribed to, the emphasis on remembering and mental knowledge as keys to the unconscious. An emphasis on the work of Bergson and Henry returns us not to Oedipal mental representation, but to immanence of lived affect. Dissociation, in Bergson's view, comes first and generates new associations. When dissociation is fixed, especially when it is stuck in an overly intel-lectual tension or representation, it becomes defensive and hysterical. But dissociation is also how we dream our realities; it is how we move within lived time. Not only does it allow for self-states to function optimally, but also it is the very means in which multiplicities of lived duration are brought into being in their necessary and creative tension between real and dream worlds. Freud's Oedipal opposition, between phallus and maternal body, language and the body, is overcome in Bergson's emphasis on the duration or flows between imaginary and real; a duration which is also known as the hypnotic trance. Whereas dissociation as a defence is an encysted hypnoid state, split off from other multiple flows of being, we can also see the hypnotic trance, in its ability to traverse the space between reality and sleep, as the very creativity of our multiple differences of being.

Freud's Oedipal Complex and his later theory of a dynamic repressed unconscious emphasises repression as the ego's defence against unwanted thoughts and wishes: the unconscious harbours what has been energetically rejected. In Jung's (1913) theory of unconscious projection and dissoci-ation, libido functions within a physiological energy system (incorporating hunger and sexuality); when energy is heightened in one area it has become lost and displaced elsewhere. So, whether affect is exaggerated or lacking, it displays a dissociation of our embodied relation to the world and the object. The phenomenological balance between conscious and unconscious is altered and the unconscious becomes the place where the displaced and dissociated libido is hiding.

For Freud, psychic repression also involves the rejection of the object and the world; in psychosis this repression fails completely and accordingly becomes distorted and projected. The differences between repression and dissociation, and between Freud and Jung, have been made much of within the growing institutionalisation of psychoanalysis. Although these terms were exchanged and used much more freely in Freud and Jung's early correspondence, their eventual differences led to a definition of Freud's work within a meta-psychological explanation. Dynamic repression within psychoanalysis is used to describe an intra-psychic, internal world, whereas dissociation is often used to describe a more primitive type of splitting: a situation such as psychosis, where psychic content is simply evacuated, rather than allowed storage. Repression is seen as developmentally more advanced and linked to the Oedipal Complex because it signifies the ability of the client to experience internal psychic conflict. In dissociation, there is no storage of the unwanted material and no conflict, it is simply projected and split off.

Let us consider this difference. If we think of Melanie Klein's work, then repression and splitting become less opposed. We split unwanted material into internal as well as external objects. Originally, we split between the good and the bad breast. But we can perhaps see the Oedipal Complex as just another form of this splitting. As Klein (1986) envisages the early Oedipal Complex to involve the internal parents or object that are envied, so too can we see the so-called later Oedipal Complex as objects, now placed in the external world which are desired, but more importantly envied. Children want the mother or the father because they perceive and want what belongs to their parents. This is not so much about having the parents as being them. Mimetic identification between ego and object also leads to dissociation or repression where we split off and project unconscious experience into an 'other', whether that 'other' is internal as the super-ego, or external as the parent. Freud's topography of ego, super-ego and id, Klein's internal parents and Jung's unconscious complexes are all different ways of describing the multiple selves and self–other relationships that exist within us. These selves are not necessarily signs of a pathological dissociation. In fact there is no reason why we should not see dissociation as a positive and creative process; something implicit in day and night dreaming, an essential part of the immersion in the work for the artist or genius.

Putting someone on the therapeutic couch and asking them to free-associate – Freud's basic rule – entails the client dissociating from his or her conscious reality. So maybe dissociation and free association are inextricable, one dependent on the other. If we see repression, dissociation and association as the different ways our family of selves talk to each other, then the ways that these selves communicate, just like any family, will involve fights, judgemental criticism, disappearances – creative flights in one's bedroom etc. Maybe we don't have to divide intra-psychic repression from dissociation. Maybe the early fluidity of concepts between Freud and Jung is more useful than their later divergences?

Perhaps another way to think of intra-psychic repression or Oedipal conflict in a way that does not set it up in opposition to dissociation is to see the Oedipal Complex as essentially defensive and creative. As a defence it splits in a dualistic fashion, life and death, in order to master the latter. Masculinity and femininity, activity and passivity or a sublimation of language over the body are all part of this defence. But the Oedipal Complex is also creative because it is an imaginary tied to the psychic body. As such it moves between real and imaginary worlds endlessly remaking our relationships with our parents and the world into new and creative differences.

In this model intra-psychic conflict just becomes a stage between rigid traumatic dissociation and a more creative ability to produce and move between the lived differences of duration.

What, then, would it mean to refuse the distinction between an intra-psychic world of Freudian repression and a phenomenological, Jungian world of dissociation? In the history of psychoanalysis, especially within object relations thinking, dissociation as a defensive and creative mechanism has never left centre stage. Ferenczi's late papers on 'The Principle of Relaxation and Neocatharsis' (1930), 'Child Analysis in the Analysis of Adults' (1931) and 'Confusion of Tongues between Adults and the Child' (1933) all illustrate beautifully the defensive and creative aspects of dissociation. Sullivan (1953), Laing (1960), Winnicott (1971d), Fairbairn (1952) and Searles (1977) are all thinkers who emphasise the dissociation and multiple selves that are implicit within psychoanalytic work. Whereas intra-psychic models of psychoanalysis stress narrative representation and a reflexive consciousness that occurs after the experience, phenomenological approaches to psychoanalysis (R. D. Laing's work is probably the most famous) stress a lived phenomenology of experience and time that are at the heart of therapeutic treatment. The problem in simply focusing on mental representation and narrative representation as the goal to therapy is that in the argument I have been advancing, an over-reflexive mental representation is often the very essence that characterises hysterical or psychotic disorder. It is the ability to inhabit time and a lived affectual body, not the ability for mental representation that lies at the heart of the therapeutic cure.

Lived experience in the therapy session

Daniel Stern (2004) has explored the phenomenological lived experience at stake in the therapy session. He distinguishes between the phenomenal consciousness and introspective consciousness. Phenomenal consciousness accounts for the lived moments of experience in the therapy session, the minute-to-minute experience that does not enter long-term memory. Introspective consciousness entails the reflection on experience, a verbal symbolic world that occurs after the event. The dynamic Freudian unconscious is attributed to this introspective model, whereas the negative of phenomenal consciousness is described by Stern as being non-conscious, rather than unconscious: something we implicitly know. This implicit knowing which he likens to Bollas's (1987) description of the 'unthought known' is the nonverbal domain, not only very present in the mother–baby relationship, but also present for all of us, in our relationships with others and the world. Implicit knowledge is what we know, but don't necessarily verbalise or represent; it is body language, for example facial expression or the tone of our voice.

However, elsewhere Stern suggests that phenomenal raw experience and reflective consciousness are just two moments of experience, one following on from another. If we see dissociation as the structuring principle of the psyche, then we can see how in health we can disassociate and move between self–other states that are experiential and reflexive. Such dissociation, where we move with ease between imaginary and real worlds, enables us to be constantly surprised and remade in relation to our other selves or the selves of the other. Like Benjamin's reading of Proust's involuntary memory, the unconscious is a form of affectual communication that can surprise or shock in a good way because it allows particular self-states to be undone in relation to an 'other'. Here, dissociation is creative, producing and moving between different creative multiplicities.

In defensive dissociation, or repression, such affectual memory becomes blocked off in the self-enclosed world of the hysteric or the schizophrenic. Here, whether that traumatic dissociation is characterised by a passive will to life, or an overly intellectual disposition, memory loses its lived duration, affects become deadened – a feeling of indifference – or they transmute into anxiety. In schizoid conditions affect is deadened and the relation to the other foreclosed, but in hysteria, affect is less split off and is located in the so-called conversion symptoms where the body erupts because its duration or memory is blocked.

Likewise, repression can also be traumatic or creative. Huge repression on the part of the super-ego will turn into psychotic evacuation if it becomes sufficiently invasive, just as extreme hyper-reflexivity is a characteristic of the severe schizophrenic. But repression in less extreme forms allows experiences and selves to be out of sight but still around. The problem with intra-psychic repression as an overall model of the psyche is that it returns us to meta-psychology where internal and external worlds are divided and set up in opposition. As we have seen, such division is healthy only if it can be seen as a stage in the creation of multiplicities. Defensive dissociation or repression between dream and real worlds is the monological discourse of the hysteric. I would also argue this is a fixed Oedipal Complex that can divide up only along the lines of heterosexuality and gender. In his book on hysteria, Bollas (2000) speaks movingly of the need to move out of hysteria into Oedipal exchange, but in order for this Oedipal imaginary to be enabling, it has to give up rigid dualisms and move forward in time to access new and different identifications. If Freud had been more open to Dora's need for a mobility of identifications, he would perhaps have realised she needed to be, and desire, both parents. Envying your parents is all about hoping you will become them, and if you can't envy them in a satisfactory manner, if they are too present, absent or disappointing, then your task of remaking them and yourself is going to be harder. Dora's rapt admiration, or shall we say trance, in front of the Madonna was her disappointment in her parents as sexual beings, and her hysterical need to dissociate from them. Nevertheless, her idealisation and hysterical fantasy was also what could have possibly been reworked as a more creative dissociation, providing her with new experiences.

Freud wanted to fight it out with Dora in terms of sex. She chose to ignore him and her dissociation from her lost mother was perhaps not just the definition of her hysterical pathology, but the ground where new associations could begin. Fights between fathers and daughters are important, but sometimes, as in Dora's case, the sex has to be implicit. Freud tried to fight Dora in the bedroom, but bedrooms for teenage daughters are sacrosanct, a place to dream realities. So when we think about repression and dissociation as therapists, we should also just think of how they operate in time and space. Daniel Stern argues for the importance of a social intersubjective perspective in therapy. Here, shared phenomenal experiences are mixed with a social reflective self-consciousness, 'the two experiences are intermingled but also separate' (Stern 2004: 131). Stern is concerned with the experience that is built in the therapy session in an intersubjective relationship. He concentrates on the implicit awareness and the moment-to-moment building of experience rather than reflective meaning in the therapy session. Stern's work shows that although we can divide therapy work up into implicit experience and explicit meaning or narrative, for change to take place in the clinical arena it has to be in terms of a phenomenological lived experience. We can't effect change as analysts through recourse to abstractions about meaning and narrative; we can enter into change only through the lived, phenomenological experience of the therapy session.

One way of thinking about this is to return to Bergson's and Henry's analysis of the immanence at stake in psychoanalysis. The hysteric, whether seen by Janet as too passive, or by Bergson as inhabiting a tension which is too intellectual, is someone who has become immersed in a virtual world of abstract representation and memory. The hysteric lacks the attention to life and active perception that will embody the senses and produce a meaningful response to the world. As Freud and Jung have both shown in these hysterical reminiscences or complexes, the hysteric escapes into a hypnoid state where regression into a virtual or imaginative past substitutes for the present. Opening this trance up to a movement of lived time is the realisation that the past is truly created only when the present is lived, just as satisfactory reality or object relations are achieved only when we can recreate them through affectual fantasy.

Hysterics can present in therapy as self-conscious and reflexive, clients who want nothing better than to keep telling their story, their particular fantasies, rather than to stop telling them and feel some emotions. But hysterics can also rant and rave, like the example Freud (1893b) gives in his early paper on Charcot. Here, Freud describes a patient who screams and cries from painful affects, but does not know why. In this case it is not body affects but mental representation which is forgotten, so memory expresses 'its affect by means of bodily phenomena without the other mental processes – the ego – knowing about it or being able to interfere' (Freud 1893b: 20) In the first case meaning is the problem and in the second case meaning is the cure, but if we see these quite different hysterical symptoms in terms of the issues of entering lived time, then we can see how these symptoms are both about being split off from a relation to the psychic body. In the first case it is the abstraction of ideas which keeps the phenomenal, felt experience at bay. In the second case, the body repetitively speaks, but these are mad emotions, dissociated from more imaginative meaning and incapable of being shared.

Daniel Stern's important book *The Present Moment in Psychotherapy and Everyday Life* (2004) challenges the longstanding bias in psychoanalysis to narrative and verbal meaning as the main vehicle of cure. His emphasis on the enriching of lived experience through moments of intersubjective relating in therapy is a challenge to the Lacanian and Freudian psychoanalysts who still want to hold up the linguistic symbolic or a mental meta-psychology as the goal of clinical relating. However, I am unsure about the ways in which Stern wants to delineate his model of implicit experiential 'doing together' in the therapy session from a narrative model. For him, 'Both are needed. But each demands a different descriptive model' (Stern 2004: 227). But this seems to detract from Stern's overall message in the book that it is phenomenological experience and the entry to lived time that effects change within the therapy session. A distinction between phenomenology and narrative models of psychotherapy also ignores the way in which mental representation, instead of being the cure, is actually often the obstacle to change, lived experience and an attention to life – the necessary goals of the therapy situation.

I want to illustrate this chapter with a clinical story.

A young woman came to see me. She had a background of psychiatric treatment and various labels. Her preferred diagnosis was multiple personality.

'I like having four personalities,' she said, 'it makes me feel important, it keeps you interested and it means that we won't run out of things to say. Mind you there are only a couple I am prepared to tell you about.'

I could see immediately that this young woman was extremely intelligent, and indeed as the therapy progressed it became clear that this intelligence was both a help and a hindrance. It was helpful because this young woman was able to tell me her different selves and represent them all to me. It was a hindrance because it was marshalled into a massive defence and dissociation against her sense of experiential being, whether that being was her immanent desire, or her being in the world.

All the personalities had the same name but were numbered Mabel 1, Mabel 2 and so on. Mabel 1 was the favourite; she was adventurous, extreme, risk taking and could always win competitions with her mother. Mabel 2 was the opposite; she was depressed, did not want to live her life, but was too scared to take it. Mabel 3 spent her life watching video games in bed and spent the sessions telling me of the movies going on inside her head. Mabel 4 was objective and clever, so clever that she had no intention of going to university, as this was her mother's desire and meant letting her win.

At the beginning of therapy any interpretations of what I perceived might be Mabel's internal world were rejected, but they became important markers in the sense that I knew when I made them and she rejected them that we were in the process abandoning shared experience and moving along together. They became warnings that made me get back on track. In one session when Mabel 3 had been relating a particularly vivid and surreal dream, figuring women who reminded her in some ways of her mother and sister, I ventured to make an interpretation about how the women in her family, in her dream and in life, all seemed hell bent on outdoing each other. She just replied, 'I can't really hear you. It's like I'm far away, I'm on the ceiling.'

Telling me she was on the ceiling became Mabel's way of informing me when she had stopped sharing experience with me, and I learnt not to make interpretations around meaning, but to follow her stories. Most of her stories were imaginary ones that were enacted in her head; the ones in real life were normally traumatic or at times life threatening. The real-life stories enacted by Mabel were terrifying, stories about her getting high on drugs, booze and being abused and raped by men. The imaginary stories often told by Mabel 3 were the experiences she felt safe in, as she told me right at the beginning, 'I want to live the rest of my life in bed.'

I replied, 'What about living in the world?'

And she said, 'The world is a terrible place, I would rather die than go there. The only reason I like coming here is that you understand me when I say I am never getting out of bed, and you also believe me about my mother.'

Mabel had told me at the beginning of the sessions that her mother was mad, but that no one believed her. Her mother had to be mad, or else she was. So, of course I believed her. Because Mabel could not connect her imaginary and real worlds she could not separate them either. Mabel could never really decide whether she was pretending to be mad, or whether she really was ill. You never really know, when you are dealing with someone's mad mother, how real she is, but that does not make her any less persecutory.

Mabel used to dream about rooms, especially bedrooms. Her mother had once decorated her bedroom and then moved into it. Such impingements that had been regular throughout her childhood had resulted in Mabel literally living in a self-enclosed bedroom or bed, where access to other selves with herself, or in other people, was strictly limited. Sometimes, in her dreams, her bedrooms were covered in books – they were mini-libraries. In Mabel's life history, although she had been a brilliant student, her mother had often completed Mabel's homework before she got around to it. These stories and experiences informed me that Mabel could not have her own desires. Having desires were dangerous because they got stolen by your mother.

In conventional Oedipal terms Mabel would be seen to lack identification with a paternal order, her mother was narcissistically over-identified and her father was absent, collapsible and always in total agreement with her mother. Another way of thinking about these pre-Oedipal and Oedipal constellations is that they did not provide Mabel with the necessary ideals to leave home. Rivalry and envy of parents with children is downplayed, when we talk about the Oedipal Complex. As we increasingly invest in our children as commodities, they become our needs and desires. Envy is another word for what parents do when they desire their kids and can't move beyond them. A successful Oedipal Complex is one which we can imaginatively remake in relation to the world, where parents and children can both win and lose, where envy can enable us to move forward in time, not backwards into just triumph or just sacrifice. Mabel was mad so her mother did not have to be. She failed or sacrificed herself in order to beat her mother, but also because triumphing over her felt so unbearable. Mabel could suffer from envy and from her desires, but she could not be satisfied by them, for that would mean acknowledging the mother's failure; it would mean leaving her behind.

Staying in bed and not going to university was one way of beating her mother, and of course it was another way of letting her win. At the beginning of the therapy I did not insist on Mabel leaving her bed, or the hysterical or the enclosed self-state she was so attached to. But wanting to come to therapy – and Mabel did want to – meant leaving her bed at least twice a week. A gifted and intellectual student, Mabel read literature and philosophy voraciously. It was something we began to discuss and share on a regular basis. The friends that Mabel had did not take reading seriously and would have laughed at this secret desire.

She spent four years with me in therapy. During that time she left her home and found a boyfriend who also liked to live in bed. They got looked after by his mother. Mabel never managed to make any appointments, except for therapy. She came twice a week like clockwork. Coming to the sessions was important for Mabel because, in her words, 'This is the only place I can come, where I don't feel mad, and where I don't have to pretend to be mad.'

I waited and emphasised I was with her by saying uhum.

She said, 'This is where I can be myself.'

'I wonder what that means to you?' I replied.

She said:

> Well, I can be all four Mabels here, except I don't do extreme things here like extrovert Mabel. Normally, when I am at home or in bed, I am completely divorced from everything. It's like I am outside of myself watching whichever Mabel is there. Or, like the way I watch movies in my head, it's interesting but there's always two of me, the one watching and the one doing. Here, except when I feel on the ceiling, I don't get that strange sensation of watching myself.

There are many ways to describe these dissociated split-off states that Mabel experienced. This out of your body feeling is quite common for psychotics, but Mabel wasn't like this all the time. Sometimes she would say, 'You know I like living in my head and in my dreams, it's much more interesting and far less scary than real life, and I always know when to come back.'

I would laugh and say, 'But it's important we acknowledge that you have to come back. If you stay there too long, your dreams turn into nightmares.'

Mabel was dissociated in a defensive way. In these states she inhabited a virtual dream world, split off from more active perception, a space where part of her was on stage and the other part watching from the ceiling of the theatre. Perhaps the most important experience or self-state that Mabel talked about was the part of her that felt depressed and sad, the Mabel that felt totally insignificant and did not really want to live. This Mabel was never on stage, so to speak, and for that reason it was vital we never lost sight of her. Extrovert Mabel got drunk, high, and cut herself, colluding with situations where she was sexually abused and often physically harmed by men. And yet this was the Mabel she preferred, because she felt more alive and desirable, she was more popular with other people. Feelings were hard for Mabel to acknowledge and I could never ask her what she was feeling, because she just went blank.

But if she seemed particularly sad or angry and I noticed it, then it was easier for her to own the feeling as belonging to her. As the therapy progressed, Mabel began to procure animals – a cat and some rabbits.

Looking after them seemed beneficial. Sometimes we talked about transference onto her mother and onto me, and of course I was the ideal mother or the success story, because in Mabel's mind I was a mother who could share. In this split Mabel would talk about how she always had to forget my telephone number, so she would never be tempted to use it. Her fantasy of that need was that it would be 24/7. Her aggression got acted out outside the session and got brought in with all the destructive things she told me she did to herself. However, therapists are not just Hollywood repeats of our mothers and fathers; they also represent different selves and futures. If Mabel needed to learn how to beat me in a satisfactory manner, then sharing and winning needed to go hand in hand. What was most important in these sessions was what Stern (2004) called the building of moments of experience, the getting along together: the fostering of a space where Mabel could share something of herself with me. Gradually, in agreement with the psychiatrist, she came off her drugs. Then, one week she came into the room to tell me she had been discharged from psychiatric care.

Some time after that Mabel began to wonder with me about her desires and what they would be, if she ever decided to risk having any.

'Maybe,' she said, 'I want to be a therapist like you. I know I want a boyfriend who I can desire and keep on desiring.' (Boyfriends were normally desirable only when they were completely unavailable.)

I said, 'To become a therapist you'll have to go back to university.'

Mabel said dismissively, 'Fat chance of that.'

And then I said suddenly, in a challenging sort of way, 'Why can't you go? What is so terrible about competing with your mother? Why can't it be for you?'

'Because it wouldn't be for me, it would be just so she could show off in front of her friends. I can't face all those awful middle-class students. They are shallow and successful like my sister.'

Conversation about competition with her mother moved to discussion of her elder sister, who was now in a very successful job working in television. We talked about how Mabel's fear of meeting up with students at the university would put her in direct competition with a sister whom Mabel had perceived to have beaten her to being the good daughter and the ideal success. I wondered with her about the different selves at stake in this. How going to university and being a success not only would make her more like her sister, but also meant losing out to her bad self Mabel 1, the extrovert, who smashed all her ideals. Mabel admitted to me that she secretly liked Mabel 1, because she was mad and bad.

I said, 'So going back to university is pulling the rug from the Mabel you like?'

'Yes. At least when I'm ill, I'm different. I don't want to be good like all the other students, they are so compliant – you know, are the right brands, all heading to be media personality of the year.'

I said, 'But perhaps you don't have to give up extrovert Mabel to go to university, maybe you can be a bit like the students, but hang on to the extrovert side you like. You say that you are too bad, but what if the problem is that you are too good?'

'What do you mean?' she asked.

'I wonder if the Mabel that always goes too far in getting out of her head or being self-destructive is actually too good; the sacrificial Mabel that won't leave her mother. How about being bad *and* not being sacrificial? What if going to university could be a success story for you?'

Adam Phillips discusses how success is a paradoxical thing from a psycho-dynamic point of view, because our different selves or characters have differing agendas. What signifies success for one part of ourselves means failure for another (Phillips 1994: 50). To act in the world, Mabel had to feel able to choose her ideals, or the fantasies that she wanted to make real.

Her illness was an angry rebellion, but it was also a retreat into a negative rivalry with her mother both pre-Oedipal and Oedipal, where nothing could be won or lost. This retreat out of lived time was a flight, like Freud's early hysterics, into a virtual world of the imaginary. It meant that Mabel could not act on any of her envious fantasies or ideals; her sacrifice was about not making any of them real.

Mabel did eventually go back to university. And I was not in the least bit neutral about this. There is no competition between living in the world (however hard) and being killed by dangerous men you meet in the pub. In a phenomenological sense Mabel had withdrawn from the world. Her immanence of being and her being in the world were synonymous; one was dependent on the other. Therapy had been a halfway house, somewhere she could withdraw from the world and regress, but it could not become a permanent refuge. Therapy, like the Oedipal Complex, is a success only when we can remake it and move on. Mabel had to grow up and take her place in the world, and universities are, on the whole, better halfway houses than therapy couches.

Chapter 3

Hysteria and hypnosis

Freud describes the non-verbal identification between persons, initially between mother and child, as a mimetic principle. Crucial to Freud's explorations of identification and mimesis is the idea that mimesis is not only cognitive, but also based on affect. This mimetic principle is present as the origins not just of psychoanalysis but of dynamic psychiatry and the beginnings of all psychotherapy, and is manifested as hypnosis, trauma and hysteria. Now, these terms have been differently contextualised at differing historical moments and do not represent any timeless meaning. However, the mimetic principle in psychotherapy overall can be traced back to hypnotism associated with Anton Mesmer in the 1700s, who was arguably the founder of modern psychiatry, and his disciple the Marquis de Puységur. Whereas Mesmer invented a physical theory of animal magnetism, a magnetic and electrical fluid that passed between hypnotist and patient, Puységur discovered magnetic sleep and artificial somnambulism, realising it could be controlled to explore the unconscious psychological world of the hypnotised patient. Crucial to both these early hypnotisers was the notion of clinical rapport between hypnotiser and patient, although it was Puységur who emphasised how hypnosis should be used only for therapeutic purposes, and not, as Mesmer had done, for experimentation and exhibition (Ellenberger 1970: 92). We can see in Mesmer and Puységur the origins of two traditions in hypnosis: the fluidists who emphasised the physiological basis to hypnosis and the animists who concentrated on the psychological component of hypnotism. In the nineteenth century we can trace these two traditions of hypnosis in relation to not only the neuro-physiological investigations of Charcot and his pupil Janet, but also the more psychological emphasis on suggestion elaborated through Bernheim and the Nancy School and developed by Freud and Breuer in their early psychoanalysis with hysterics. This duality is a crude distinction, for Freud's work contains an early neuro-physiological narrative, in tune with Charcot, just as Janet pioneered the psychology of working with hysterical patients. However, this dual narrative of hypnosis is helpful in discussing how hysteria and indeed neurosis in general went on to have a contested career with its origins located in either suggestion/simulation or as traumatic aetiology.

Early dynamic psychiatry, therefore, understood hypnosis as related and central to the characteristics of, on the one hand, dual consciousness, sub and multiple personalities, and on the other, a notion of nervous illness linked to mental fluid and then energy. Interestingly, Bergson and Janet brought these ideas of physiological energy and dual consciousness together. Alongside these phenomena the clinical picture of hysteria and somnambulism presented itself. Therapy relied on the methods of suggestion and hypnotism. I want to suggest that the notion of affectual and suggestive mimesis can be also seen as the main principle of identification in play here, between therapist and patient, self and other, or ego and object.

The debate of whether we return psychoanalysis to a thesis of representation, an Enlightenment ideology of knowledge and reason, or whether we understand it in terms of lived affectual experience has been a fraught one. Lacan was scathing of those analysts who believed in lived affectual relations and compared them to dogs sniffing each other. In his doctoral thesis Lacan (1932) warned against the army of Bergsonians who advanced this notion of lived affect, and in 1953 he noted that the very identity of psychoanalysis depended on the conscious exclusion on the part of the analyst, of hypnotic affect from analysis. He says:

> I do not deny, any more than Freud himself did, the psychophysiological discontinuity manifested by the states in which the hysterical symptoms appear, nor do I deny that this symptom may be treated by methods – hypnosis or even narcosis – that reproduce the discontinuity of these states. I simply repudiate any reliance on these states – and as deliberately as Freud forbade himself recourse to them after a certain time.
>
> (Lacan 1977: 48–49)

For Lacan affectual hypnosis must be excluded because the goal of analysis is to discover the 'trans-individual' meaning of the subject in the domain of speech. Analysis is discovering the operation of the signifier and the symbolic interaction of signs. Michel Henry (1993) and Mikkel Borch-Jacobsen (1992) have both challenged Lacanian doctrine with their arguments of affect and mimesis. Henry deconstructs the Freudian project to reveal the truth of psychoanalysis in lived affect. Although Freud never escaped from his Enlightenment project of analysis as the recovery of memory, knowledge and representation (he always conceptualised the unconscious in terms of repressed representations), this did not stop him from realising that no memory is effective if it does not lead to the recovery of lived affect. The unconscious as a theory of knowledge masks this ontological lived affect which by its very nature defies representation, as it can experience itself only as self-immanence (Henry 1993).

Borch-Jacobsen also challenges Lacan's subject of representation, but instead of seeing affect as self-immanence he sees it in terms of a mimetic relation to the other. Subjectivity, for Borch-Jacobsen, is based on a mimetic identification: Freud's expression 'I am the breast' sums up this primary affectual tie, before any differentiation into ego and object. The unconscious as mimesis is an affective link with others based on a self-forgetting or hypnosis where the ego always plays or mimes the role of the other.

Mikkel Borch-Jacobsen famously takes up the mimetic hypothesis in relation to Freud's work. In *The Freudian Subject* (1988) and *The Emotional Tie: Psychoanalysis, Mimesis and Affect* (1992), Borch-Jacobsen returns to the 'pre-history' of psychoanalysis and the understanding of hypnosis that Freud abandoned prior to constituting his theory of psychoanalysis. Hypnosis, Borch-Jacobsen tells us, did not disappear from psychoanalysis. Quite the contrary, it reappears as the heart of psychoanalysis in the transference. Because transference is identical to hypnosis and because both figure the indissolvable emotional tie that constitutes the subject between self and other, ego and object, then the transference can never be ended. The subject is formed out of the relation between ego and object. Not only is psychoanalysis originally rooted in the power of suggestion (from the other), but also the subject is constituted between self and other, and therefore between the internal fantasy world and the outside external relationship or event. The ego, in this account, is bonded to the object and therefore indistinguishable from it. Borch-Jacobsen makes a claim against Lacan that the unconscious is neither representable nor memorable. Prior to any reflexive representation of the subject, this unconscious as affect can only be repeated and acted out.

Desire then is identificatory mime from the beginning between ego and object. This narcissistic mime or mimesis is thus:

> The matrix of desire and, by the same token, the matrix of rivalry, hatred, and (in the social order) violence: 'I want what my brother, my model, my idol wants – and I want it in his place.'
>
> (Borch-Jacobsen 1988: 27)

Borch-Jacobsen, therefore, replaces Freud's repressive Oedipal father with a Kleinian notion of envy. The root of fantasies and wishes is to be found, not in sexuality, but in jealousy, envy and rivalry; a mimesis of the other, whom one does not wish to have but to be. In this way, Borch-Jacobsen disposes of the need to explain the relation between the psyche and society in terms of the life and death drives. Desire does not have an aim such as pleasure or unpleasure, because being mimetic it is without aim. Children playing at *being* Mummy and Daddy are not playing out their desire to be grown up. They are simply playing and miming because they identify. Their playing constitutes desire, it does not represent the desire to seek or have a goal or object.

More recently Borch-Jacobsen (1996) has dramatically renounced this earlier reading of mimesis, where the tie between patient and therapist is one of blind hypnosis, and where the patient is unconsciously identified with the other. In place of this thesis, he emphasises the hypnotic bond between analyst and patient as one of conscious suggestion and simulation. Exposing Breuer's famous patient, Anna O, as a hysteric engaged in a game of mimetism, producing all the symptoms the doctor was looking for, he writes: 'Her illness was clearly a mimesis a "private theater", a dramatic performance put on for her physician' (Borch-Jacobsen 1996: 87).

In order to evaluate Borch-Jacobsen's recent theory we have to recall in a bit more detail the case of Anna O. In 1880 Josef Breuer started treating Anna O, a hysterical young woman he diagnosed as having a double personality disorder. Anna's real name was Bertha Pappenheim and she came from a high-class Jewish family in Vienna. In her later life Bertha became a famous social worker, feminist and philanthropist. A wide gap distinguishes this independent woman from the mad and hysterical patient who was treated by Breuer. According to Breuer, Anna O was intelligent and attractive. She was strong-willed and imaginative and was confined by her monotonous domestic existence. Her daydreaming as a response to this stultifying life led to illness, which manifested itself after a period of nursing her dying father, whom she loved. She suffered all sorts of psychotic and hysterical symptoms such as paralysis of her right side, loss of vision and of hearing. Her symptoms got worse after the death of her father when her personality became noticeably split between a 'real self' and an 'evil self' – selves Breuer could make her switch between by holding up an orange. In the second year of her illness she also began to alternate between a present self and a self that had existed exactly one year before. She relived the exact day-to-day existence of the previous year and Breuer confirmed the accuracy of these memories through the diary of Anna's mother. Anna was visited every day by Breuer and he devised a method where she would put herself into a state of auto-hypnosis and talk about the origins of her symptoms, until one by one they disappeared. Breuer noted that 'when a symptom was being "talked away": the particular symptom emerged with greater force whilst she was discussing it' (Breuer 1895a: 93).

Anna was over-identified with her father and during treatment this hysterical mimesis became transferred to Breuer. The end of Anna O's treatment is a subject of hot debate. One story propagated by Freud and Ernest Jones is that the treatment eventually collapsed with Anna fantasising she was pregnant with Breuer's child. Horrified, Breuer fled to embark on a second honeymoon with his wife. Borch-Jacobsen denounces this story as a false myth, propagated to advance Freud's thesis of the sexual aetiology of neurosis, and then proceeds to reveal another story that has lain hidden in Marie Bonaparte's journal. In this story Breuer ends Anna O's treatment abruptly as a response to a suicide attempt by his jealous wife (Borch-Jacobsen 1996: 460). It would seem that, whatever the myths surrounding the hysterical birth fantasies of Anna O, the erotic transference between Breuer and Anna O was real enough.

Borch-Jacobsen's (1996) reading of Anna O sets out to discredit psycho-analysis and its theory of the unconscious. His critique is interesting, not least because it contradicts his earlier discussion of the hypnotic identi-fication and unconscious mimetic transference that lies, for him, at the root of the psychoanalytic project. I think that many of Borch-Jacobsen's criticisms are right, but unlike him, I do not think they lead to a rejection of the unconscious. Alternatively, I see them as providing weight to a more creative account of the unconscious as affectual memory and becoming. It is true, as Borch-Jacobsen (1996) points out, that Anna O was not pro-fessionally abandoned by Breuer. She was hospitalised after her analysis and was subsequently in and out of the same clinic for several years still suffering from hysteria. But we also know that Anna O eventually made a complete recovery and went on to have an independent and successful life. How much her recovery, if any of it, was due to her therapy with Breuer is a mystery because we have no account from Anna about her cure, either at the time or later in her life.

Borch-Jacobsen (1996) equates Anna's hysteria with the hypnotic trance, but because he now subscribes to a social-psychology interpretation of hypnosis as *conscious* simulation, he uses the fact that Anna and Breuer were both involved in hypnotic suggestion and simulation to discredit the notion of the unconscious. According to Borch-Jacobsen, the relationship between the analyst Breuer and the hypnotised Anna was a game of simu-lation or a specular game, which both parties were consciously aware of. Anna faked her symptoms as a childish game in relation to Breuer's suggestions. Borch-Jacobsen rejects, here, his earlier hypothesis of hyp-nosis as an altered state of consciousness, aligning himself with a social-psychological interpretation of hypnosis. Following the cognitive beha-vioural approaches of Theodore Barber (1969) and Nicholas Spanos (1989), Borch-Jacobsen argues that however involuntary hypnotised subjects might appear to be, they are in fact consciously in control, and playing a role. This social psychology model understands hypnosis dramatically; Borch-Jacobsen uses Diderot's (1957) ideal image of the actor as one who remains detached from the emotions he acts on the stage.

Now it is interesting at this point to wonder why exactly Borch-Jacobsen wants to reject the notion of hypnosis as an altered state of consciousness, something his earlier work on mimesis subscribed to. Ruth Leys (2000) states that Borch-Jacobsen simply moves from a theory of hypnosis as altered consciousness, that was present at the turn of the nineteenth century to a present-day understanding of hypnosis as conscious role-play. But the idea of hypnosis as an altered state of consciousness is still as strong now as it was in the 1890s. If anything, the evidence for it has become even more compelling, now that neuroscience can prove the existence of altered brain activity in hypnotic states.

The cognitive doubters of hypnosis as an altered state have, since the 1950s, relied on Barber's (1969) position that hypnosis is simply suggestion and that we have known since Bernheim that people in a relaxed state, especially if they are a bit fantasy prone, will be susceptible to suggestions. These doubters argue that hypnosis is simply goal-directed fantasy or imagination. But of course if we think about this, the fact that hypnosis is fantasy or imagination does nothing to change its also being an altered or unconscious state – quite the opposite. What is so interesting and inexplicable about Borch-Jacobsen's (1996) argument in *Remembering Anna O* is that it draws on the work of Ernest Hilgard (1968) and Milton Erickson (1980). Both of these thinkers see hypnosis as dissociation, in other words as an unconscious state! Describing Ernest Hilgard's (1968) research, Borch-Jacobsen comments on how there is 'always a "hidden observer" who is present at the spectacle of the trance' (Borch-Jacobsen 1996: 89). The hypnotic subject lets him- or herself pretend and imagine, but the hidden observer always knows the reality of the situation.

Now this is not actually Hilgard's argument. Hilgard's experiments were seen by him as evidence of dissociation, the idea that one part of us might remain aware of an altered state of consciousness. This is a bit like the experience we occasionally have in dreams when we become aware we are dreaming. It is a very common feature of the extreme dissociation we witness in people suffering from schizophrenia or multiple personality disorder. Dissociation, however, can also be a creative phenomenon – the trance-like states that we move in and out of when we daydream, listen to music or actually craft something, as in painting and writing. The hidden observer in a trance state is the part of us that is aware of the outside world and what is going on. This observer is a kind of gatekeeper to the conscious world, allowing other parts of ourselves to slip into a more unconscious state.

It seems strange that Borch-Jacobsen would use Hilgard of all people to back his argument for hypnosis as conscious simulation. He argues that Anna O was not lying or faking, but that her simulation was real. Quoting Milton Erickson, he writes:

As Milton Erickson so neatly puts it, 'The best simulation is an actualization': the best way of simulating hypnosis is to fall into an hypnotic state.

(Borch-Jacobsen 1996: 91)

So, Borch-Jacobsen is arguing here for Anna O's simulation as both real and surreal, a role pushed to the point where the body incarnates a new reality, to the point where we can't tell the difference between simulation and hypnosis. To put this forward as an argument against the unconscious simply does not hold up. Erickson's view was that simulation can easily fall into an unconscious hypnotic trance; such are the dissociative powers of the mind. He was not suggesting that simulation is always conscious role-play.

So why does Borch-Jacobsen back up his argument with views from Hilgard and Erickson, who are clearly on the side of hypnosis as dissociation? Why not explicitly refer to the work of Spanos and Barber, who have made the case for hypnosis in cognitive terms? Borch-Jacobsen clearly wants to use the idea of hypnosis as conscious simulation to renounce the discourse of psychoanalysis. It is unfortunate, given his earlier brilliant thesis of mimesis as hypnotic dissociation, that his recent theory for debunking Freud's work is so flawed.

This is not to say that Borch-Jacobsen does not make some very good criticisms of the Anna O case. But whereas he uses these critiques to reject wholesale the theory of the unconscious, I think they should be read as more evidence for a theory of the unconscious based on dissociation, rather than Freud's repressive Oedipal meta-psychology. For example, like Borch-Jacobsen, we can link the following passage from Breuer's case history to Hilgard's theory of the hidden observer. Breuer writes that the manifestation of Anna O's split or double personality, where she exhibits a normal and mad 'self', is accompanied by long spells of somnolence and being a clear-sighted observer:

> Nevertheless, though her two states were thus sharply separated, not only did her secondary state intrude into the first one, but – and this was at all events frequently true, and even when she was in a very bad condition – a clear-sighted and calm observer sat, as she put, in a corner of her brain and looked on at all the mad business.
>
> (Breuer 1895a: 101)

Borch-Jacobsen takes this as evidence of Anna O's conscious simulation, but if we want to link this strictly to Hilgard's ideas then we must take it as evidence of dissociative mental states. Charcot (1991), and later Lawrence Kubie (1975), both argued that hypnosis is mimetic and mobile in its ability to move across and between psychological and biological processes. Hypnosis bridges states of wakefulness and sleep, and of neurosis and 'health'. As a trance state, hypnosis is a simulation but it involves all stages of consciousness, pre-conscious and unconscious phenomena. As an experimental state it can be used in therapy to explore all these different crossings between conscious and unconscious worlds. Breuer is struck with how Anna's clear thinking, which is going on at the time of the psychosis, is also linked to her sense after the attack has passed that she has made her illness up. Only when Anna has gained a more unified sense of herself does she seem struck by the idea that she has simulated her illness.

> When a disorder of this kind has cleared up and the two states of consciousness have once again become merged into one, the patients, looking back to the past, see themselves as the single undivided personality which was aware of all the nonsense; . . . thus they feel as though they had done all the mischief deliberately.
>
> (Breuer 1895a: 101)

Anna's clear-sighted observer is evidence of her trance state, but we can also link it, together with her sense of simulation, to the extreme hyper-reflexive dream state inhabited by psychotics. The sense of being inauthentic is often experienced by neurotic patients, but it is even more acute in psychotic conditions where patients are autistically split and self-conscious – watching themselves playing a role. Many borderline patients also have a sense of making their illness up, and this goes together with a sense of being inauthentic and unreal. Rather than attributing 'the hidden observer' in Anna O to conscious game playing or an undivided consciousness, we can link it directly to Henri Bergson's (1908b) description of a double consciousness. This is the mirror scene of false recognition, where perception and memory are present as separable streams. Here, the virtual and imaginary world of memory and being mirrors and haunts the actual perception. The person has an uncanny awareness of seeing themselves as an actor playing a part: one free spectator and the other 'automatically playing his part' (Bergson 1908b: 149). Bergson thus emphasises the hypnotic role as a virtual world of unconscious being which mimetically tracks more conscious perception. Such hypnotic doubling is characteristic of a weaker 'attention to life', but paradoxically it is also an awareness of this other unconscious self or double which can creatively help to expand consciousness.

If we understand the unconscious to be a creative and mimetic immanence then suggestibility lies at the heart of memory and consciousness. Borch-Jacobsen's (1996) later attack on Breuer's and Freud's treatment of Anna O assumes that she in a sense made up her hysterical trauma as a kind of game. He therefore extends his criticism of Freud and Breuer to all exponents of a dissociated unconscious. Borch-Jacobsen observes that the role of traumatic memory attributed by Freud to Breuer's case was self-serving. In his view, Freud arrived at his theory of pathogenic memory as a response to Charcot's teachings that he became aware of after Breuer's treatment of Anna O. This retrospective theory then falsely attributes the role of traumatic memory to Anna, for although Breuer writes of fantasies and 'psychic excitation' he does not mention 'psychic trauma', 'dissociation of consciousness', or 'reminiscence' (Borch-Jacobsen 1996: 56).

Referring to the later stage of treatment, where Anna O remembered and repeated events exactly from the year before, Borch-Jacobsen remarks that these were not real memories of events, but the 'stories she told Breuer during her trancelike states'. Anna O, therefore, repeated the same trance or self-hypnosis of the year before. Now I think this is a very plausible explanation, but instead of seeing Anna O's self-hypnosis and fantasy as conscious role-playing, a game that puts paid to a theory of the unconscious, let us consider how it merely strengthens a particular argument for an unconscious structured in relation to suggestion and dissociation.

In Chapter 2 I proposed that the hysteric's defensive dissociation splits her into a virtual fantasy world that cannot penetrate reality, and an over-reflexive consciousness of fixed thoughts and ideas, where affects are alienated – displayed in symptoms of delirious anxiety or indifference. Anna's hysterical memories were the fixed ideas or stories of suffering she hypnotically transferred onto Breuer. They were also virtual fantasies: the images she needed to forget and the images she needed to transform into a more active attention to life. Being able to stop telling her hysterical stories to Breuer would have liberated Anna's affects, returning her to a more mobile psychic body. Losing her fixed ideas would also have entailed the transformation of virtual fantasies into a more active perception. Anna's doubling was a symptom of her mental illness, but as virtual fantasy, her double also held the key to her future identity. Bergson, and a later Freud, both agreed that virtual unconscious memory changes into something else when it becomes conscious.

To call Anna O's reminiscences simply conscious imagination, or memories of real events, is to miss how these images which are so bound up with an alienated affect are a defensive dissociation, a doubling which can be creatively put back into movement through therapy and self-hypnosis. We know that Anna O was helped by hypnotic treatment, even though she was not cured by the end of her therapy with Breuer. The primary role of mental representation and recollection in the therapy situation takes centre stage in Freud's writing only after his discovery of the Oedipal Complex. However, in the early case study of Anna O, reminiscences are seen by him as affectual fantasies that are both abreacted and transformed by the therapy situation. It is not true to say (as Borch-Jacobsen 1996 does) that Breuer fails to refer to a 'dissociated unconscious'. He might not use this exact term, but Breuer's case study is littered with references to Anna's double consciousness and her auto-hypnotic states that, unless we believe Borch-Jacobsen's cognitive account, are clear evidence that Breuer thought in terms of unconscious dissociation.

Anna's reminiscences and reproductions of past trance states were auto-hypnotic fantasies and fixed ideas. They were not necessarily traumatic memories of real events, but evidence of a traumatic dissociation. In this defensive doubling, conscious and unconscious worlds were incapable of being translated – they were unable to move in relation to each other. We are left, of course, with the question of Anna O's cure at the end of her treatment with Breuer, but then the question of therapeutic cure is not a simple one. I will come back to this point later.

If we consider Borch-Jacobsen's (1996) account of hypnosis as conscious role-play, against the work of Bergson and Janet, we can see how limited it ends up being. Reducing hypnosis to consciousness and so getting rid of the notion of the unconscious leaves the creative and phenomenological immanence of the psyche out of the picture. We need to consider what we think the relation between affect, the unconscious and consciousness consists of. In Bergson's account of the doubling between a virtual past and an actual present, unconscious and conscious states are not strictly delineated. The pure past is virtual for Bergson, actualised in moments of duration or becoming. Duration or attention to life actualises memory, but because movement from virtual to actual is a differentiation, then the unconscious past is a past, as Derrida (1984) says, that has never been present, and never will be. Duration is the constant movement and actualisation of the virtual, within the actual, and these transformative moments of duration are understood as differences. Memory is for Bergson bodily movement. So, the unconscious lives as a virtual past which is also real and affectual. Duration is the embodiment and difference that occur through the actualisation of the virtual, and this creative evolution moves us forward in time. In this account real and imaginary are not separate and the unconscious as memory is not some internal container, but bodily movement, for example hysteria, although, as I will argue, hysteria is actually a sign of how the body is stuck and unable to move forward in time. Hypnosis reveals this hysterical affectual memory as a doubling or mimesis that passes between self and other.

Like Freud, Pierre Janet was unhappy with Hippolyte Bernheim's (1897) notion that hysterical illness was caused only by suggestion. But whereas Freud saw the issue as a refusal to remember past, psychic traumatic events, Janet thought that purely psychological explanations were inadequate and that the cause of what he called the hysteric's narrowed consciousness also lay with his or her weakened physiological disposition. Nevertheless, it would be a mistake, as we have seen, to position Freud's thinking on hysteria as very far from Janet's. We can bring both Freud and Janet's thinking on hysteria together if we frame them together, within Bergson's ideas of creative life.

Hysterical reminiscences are a kind of misrecognition or weakened attention to life, where suggestion has become defensively fixed in terms of a certain neurotic suffering, which is transferred onto an all-powerful other. But suggestion is not just the hysterical mimesis onto an ego ideal. Suggestion, as Bergson tells us, lies at the root of the psychic creative body and it is how we recreate ourselves in relation to both art and nature. Suggestion and dissociation characterise the defensive doubling of the hysteric; but they are also key to a more creative transformation of our psychic self-states, where we live a more embodied time.

Charcot's degeneracy theory of neurosis and his fame associated with the Salpêtrière clinic began to wane during the 1880s, partly as a response to Bernheim and the Nancy School, who challenged the nervous aetiology of hysteria. According to Bernheim (1897), it was not necessary for an actual physical trauma to trigger hysteria. Such was the suggestibility of the patient that just thinking of some trauma or accident was enough to produce hysterical symptoms. This then heralded a move towards a more psychological understanding of the illness. Charcot's technique of hypnotism, one where he would make hysterical symptoms appear and disappear, was originally taken up by Breuer and Freud in their original 'trauma' theory of hysteria. But then Freud abandoned degeneracy theory and the neuro-physiological explanation for disturbed psychological states in his belief that repression of traumatic, sexual memories relating to childhood was the central terrain. Freud also abandoned his techniques of hypnosis for free association, aware of the non-lasting effects gained under hypnosis because defence mechanisms, the repression and its relief, remained unconscious.

In Freud's 'Autobiographical Study' (1925), he admits the influence of Bernheim but insists that he always used hypnosis in another manner, distinct from suggestion: 'I used it for questioning the patient upon the origin of his symptom' (Freud 1925: 19). Of course this claim is false. In his early paper on 'The Psychotherapy of Hysteria' (1895a), we see Freud worrying because his patients cannot recollect the interpretations of unconscious thoughts he offers them. His real anxiety, here, that these thoughts had never come about, 'merely had a possibility of existing', shows the power of his suggestion in operation (Freud 1895a: 387). In his auto-biography Freud also distances himself from Breuer, saying that *Studies in Hysteria* was essentially 'the product of Breuer's mind'. But then Freud contradicts himself, saying he was partly responsible for the theory, 'to an extent which it is today no longer possible to determine' (Freud 1925b: 21). Freud goes on to say that he was concerned with the description of hysterical symptoms and their origin, but he never established the nature of hysteria. Maybe that was because hysteria is so indicative of a theory of the dissociated unconscious, inseparable from the processes of hypnosis and suggestion? Such a theory makes perfect sense of Anna O's case history but creates a more serious challenge to Freud's later Oedipal meta-psychology.

Freud's early emphasis on memory was not the same as Breuer's. Freud centred on the idea that hysterics did not want to remember past traumas rather than that they were incapable of remembering. Hysterics did not remember past traumas, according to Freud, because they were repulsive scenarios of incestuous sexual abuse. Breuer's work always differed from Freud in that Breuer stressed dissociation rather than repulsion. In this

Breuer was much closer to the work of Charcot's student, Janet. However, he disagreed with Janet's explanations of hysteria as a weak disposition that therefore gives rise to fixed ideas. Breuer saw hysterics as suffering from affect that is both in excess and blocked. He writes:

> Janet regards a particular form of congenital mental weakness as the disposition to hysteria. In reply, we should like to formulate our own view briefly as follows. It is not the case that the splitting of consciousness occurs because the patient is weak-minded; they appear to be weak-minded because their mental activity is divided and only a part of its capacity is at the disposal of their conscious thought.
>
> (Breuer 1895b: 311)

But if we follow Janet's thinking closely, especially as it relates to Bergson, we can see that Janet agreed that the lack of psychic tension in hysterics was due to their double personalities: a doubling between virtual memory and actual perception. Setting himself up in contrast to Janet, Breuer states that hysteria is not about a weakened constitution and is more likely to occur in people with lively dispositions who are bored and unstimulated. And yet we can see this as an excess of mental energy occurring in bored young women in the late nineteenth century who are denied precisely the psychological and physical actualisation of their fantasies. In other words, Breuer's over-stimulated hysterics and Janet's weakened ones both lack the same central ingredient which is an embodiment of their consciousness within lived time: the vital attention to life, Bergson's '*attention à la vie*', or what Janet called '*fonction du réel*'.

Breuer was right to understand dissociation as a splitting of the mind, but Janet's work was also correct in establishing not just the dissociation of ideas, but also the accompanying dissociation of the body. Janet documents the loss and imbalance of sensibility in his hysterical patients, who lose the sensation of limbs, become paralysed etc. He writes:

> These great systems of sensations and images are at the same time anatomical systems, which have a unity in the brain and in the spine. I do not deny it by any means; the fact that a system is psychological should not cause us to conclude that it is not at the same time anatomical. On the contrary, the one involves the other.
>
> (Janet 1920: 179)

The differences between Breuer and Janet are smaller, on examination, than history has made them. Both men were clinicians treating hysterics at the end of the nineteenth century and both saw the problem of hysteria as linked to affects. For Janet, the issue was a weak constitution, whereas for Breuer the issue was not too little energy but too much: affects which had become strangulated and blocked and hence needed the cathartic method in order to encourage them along the right path. Both men, therefore, followed Charcot in basing their methods in the realm of physiology, but they also followed Bernheim's ideas of suggestion in terms of their therapeutic endeavours. Breuer thought that hysterics were so open to suggestion because they want to be elsewhere: they want to escape. At a later date, Sandor Ferenczi, Freud's disciple, agrees with this point but goes beyond Bernheim's idea that the hypnotist can simply introduce suggestion and dissociation. Ferenczi emphasises that suggestion works only because there are potent psychical forces of dissociation and suggestion already present in the subject or patient. He writes:

> Psychoanalysis allowed us to establish with certainty the fact that the hypnotist is relieved of the effort of evoking that 'dissociation condition' (which effort, by the way, he would scarcely be equal to), for he finds dissociation ready . . . also in the persons who are awake.
>
> (Ferenczi 1952: 59)

This is of course also Bergson's thesis. Hypnosis was, as I have already discussed, very much part of Freud's early clinical investigations, and contrary to his own declaration of having abandoned hypnosis as a method, it never really departed from either Freud's practice or his ideas. If we follow Freud's autobiographical account of his move away from hypnotism and hysteria to his ideas of repressed sexuality, we see that he documents the usefulness of hypnosis in the cathartic technique, but then begins to doubt it as his understanding of transference love deepens:

> Increasing experience had also given rise to two grave doubts in my mind as to the use of hypnotism even as a means of catharsis. The first was that even the most brilliant results were liable to be suddenly wiped away if my personal relation with the patient became disturbed. It was true that they would be re-established if a reconciliation could be effected; but such an occurrence proved that the personal emotional relation between doctor and patient was after all stronger than the whole cathartic process, and it was precisely that factor which escaped every effort at control.
>
> (Freud 1925b: 27)

Freud goes on to describe a patient for whom hypnotism has yielded 'marvellous results', who after waking from her trance threw her arms around Freud's neck. Understanding this to be a transference love that did not properly belong to him, Freud realises that he must isolate this 'mysterious element that was at work behind hypnotism' and so must abandon the hypnotic method. Reflecting on Bernheim's perception that when encouraged through pressure to the forehead, a patient can remember what had happened under hypnosis, Freud decides that the patient must already know everything recovered under hypnosis. Thus, it follows that other more conscious methods can be used to aid memory. Freud writes: 'My expectations were fulfilled; I was set free from hypnotism' (Freud 1925b: 29).

According to Freud, his theory of sexual repression and his technique of free association had an advantage over hypnosis because

> It exposes the patient to the least possible amount of compulsion. It never allows of contact being lost with the actual current situation, it guarantees to a great extent that no factor in the structure of the neurosis will be overlooked and that nothing will be introduced into it by the expectation of the analyst.
>
> (Freud 1925b: 41)

Freud seems to ignore that, for the analyst, his suggestibility remains a potent force whether or not he actually tries to force such memories and associations. We can see that Freud's new method of free association allows 'interrelated material to make its appearance at different times and at different points in the treatment'. Nevertheless, free association as the basic rule strengthens the transference and the hypnotic bond even more, because it encourages patients' phantasmatic history, allowing them to transfer all their past relations to the Other. Patients transfer, in other words, all the images, desires and wounds that have constructed them, onto the analyst. So, in place of the analyst's actual suggestions, we have the patient's fantasies of that suggestion and knowledge – as the one who is supposed to know. Free association is not distinct from hypnosis because it increases the hypnotic transference onto the analyst. It also develops clients' ability for self-hypnosis, their ability to disassociate and associate, thereby opening up their fantasy world.

Ferenczi is probably the most famous disciple of Freud who was interested in hypnosis. Ferenczi saw the Oedipal Complex as the heart of hypnotic affectual relations, with the relation to the mother figuring as a nurturing hypnotic transference, and the father as the more authoritarian and frightening. He was contradictory over the question of suggestion and hypnosis throughout his career. On the one hand he wants to distinguish suggestion and hypnosis from what he sees as the proper analytic method: the overcoming of Freudian notions of sexual repression and resistance. He writes:

> It is necessary to lay stress on this, as many people hold the mistaken view that even to-day analysis, as in Breuer's time, is nothing else than the recalling of memories and the abreacting of affects in the hypnotic state. There is no question of this; on the contrary, the patient must be

awake in order that his intellectual and affective resistances may display themselves in their entirety and be overcome.

(Ferenczi 1912: 66)

However, elsewhere, Ferenczi (1919) writes of the abuse of the free-association technique and the dangers of simply allowing the patient to free-associate as a way of confronting difficult material. He realises that one of his patients uses the basic rule to simply break off trains of thought that are leading to unpleasant feelings and memories. Ferenczi in an authoritative way *suggests* that the patient complete every sentence he has begun (Ferenczi 1919: 181). Here we can see how Ferenczi *suggests* that the patient follows the path of his own *suggestions* to creative actualisation, rather than using dissociation in a defensive way. In another essay Ferenczi (1920) notes the passivity of psychoanalysis and the importance of active interpretation and technique in interfering with the patient's psychic activity.

Free association is important because it can elaborate the hypnotic transference onto the analyst; but it also elaborates a self-hypnosis, the multiple fantasies or possible 'selves' we can become. Free association opens up our dream world. However, as Ferenczi notes, free association that is not negotiated between two people in the analytical relationship simply takes the client back into a solipsistic dream state – a hysterical world of uncanny doubling where patients observe themselves in a detached manner.

Freud first discovered free association in his work with Frau Emmy Von N. A careful reading of this case study shows that although Freud lets Emmy follow her own meanings within the session, he allows this only after she has got angry with him for interrupting her with his suggestions:

> Her unruly nature, which rebelled, both in her waking state and in artificial sleep, against any constraint, had made her angry with me because I had assumed that her narrative was finished and had interrupted it by my concluding suggestion.
>
> (Freud 1895b: 118)

As Bromberg (2001) has suggested, the lesson Emmy teaches Freud is not one of technique but one that illuminates the analytic relationship (Bromberg 2001: 125). Free association disseminates unconscious meaning between two people; it opens up a more fluid relationship between imaginary and real. The difference between a self-hypnosis that is hysterically fixed and one that can communicate and transform itself in relation to 'other' self-states is one which is dependent on the therapeutic relationship. In the right therapeutic transference the analyst is an 'other' who functions not only as the unconscious double for the client, but also as a real and separate presence in the world. We all return to the scene of the other (in a therapy that works). We return to a hysterical doubling of virtual representations and affects. But what eventually brings therapy to a desirable end, what cures the client, is the ability to move between fantasy and real worlds, past and present: the remaking of our identities in relation to a lived temporality. The hysteric is stuck in idealistic fantasy and is also stuck in a literal repetition of his or her body – the strangulated affects that accompany fixed stories of suffering. The hysteric is unable to access the different temporal flows between virtual and actual.

Dreaming and daydreaming is pathological if it ends up being all we do, but without it, we can't explore the fantasy world that holds a key to who we can possibly become. The hysteric is stuck – in dreaming all the time, or not being able to have a fantasy, it amounts to the same thing. Hysterics are the people in life who can't make a choice, like Esther in *The Bell Jar* (by Sylvia Plath) who imagines herself sitting in the crutch of a plump fig tree. The figs represent all the different things in her life that she wants, like marriage, or a brilliant academic career. Choosing one means losing all the others and because she can't choose, she is starving to death. So she sits in the tree, a twilight tree of fantasies and reminiscences, and watches the figs 'wrinkle and grow black' as they drop one by one to the ground.

Severe hysterics can't even have fantasies; they have hallucinations. To have a fantasy means you have to admit on some level to the possibility of its becoming actual. You have to own a fantasy as something that belongs to you. Choosing also means sharing; if we share everything with an all-powerful mimetic other, analyst or mother, we are not sharing, for they become the fig tree, the repository of all our desires, selves and wants. The hysteric sits in this fig tree wanting it all and choosing nothing. But the good-enough analyst knows how to be a fig tree *and* just another person sitting in the branches. In other words the analyst remains in this function as the all-powerful other, but he or she also remains a real person in the world.

Ferenczi (1951) sees that hypnotic suggestion and free association are not enough by themselves. They have to be negotiated in a meaningful relationship between two people. He realises that the therapist has to be a transferential other but also has to be active in terms of the world, thus enabling the hysteric to fantasise about the figs, but also allowing him or her to choose some and reject others. Choosing certain figs and selves means acknowledging all the pain, envy and jealousy involved in separation. Choosing figs also means acknowledging that you are also a fig tree for someone else, being chosen and ignored, being the withered figs that drop to the ground. Finally, choosing some figs, and not others, like the story of Eve, means getting out of the tree or garden and waking up to your embodied, active being in the world. Children, as Adam Phillips (1994) notes, have to bear their triumphs; they have to learn to share without sacrificing their passions. But sharing also means selecting the fantasies you want to make real for yourself, and in therapy that entails the therapist being the fig tree, but also becoming, over time, another real person sitting next to you.

Suggestion, on the part of the analyst, is about deepening the transferential associations, but it also involves, as Ferenczi has shown, an active technique on the part of the analyst, making clients confront fantasies and realities they might rather avoid. In later years Ferenczi and Rank (1925) challenged Freud in relation to his exclusion of hypnosis from analytical technique. They criticised what they saw as an overemphasis on interpretation. Rather than dividing hypnosis from analysis of the transference as Freud had done, they suggested using both techniques. Introducing hypnosis back into therapy meant that the analyst would actively take up a hypnotic position – he would actively repeat with the client and participate in a real actualisation, but he would also disengage from that role.

So in *The Development of Psychoanalysis*, Ferenczi and Rank (1925) write:

> If one could, for example, combine the inestimable advantage of the technique of hypnosis with the advantage of the analytic ability to free the hypnotic affect situation, a tremendous advance in our therapeutic ability would be achieved.
>
> (Ferenczi and Rank 1925: 61–62)

They go on to say that the final goal of psychoanalysis 'is to substitute, by means of the technique, affective factors of experience for intellectual processes' (Ferenczi and Rank 1925: 61–62). In Freud's day psychoanalysis was seen as the liberation of repressed desires from an ideology of the Enlightenment. But nowadays things are very different: ideology does not repress, rather it produces such desires for consumption. Perhaps repression of sexual desires was never the central issue and it is Breuer's ideas that we have to attend to. What is at stake in the clinical transference is the acting out of affectual relations, the dramatisation of our affectual mimesis with the other; an emotional mimetic bond that was somehow denied to us in childhood. But then this brings us to a discussion of what the transference is and what the difference is between hysteria and the healing transference. Or what distinguishes hypnosis and a mimesis that produces neurosis from one that can open up the neurotic to lived time and future possibilities?

François Roustang (1996) begins to answer some of these questions in his astonishing book, *How to Make a Paranoid Laugh: Or, What is Psychoanalysis?* Using Freud's example of the woman throwing her arms round his neck, a woman whom he had supposedly just cured, Roustang asks what this demand of transference love signifies. The love is addressed to the analyst as 'Other', the one who is supposed to know. This Other, Lacanian analysis insists, must remain a Nobody – of Oedipal Law to which the analysand's imaginary desire is directed. Expression of transference love is then a refusal of this Nobody position of the analyst, and it can signal the end of analysis and the transference, as the patient learns to substitute the all-imaginary Other with other identifications and desires in the representative Symbolic.

Roustang challenges this Lacanian practice – itself a model of classical Freudian technique – and suggests that the demand of transference love is not necessarily a demand for the end of analysis, but a demand for the analyst to move his or her position. He asks us to consider that transference onto Nobody and the Oedipal Law actually produces the hysteric. The hysteric is Nobody's mimetic other. In order for this hysterical transference to be broken, the analyst must implicate him- or herself as a somebody as well as Nobody. For hysterics to resolve their transference onto the Other, or the one who knows, they have to perceive the analyst as a real somebody. Not that real, for that would paralyse any projected fantasies, but not completely imaginary either. The hysteric is not really asking for love, but is asking for the analyst to partially disengage from his or her function as an analyst, so the hysteric can glimpse the analyst as a person. The hysteric is asking the analyst to implicate him- or herself into the procedure:

> She does not ask for love, that softening of the irreparable; rather, she asks that the enchanted circle be broken . . . and thus that the analyst stop being Nobody, but that he not be in love either. In other words, *her love is a request not for love, but for implication.*
>
> (Roustang 1996: 4, original emphasis)

Perhaps this was also Anna O's demand to Breuer? Nowadays we know that reproduction of neurotic transference onto the therapist has to be followed by the therapist also modifying his or her position as the patient's other. By all accounts Anna O was not cured at the end of her therapy with Breuer.[1] Maybe termination of the treatment with Breuer – whether that was prompted by Anna's phantom pregnancy or a suicide attempt by Mrs Breuer – enabled Anna to modify her transference in a more enabling way with her next physician. Of course we can't really know this, but the fact remains that Anna did make a complete recovery. And unless we believe Borch-Jacobsen (1996) that Anna's illness was simply a childish game, then we have to take seriously the therapeutic work she undertook with Breuer. Henri Ellenberger notes that Anna's illness was 'analogous to the great exemplary cases of magnetic illness in the first half of the nineteenth century' (Ellenberger 1970: 484). If we don't want to reject the notion of an unconscious then we have to read, in Anna's case history, the central place allotted to dissociation and hypnosis in the transference.

The mimetic and hypnotic bond that we transfer onto the analyst is a repeat of all our neurotic identifications: our loves and sufferings. As clinicians know, this is a projection onto the Other in the transference, of our desiring and emotional relations, enabling the patient to become more aware, through repetition, of what these neurotic bonds are. But if transference is neurotic, if it creates the hysteric in his or her hypnotic thrall to an all-powerful other, then how can this transference be dissolved or replaced with a mimesis that opens the hysteric up to new and different possibilities? Freud was well aware of the resistance to the treatment that transference love represented. He describes how the hitherto compliant hysteric suddenly discards all attempts to reflect and work in analysis and becomes immersed in her love for the analyst. Often this is right at the point of a particularly difficult or distressing resistance. Freud notes how the

> Resistance is beginning to make use of her love in order to hinder continuation of the treatment, to deflect all her interest from the work and to put the analyst in an awkward position.
>
> (Freud 1915c: 381)

Freud's advice, here, is for analysts to stand fast in their analytic function against this 'ungenuine love', a stance that not only enables hysterics to overcome their pleasure principle and infantile fixations, but also leads them to acquire a mental function and freedom over the unconscious.

For Freud here, as for Lacan, the goal is mental representation or Oedipal identification with the paternal principle of language and culture. However, if the (female) hysteric identifies with the (male) father analyst out of rivalry and her desire is to topple him from his position, then how does this hypnotic identification with the One become modified through representation? In Freud's view, affects becomes repressed and attached to the wrong representations. Thus the aim of therapy is to give back to patients the right meaning and representation of their drives and desires.

According to Roustang, 'Neurotic suffering derives from the fact that affect is constantly in a state of inadequacy and consequently seeks to tie itself to representation' (Roustang 1996: 78). In other words, representation is an alienation of affect. For affect to be returned to its dormant state and its natural force, it has to leave the scene of dramatic representation. In therapy, then, patients would no longer need to tell their story or project their fantasies in a dream-like way onto the analyst. Roustang calls this a form of self-hypnosis, 'where affect is now unlinked from representation, it recovers the strength that is distinct to it' (Roustang 1996: 78).

But what does this mean? According to Roustang the hysteric's suffering is not so much located in the body but in its representation. One way of understanding this phenomenon is to return to *Studies in Hysteria* and examine what Breuer (1895) meant when he said that hysteria was caused by hypnoid states. Although Freud thought that hysterics were suffering from deliberate amnesia as a defence, Breuer thought that hypnoid states occurred naturally. This accounted for the natural suggestibility of patients. Breuer and Janet saw these hypnoid states as a splitting of the mind and evidence of a double consciousness. Nowadays the idea we have multiple states of differing degrees of consciousness is much more recognised. The notion that we carry a multiplicity of selves within us that are discontinuous and dissociated is not seen as necessarily pathogenic. Freud turned away from the notion of hypnosis and dissociation after writing *Studies in Hysteria*. This might have given him the distance he wanted from Breuer and Janet – his unique Oedipal theory, but we can see that in reality Freud never gave up on hypnosis – free association and hypnosis *are* inevitably linked.

Breuer did not just see auto-hypnosis, or dissociation, as pathological; he also saw it as a natural creative ability. As an 'absence of mind' this dissociation occurs in the thinker or the creative artist as a state of abstraction or dreaminess. It is only when reveries becomes filled with affect that they become pathogenic. Thus neither 'absence of mind' during energetic work nor unemotional twilight states are necessarily signs of mental illness, whereas reveries, filled with emotion and states of fatigue arising from protracted affects, are neurotic. Perhaps we can see these pathogenic reveries as affects that are constantly seeking representation, and are thus alienated. Breuer gives examples of pathogenic reverie as the rapt longing for an absent lover, and the quiet concentration of the sick-nurse on his or her object. These examples are interesting because they are hysterical in the sense that the fantasies at stake are transmitted onto an unavailable other, who like the analyst becomes the seat of all our projected fantasies. It seems, then, that hysterical reveries are strangulated in terms of affect, stuck in relation to an all-powerful other, without being able to move forward creatively in time.

I suggest that the hysteric remains split between a virtual 'past world' of fantasy representations and an over-conscious presence of certain representations which are strangulated with affect. Here, one fixed idea or fantasy, one dissociated self-state, takes over, preventing the hysteric from entering a creative actualisation of differences and of making associations with other 'selves'. Now, as I have said, this is not because the hysteric has one fantasy, in fact the hysteric has many, but these multiple fantasies or other selves remain dissociated, incapable of being actualised within the world. Consequently, the hysteric can choose only one fantasy 'self' to become in the world, and often this 'self' has to be embodied by someone else. This is often why therapists talk about hysterics being unaware of their unconscious; they cannot have access to a more fluid and multiple sense of self. If the neurotic can choose only one, the psychotic has many 'selves' but chooses to share none. This accounts for the accepted difference in therapeutic technique. With neurotics the aim of therapy is to make associated fantasies available to the patient through the analyst's function. The implication of the therapist as a real person then enables hysterics to select from their gallery of fantasies and negotiate through the analytical relationship a more embodied action in the world.

For the psychotic the associations do not have to be searched for: they are massive, in an overpowering transference onto the other. Here, the analyst must start from the reverie but because the psychotic does not wish to share or make any fantasies real, the analyst has to be more careful. Instead of taking up the position of the patient's other, being the repository of unconscious fantasy, the analyst has to enter the self-enclosed fantasy world of the psychotic and try to share one fantasy with the patient. Whereas with the neurotic the aim is to open up, through free association, a more multiple world of possible selves, with the psychotic the more basic work of communicating the fantasy between two people has to be established.

Bromberg (2001) describes how Emmy Von N's symptoms of agoraphobia and abulia (loss of will) were linked to her dissociation. This dissociation happens when the mind is split from (what Winnicott (1949) calls) the psyche-soma. Emmy's anger with Freud was with his suggestions that simply attended to one dissociated self-state through hypnosis, but ignored the others. Freud tried to erase some of Emmy's picture memories through suggestion and hypnosis through applying pressure to her forehead. This did not last, and was partly the reason why Freud gave up a direct hypnotic technique; he eventually realised that Emmy had to learn to choose or eat – for herself. In order for this to happen, Freud had to listen and acknowledge all her dissociated fantasies. Emmy's anorexia and abulia resulted from one dominant self-state taking over; consequently she was restricted in her modes of relating to the object or the outside world. In health, we all have contradictory and plural ways of experiencing ourselves, others, and the world we live in. This is problematic for the hysteric, what Bromberg (2001) would describe as a personality dynamic, where the hysteric is excessively wilful in certain areas, and completely inhibited in others. Eating disorders are a common example of this. We can also think of this dynamic in terms of dealing with trauma in the therapy situation. The hysteric brings with him or her the fear and dissociated states that have been split off and petrified by past traumas, but finds it difficult to bring these past traumatic experiences and selves into dialogue with the more trusting feelings he or she has towards the therapist, in the here and now situation.

Therapy entails understanding how the past is relived in the present situation, within the current intersubjective context. Again we can see this in terms of the analyst's ability to be a transferential object, and a real, active person. But we also have to consider how affect and auto-hypnosis present in this scenario. Hypnotic transference onto the therapist opens up the hysteric's auto-hypnotic dissociations, his or her petrified affectual fantasies. Free association between analyst and patient allows these petrified fantasies to find a meaningful relationship with other multiple self-states that exist in the patient and within the analyst. Like Breuer's (1895c) examples of pathogenic auto-hypnosis, the cure cannot happen as long as the client remains lovesick for the therapist, or if the therapist is too preoccupied with hugging a sick patient.

For pathogenic auto-hypnosis to return to its creative function, affects have to be released from their representation to an all-powerful other. Transference has to be modified. Mimetic hypnosis shows us that transference is never dissolved, but it does have to move forward, away from a fixed hysterical representation, towards a creative evolution of difference. The analyst facilitates this by being a fantasy other and a real person. The hysteric has to learn to actualise and make real his or her fantasies, moving from a projection onto the other to the production of that affectual relation as a difference.

At the end of therapy, transference is modified and allowed to creatively evolve away from the analysis and onto the world. But a question remains. Are affects in this situation really returned to an auto-affection or self-immanence, as Henry (1993) suggests, or is it that affects are released into a productive immanence in relation to the other? I suggest that modification of the transference entails the latter. This would mean, in Borch-Jacobsen's (1992) terms, that the client can identify as the breast, 'I am the breast', but also I am the breast differently. I am you and I am also elsewhere. This latter account would not mean making a radical separation between the registers of affect and representation. Instead, affect would be liberated in a new production of flows between fantasy and the real.

Classical Freudian readings define hysteria as a return to the pre-Oedipal body, a refusal of incest prohibition, and the paternal symbolic order. The task is then to make conscious through representation and language the hysteric's unconscious affects. This reading privileges an Enlightenment ideology of the unconscious and the efficacy of knowledge, where the unconscious is seen as an issue of memory and recollection. Alternatively, a conception of the unconscious as mimetic affect sees the hysteric's cure as the liberation (and separation) of affect from representation to the Other. Hysterics get better when they no longer need to tell their stories to an imaginary One. Release of affect from fixed ideas enables the translation of fantasy into new experiences.

Freud was well aware that in the transference, hysterics repeat – because they cannot remember – affects that have never been conscious. The task, here, is to liberate affects from a virtual and real world that have become fixed and split off from each other, so they can access lived time and an immanent becoming in relation to different others. This immanent becoming is a mimesis that is psychologically embodied in relation to the world. It is what Pierre Janet calls an 'attention to life' or the phenomenological life force, characterised by Nietzsche's (1967) 'will to power' and Bergson's (1911) *élan vital*. This immanence of the body is not self-evident experience; it has to be forgotten in order for the hysteric to move forward within lived time. Neither is it simply self-immanence. We move from one dream to many. Forgetting the body is also implicit in creating it anew somewhere else. I am the breast and I must forget it in order to create it again and again differently. In this sense we can say, as Freud and Lacan did, that the ego is a fiction. We are, as Borch-Jacobsen reminds us, born in relation to the other and that emotional identification and tie – our earliest bond – is primary. The transference repeats this early hypnotic bond and within it the client plays at being the mother, the father, and the breast in identification with the analyst.

However, healthy children don't just play at being Mummy and Daddy, they also play at being objects such as trains, trees and aeroplanes, and it is their identification with a plurality of others which moves them forward in the world. In other words children, who are more at home moving between fantasy and reality, have the ability to forget their dependence on the other; they use fantasy to forget and kill it off in a variety of ways. And this ability allows them both the fantasy and the reality of creating themselves and the object anew. The child plays at being Daddy and the next moment Daddy is killed off as the child becomes something interesting and new. This forgetting of our representation to the Other leads to a liberation of the affectual body. The moment we actualise our fantasy of someone, who of course is also our fantasy double, then everything changes. That fantasy relation is forgotten as we live the time of possible different selves. Perhaps the sadomasochistic relation, like the hysterical one, is the one most likely to keep on representing the same old identification, of Mummy, Daddy, Breast, in its refusal to live the affects of lived time and possibility.

Forgetting hysterical fantasies and representations cannot be achieved through the analyst's didactic interpretations because the analyst just turns up as another, more powerful, sadomasochistic fantasy. It failed for example when Freud tried to sweep Emmy's reminiscences away through suggestions which set himself up as the expert. Returning affects to the body and gradually forgetting their representation has to be the result of a meaningful relationship between two. The consequence, when a client's decision to move out of self-conscious narcissism and be creative, means that the world becomes more interesting, something else we could be. The definition of a hysteric is the person who can't stop representing his or her stories in therapy, or indeed, it is the analyst who is too into his or her role.

He sits opposite me. It is the first session and he stares me out till I am forced to avert my eyes. He grabs his head and makes deep guttural noises.
'I am really mad at people all the time, especially women,' he says and I wonder, slightly alarmed, whether he is mad or just pretending to frighten me. At what point does anger become madness?

'What maddens you about women?' I ask.

'Women are like cats, they are never what they seem. They are always one step ahead of you. You know, cunning. Not like men, men are like dogs, straightforward, faithful, you know where you are with them.'

'I wonder why you chose a cat to be your therapist?'

'I need a woman to understand who I really am – to understand the nature of my being.' He became quite menacing again. 'Women are full of shit, they just play games with you; you never know what they mean.'

I said, 'I wonder if you feel that women ignore you?'

'My last girlfriend left me, she said I frightened her.'

I said, 'Maybe bullying women is one way you don't have to be frightened of them. Maybe it's also a way of not having to deal with the things they might have and you don't?'

He said impatiently, 'I don't understand women.' And then his eyes filled with tears. 'There is one thing that I think women have, that I want, but only one thing.'

'What's that?' I asked.

He said, 'They know how to be.'

This man's life was not, as it happened, so much a search for being as a search for meaning. He was purpose incarnate. The predicament in the therapy centred on this man's search for identity. On one level he was certain, far too certain, active and angry. He had an idealised, quite magical sense of who he was, an ego ideal that never matched reality. He spent his life travelling the world, living on the fringes of society, trafficking drugs, doing the festival circuit, taking odd jobs. Currently he was working in an organic food store. His upbringing had been in working-class, suburban conformity and not fitting in was this man's impetus for living. As he told me, he had spent his life literally and metaphorically driving over people's front lawns. He had come to therapy, he said, to understand the meaning of his life; he wanted the key to who he was.

He told me about his parents, that his father had died quite suddenly of cancer when he was a boy. Up until then he couldn't remember much but he supposed he must have been really happy. After that he got into fights with everyone, with his brothers, with the boys at school and that was when he had started getting really mad at his mother.

I keep wondering when I am going to get over my father's death. I get so mad with my family especially my mother because they don't feel what I do about him. My mum knows all this stuff about him and she just won't tell me. They think I should get over him, they think I'm fucked up. I'm not fucked up, it's them! Robots – living their fucking normal lives, no minds of their own. I'm sick of this society. No one is real. Everyone just pretends. Do you think I should just get over my Dad?

I told him that I thought losing his Dad had been every bit as unfair and terrible as he felt it to be. I said, 'Maybe you need your Dad's stories so badly because they are a key to who you can become as a man. Women hold the key because they are like your mother, they know but they don't tell.'

'What is your favourite film?' mused the man, not changing the subject. 'I like all sorts. My favourite actor is Russell Crowe.'

'Why do you like him?' I asked. He began free-associating about the actor. "I like him because he is fearless. I like him in the *Gladiator* because he is authentic fights, for what he believes; he saves people. A lot of my friends think I look like Crowe.'

'You do,' I said. 'Maybe being a gladiator is what you do, maybe that's your story of masculinity.'

'I like it,' he said, 'and so do women. My girlfriend's not scared of me, well most of the time. When I lash out at her, she fights back.'

'Maybe she's a gladiator too. She communicates with you, unlike your elusive, unknowable mother.'

'We have an understanding,' he replied. 'She defends herself, I like that.'

But often this man would come to therapy in a speechless rage about his girlfriend, whom he loved, because she did not always understand him, he felt ignored or demanded from. The relationship was always at the point of disintegration because of his aggressive, bullying behaviour. He wanted to discuss the meaning of life and she just wanted to know if he could look after her children on Saturday. They would have violent fights. If he was too violent she would collapse. Often he would say, 'I'm better off on my own, I prefer it.' I acknowledged the disillusion with other people. 'Maybe it's about the degree, just how much of a disappointment they are, and what you can bear. I wonder if being angry, like a gladiator, is all about communicating meaningfully with other people. If you are not angry they won't listen.'

'I challenge people,' he said, 'make them realise when they are just full of shit.'

We talked about how not getting over his father and being angry produced the gladiator. 'I wonder if being a gladiator is a good defence against finding out about women and what they might really want from you.'

'They don't let you know,' he growled. 'My girlfriend puts on this strong act, but inside she is all broken.'

This man's gladiator act, his masculinity, was a hysterical performance that covered over extreme vulnerability. His aggression, and his inability to be anything but authentic with people, was an overarching mode of relating which cut him off from other parts of himself and his psychic experience. Radically excluded from the parental couple when he was young and in fierce rivalry with his older brother, this man carried his rage and grief for his father as a kind of battle-cry which dominated his search for meaning in life.

Another way of describing this man would be to say he suffered from a dissociated self-state of ideal manhood, triumphant and vengeful, where all his vulnerability got split off into the women he tried to bully. Compromise meant compliance and he was forever taking his revenge on the Oedipal figures in his life, mothers, or partners, institutions that extracted such obedience. If compliance was being good, then transgression through rage was being bad – an addiction to his self-ideal he could not give up without humiliation.

He said, 'I'm sick of trying to be good. However good I am it's never enough.' Being badly behaved got this man noticed and remembered. We talked about the parts of him, the depressed and vulnerable bits that being a gladiator protected him from. His mother had wanted a strong son and he had always been told to cope whenever he expressed vulnerable feelings. Frightening his mother had been this man's way of stopping her managing his emotions. And so this man's anger was all mixed up with a part he played as a hero, or anti-hero, an act he staged again and again in his life and in therapy. Often, the telling of these weekly dramas became an event in itself. Not representing himself in this melodrama became gradually congruent with an ability to have other feelings of vulnerability, sadness and fear, an acknowledgement of unbearable responsibility and loneliness.

Over time therapy became important to this man because it was a place where he could feel heard without having to get mad. Therapy was also the place where he could have those 'meaning of life' conversations which became mixed up for him with his dreams and fantasies. Exploring those fantasies with me often turned me into his dream woman. But when I failed to understand him, or pointed out the reasonable compromises demanded of him, or his cruelty to women, when I became a bit more real in my behaviour, then he became wild with anger. These were important moments to acknowledge both his hurt and the need to compromise. Managing not to humiliate each other became a route out of sadomasochistic relating.

After one session that had felt quite mad and surreal, he said, 'The trouble is I don't want to settle for an ordinary life, that's why I experiment with so many drugs. Everyone wants these little lives and I want the whole world.'

I said, 'That sounds terrifying.'

He said, 'Yes but it's also exhilarating.'

'Maybe your desire to drink in the whole world can also make you feel quite mad. It's exquisite and unbearable. Perhaps the reality is that you have to bite it off in manageable chunks. You can bring your dreams here, but you also have to negotiate with what your girlfriend wants, without getting too mad at her.'

'Don't think you are telling me anything I don't know,' he replied crossly.

Just as I had to learn to move out of my analytic function of the one who knows, his dream other, the person he transferred his various unconscious histories onto, so I had to implicate myself as real and not the only thing in his life.

One day he brought a vivid dream. He was in the forest with me, and then with a man who was a spiritual healer. He went back to the man's flat and the man gave him some oak, Bach flower remedy. Then he was somewhere else in a strange town. He went into a second-hand record shop and whilst he was in there his bike got stolen. He went into a panic and became very angry with everyone.

We talked about the dream and I asked him to describe the forest and he said it was full of oak trees and beech trees, men and women, but they had no leaves. The references to the bike and the records were about his father, who had been a second-hand record collector and had given him the bike a short time before he died. We discussed the different meanings of the dream, in relation to his father and himself. He talked about how his father had been stolen from him. I said the oak trees seem important. Oak trees aren't gladiators. They hold meaning but not in a confrontational way and they don't disappear. He talked about feeling more grounded in his life. But he still found it particularly difficult that his girlfriend could be a gladiator but just wasn't interested in the soul-to-soul discussions he searched for.

'I've always loved trees; we were always out in nature as kids.' He paused. 'Do you think my search for being is a waste of time? People think I'm just mad.' 'On the contrary,' I replied, 'I don't think you should ever give up. But it's interesting that your way of searching for meaning with other people is so sabotaged by your aggression.'

We can talk about this man's story as conventional Oedipal rivalry, or even analyse it in narcissistic borderline terms, but I am interested in how this man's hysterical identification with his lost father can also be seen as a hysterical defence against lived time and possible future selves. This man's raging melancholia, his gladiator melodrama, was a self-idealised mode of

relating which dissociated him from other parts of his experience. Consequently, it also split him off from being able to negotiate different fantasies and
needs with other people.

Chapter 4

Death, life and the double

Foucault (1976) suggests that sexuality in the nineteenth century was a product of disciplinary power that regulated women's bodies, subjecting them to a hysterisation that qualified and then disqualified them. This hysterisation saturated women's bodies with sexuality, integrating and pathologising them within a medical discourse. At the same time, the hysterical female body was placed in relation to the social regulation of reproduction and as the guarantor (in the guise of the nervous mother) of the spiritual sanctity of the family. The hysteric was both the embodiment of sexuality and the personification of its lack. As the movement of sex, hysteria was both 'whole and part', one and the other, angel and whore (Foucault 1976: 153).

The hysteric is then the very personification of the double, 'she' is both the sexual whore and the sacrificial mother, 'she' is also the mad patient that grounds in a sense the Oedipal doctor of psychoanalysis. As I shall go on to discuss, the hysteric's mimesis is indistinguishable from Oedipal rivalry. Pierre Janet (1920) theorised hysteria as a double personality with a subconscious automatic existence that manifested itself in attacks, accidents and what Janet called 'stigmata' or permanent symptoms. Whereas hysterical accidents resulted from fixed ideas, the deeper 'stigmata' arose from a narrowing of consciousness and lack of psychic strength:

> The hysterical personality cannot perceive all the phenomena; it definitely sacrifices some of them. It is a kind of autotomia, and the abandoned phenomena develop independently without the subject being aware of them.
>
> (Janet 1920: 375)

Janet distinguished hysteria from 'psychasthenia', a term for what we would now call obsessive conditions and phobias. Jung, who studied under Janet, developed these neuroses and made them into the prototypes for his extroverted and introverted personalities. Jung centrally developed Janet's notion of fixed ideas into his theory of unconscious complexes. As we discussed in Chapter 3, the hysterical double in Janet's thinking is mapped by Bergson as a kind of false recognition, a weakened attention to life where virtual unconscious memory appears as a double to the more active, conscious and willed self.

But the notion of a double personality in Jung's work is also indebted to the philosophy of Nietzsche. Nietzsche's philosophy in a big sense can be seen as the origin for much psychoanalytic thinking. Freud famously denied Nietzsche's influence, saying he could not understand him. But for Jung, Adler and Rank, Nietzsche was second only to Freud in inspiring their ideas. Nietzsche's ideas centre on the notion of instincts – of aggression, pleasure and a will to truth and knowledge. These instincts gradually became formulated as one force or will to power. For Nietzsche everything we think and feel is rooted in unconscious self-deception. Unconsciousness and dreams are our cultural thoughts and feelings and they are also re-enactments of our individual and collective pasts.

Central to Nietzsche's will to power was the notion that humans, caught between their aggressive animal instincts and a false morality, must experience their animal nature to the full and overcome it. Only by expressing these unconscious, affectual desires can humans rise above them in a true way. Such individuals – the epitome of self-made value and strength – are those capable of grasping the highest morality, that of the eternal return. These individuals live their lives as ones of eternal return. The idea here is that life is always a repeat; we return to this very life or moment and live it again and again. Because everything is this eternal and cyclical repetition, there is no linear movement of time. There is, then, no escape and we have to take absolute responsibility for this life – or moment, which is our present, a present eternally recurring. To sum up Nietzsche's argument, eternal repetition is how we live time.

Many of Freud's central ideas can be traced back to Nietzsche, for example the repression of an unconscious instinctual id and the conflict of instinctual drives. Freud's *Civilisation and its Discontents* (1930) echoes Nietzsche's *Genealogy of Morals* (1967) with the idea of civilisation demanding that humans give up instinctual gratification. Nietzsche argued that the repression of envy and hatred leads to false morality or consciousness. This can be seen as a forerunner to Freud's notion of neurotic guilt and the super-ego.

In contrast to Freud, Nietzsche emphasised not repressed sexuality, but repressed aggressive and self-destructive drives. Although Freud denied Nietzsche's influence, Jung, Rank and Adler attributed their main influence (after Freud) to Nietzsche. Jung gave a series of lectures on Nietzsche's famous text, *Thus Spake Zarathustra*, a story of a prophet and his teachings (Jung 1989). Relating Zarathustra to Nietzsche's second personality or double, Jung analysed the text as a study in unconscious archetypes. For Jung, like Nietzsche, it is only by exploring our unconscious double or shadow self that we can expand our consciousness of archetypes, thus creatively overcoming the unconscious force they exert over us.

We can link this doubling between conscious and unconscious affect to Bergson's and Janet's ideas of the mind as a hypnotic, double temporality. If we think of this in terms of a phenomenological unconscious then the hysterical double inhabits a world of virtual fantasy and memory, split off from conscious perception and activity. As in Bergson's account of the virtual mirror stage, hysterics are dissociated from their active, experiential self. However, I also want to suggest that because hysterics are split between their virtual and actual worlds then they also perform the bodily real in an over-literal and exaggerated way. The conversion symptoms of hysterics, their physiological symptoms and their extreme anxiety, are manifestations of affects that have become blocked off from the imaginary flows of the virtual. Affects, here, are alienated in relation to fixed representations and so they repeat, as split-off bodily symptoms that accompany a conscious perception that is divorced from the psychic body. The hysteric is split between real and imaginary worlds. This pathological doubling manifests itself in the hysteric as a weakened indifferent state where virtual dreaming has taken over. Alternatively hysterics might present with an overly intellectual disposition, or they might display bursts of labile emotion and deliriums so characteristic of Anna O.

However, the unconscious world of the double is also creative, but creative doubling is dependent on the virtual and actual being able to flow together in what Bergson calls a lived duration. Memory is virtual being but it is also real and affectual. Paradoxically it is hysterics who display this movement of our body as memory because, for them, bodily memory has become fixated. As Janet says, nothing is lost in the unconscious. Hysterics are split between their conscious perception and their virtual world. This is why hysterics can manifest in their dissociated state as seemingly too full of consciousness. Juliet Mitchell writes that 'there is too much consciousness in the hysteric' because he or she lacks the protective capacity for memory (Mitchell 2000: 292). However, the hysteric also presents as lost in an uncanny virtual world of fantasy that cannot be actualised as desire. Bergson tells us that *memory arrives only* with our actualisation of life in the present. In a sense, then, hysterics are both too present and too absent because their virtual and actual worlds do not flow in relation to each other.

A phenomenological tracking of what hysterics are saying with their body is important in the therapy session. It is not merely a question of how hysterics represent themselves to the other, or whether they become lost in their so-called pre-Oedipal affects. Both Freud and Roustang are right. Roustang tells us that the hysteric suffers from representation, from telling the same old Oedipal stories to the therapist. But this hysterical representation is because patients are split between real and imaginary worlds. They are thus over-conscious and split off from their unconscious fantasy world, literally enacting their identifications with their body because they cannot connect them with their imaginary. At the same time the hysteric is lost in a virtual fantasy world, which is ultimately passive because these fantasies cannot be actualised in relation to the body and time. We can link this to Winnicott's (1971a) case history of a middle-aged woman who is lost in passive dissociation and daydreaming about pink clouds. In this day-dreaming the woman does not live and this is in contrast to the active dreaming she brings to therapy, where she accesses live feelings of mur-derous hate for her mother. Winnicott makes a good distinction between occupying a fantasy world and not living, and the ability to dream and live (Winnicott 1971a). In this scenario, dreams translate and transform our existence whereas fantasising is simply an escape. Anna O's hidden observer also sums up the quintessential split for the hysteric between imaginary and real worlds.

Such dissociation also explains the paradox noted by many clinicians in relation to the hysterical personality. For this character seems on the one hand to exhibit and repeat the same old dissociated self-state over and over again. At the same time she also appears to have multiple and labile identi-fications, often noted as bisexual. These multiple states are, however, not connected and swing between fantasy and the body, between masculine and feminine and between life and death in a polarised melodrama.

As I have argued elsewhere, we can see this split doubling of the hysteric as a rivalrous and Oedipal mimesis (see Campbell 2005). Borch-Jacobsen has shown us how hypnosis and hysteria make up the narcissistic and mimetic identification or (if you like) the transference that constitutes identity in relation to the other, between ego and object. This mimetic and rivalrous identification is not prior to Oedipal desire, it *is* Oedipal desire, a desire based not on identification with difference, but in relation to a 'homosexual' same-sex love. This hysterical, Oedipal same-sex doubling is at work between Freud and Jung in their rivalrous and loving relationship and letters of correspondence, the letters that precede the famous split and parting of ways, leaving Freud as sole heir to the kingdom of psychoanalysis and Jung ousted to develop his Zurich school. As Borch-Jacobsen tells it, the correspondence between Jung and Freud involves a mimesis and exchange of ideas where each lays claim to the thoughts of the other, until no discernible difference remains. Frightened by this mimetic identification that threatens to take Freud's very identity and authenticity away from him, Freud emphasises the sexuality underlying his theory because he realises that there is in reality no difference between his sexual libido theory and Jung's emphasis on a more egoistic agency and non-specific libido. Unable to extricate himself from this mimetic rivalry, Freud appropriates Jung's ego for himself, adds narcissism to sexuality, thus 'finishing off the communism of thought sharing while (re) instituting intellectual private property – that is to say the narcissistic economy' (Borch-Jacobsen 1992: 71).

No difference, then, between narcissism and object love, or between ego libido and sexual libido, or between psychosis and neurosis (except perhaps one of scale). Jung's understanding of the libido was one of energy rather than specific sexuality, a libido that becomes sexually fixated in neurosis, and non-sexual in psychosis, as the ego withdraws all cathexis from the object and social world. But if the hysterical identification and mimesis that Borch-Jacobsen (1992) draws between Freud and Jung, and between ego and object love, is more exaggerated in neurosis and abandoned or withdrawn in psychosis, then how do we understand these differences in relation to Jung's theory of projection and dissociation and Freud's theory of repression?

In Jung's theory of unconscious projection and dissociation, libido functions within a physiological energy system (incorporating hunger and sexuality): when energy is heightened in one area it has become lost and displaced elsewhere. So, whether affect is exaggerated or lacking, it displays a dissociation of our embodied relation to the world and the object. The phenomenological balance between conscious and unconscious is altered and the unconscious becomes the place where the displaced and dissociated libido is hiding. For Freud, psychic repression also involves the rejection of the object and the world; in psychosis this repression fails completely and accordingly becomes distorted and projected.

So what really is the distinction between dissociation and repression, or between Jung and Freud, when it comes to a question of the unconscious? If we return to Freud's early theories on hysteria we can see that in fact he agreed with Charcot and Breuer that the unconscious was a result of dissociation. Freud's switch from his early interest in neurobiology to Oedipal psychology was founded on the impossibility of grounding his theory in the dynamic and functional system of neurobiology, a physiological system that for him worked analogously with the psyche. Freud's hysterical identification with his early psychoanalytical brothers is then a rivalry that turns on the undecidable structural position between scientific authority and madness: the undecidable difference between Oedipal identification and hysteria. Madness is at the centre of Freud's dispute with Jung, where Jung openly admits his hysterical identifications, and with Fliess the final dissociation and split from Freud does indeed provoke Fliess's madness. Hysteria can then be summed up as a mimetic identification and dissociation that moves between ego and other; an imaginary and Oedipal identification that represses and dissociates libidinal and psychic energy. This repression or dissociation is not rooted in the past, for, as Jung states, the past is invoked as a flight from the present.

I have discussed two models of psychoanalysis and the unconscious in relation to Freud's thinking. First, is an unconscious repression of representations, where the unconscious refers to an efficacy of knowledge and memory; second, is an unconscious that cannot be remembered or represented because it has never been conscious. Now, for Roustang (1996) and Henry (1993) this latter unconscious is an unconscious that does not exist as such; it is simply life as affect, radically distinct from a system of representation. This notion of the unconscious, as immanent affect, draws on Nietzsche's ideas of a distinction between representation and will.

Following Bergson, I want to suggest the unconscious as an immanent virtual ontology. Existence is not reducible to consciousness; psychical states can exist outside conscious perception, as dormant virtual tendencies. Movement between virtual and actual is the duration of our psychic body as a state of becoming. Life is the actualisation of the virtual and affects become produced in relation to this becoming. So rather than illustrating the division between conscious and unconscious as one between representation and affect, we can see this difference more productively as one between being asleep and awake, or between dreaming and action. Bergson did not espouse either a representational or a material philosophy. For him both mind and matter are qualitative differences characterised as images and such images can be more or less conscious. Thus the mystery for Bergson is not really what is unconscious. We are unconscious of most things, the world and our psychical states that exist in a virtual way, although we remain unaware of them. These are images that we have not lived, or have ceased to live.

So affects come to life, as we do, in the duration of the psychic body that constantly translates unconscious images into actual ones. Freud is therefore right to tie the unconscious to both representation and affect, although if we accept the unconscious as virtual life, then the production of differences and new experiences is always in the movement between unconscious and conscious. This fluidity thus militates against the distinction in psychoanalysis between Oedipal representation and so-called pre-Oedipal affects, a division that in many ways can be seen to have defined psychoanalysis – privileging representation and mental meaning as the route out from the unmediated instinctual desires of the id. Bergson's ideas of lived time can allow us to understand the division between conscious and unconscious as a separation between a lived present and the whole of our past as virtual. The past never ceases to exist, but it becomes lost and is continually being reconstituted. But this does not mean that we store memories as some other repressed and psychological reality in the mind.

Memory is representational: an abstract and intellectual cutting out of time within space, or memory is the being of our psychic body. This corporeal memory of vital forces cannot be remembered or represented because it has never been consciously represented. Freud linked this bodily unconscious that has never been represented to a primary early emotional tie, a hypnotic rapport before subject and object are differentiated. This is the hypnotic bond that manifests itself as a resistance in the transference. Now if the unconscious as a lived psychic body lies outside or before conscious representation, then it is not a resistance to Oedipal, repressed desires that is at stake in the hysteric's demand of love in the transference. Although Freud did initially see the resistance to the transference as a disguised Oedipal wish or desire, he contradicted these findings in his later work of the 1920s. This is where Freud recognises that the transference cannot rest on the disguise of an Oedipal wish, because it is based on an emotional mimetic tie that has never been repressed, never been conscious. And so for that reason it can be repeated only in the present and is not available for conscious recollection.

In his later meta-psychological essays such as 'Beyond the Pleasure Principle' (1920) and 'Inhibitions, Symptoms and Anxiety' (1926), Freud poses the problem of primal repetition and compulsion. Acknowledging that traumatic dreams were not necessarily linked to the transformation of desire and wish fulfilment, Freud started to explore the defence of the ego in relation to the role of traumatic anxiety. 'Beyond the Pleasure Principle' is where Freud theorises the economic role of repetition as a death drive beyond the pleasure principle. This is where large amounts of stimulus threaten to breach the ego's protective shield. The ego's attempts to master and bind this stimulus also fail, so leading to a radical unbinding or dissolution of the ego as a death drive.

In 'Inhibitions, Symptoms and Anxiety' Freud qualifies his economic theory, also returning to his earlier theories of neurotic defence. He proposes automatic *and* defensive anxiety. On the one hand is excitement, affect and discharge as automatic anxiety, signifying a primal repression and identification with the early mother. Here, Freud is pointing to the anxiety of birth, but he criticises Otto Rank's notion that the trauma of birth is an event or experience. Anxiety, for Freud, cannot refer to an early object or event because during the child's 'intra-uterine life the mother was not an object for the foetus, and that at that time there were no objects at all' (Freud 1926: 138). Primal anxiety, therefore, refers to the early biological tie between infant and mother, which is helpless, traumatic and automatic: the repetitive, hypnotic and affectual role of physiological binding and dissolution.

On the other hand, Freud acknowledges that anxiety is not just primal. It is also a rescuing signal of danger, a response to the ego's protective defences being breached. This signal anxiety is where danger (such as absence of the mother) is threatened. Anxiety, here, constitutes a progressive move for the child towards self-preservation – representing 'a transition from the automatic and involuntary fresh appearance of anxiety to the intentional reproduction of anxiety as a signal of danger' (Freud 1926: 138). Thus Freud distinguishes between anxiety that is protective, anticipating breaching of the ego's defences, and a helpless trauma that has no such organised awareness. Situating the former with the structure of the ego, which can defend against earlier more primal losses, signal anxiety indicates a developmental history that is capable of conscious representation. Earlier automatic anxiety, however, is rooted in a physiological affect or id, a place where self-representation and delineation between ego and object is missing. But as Leys (2000) suggests, these two forms of anxiety are not separate for Freud. Loss of the mother is both a danger and a trauma. Moreover, as Freud himself declared, ego and id are never really separate – just two parts of the same entity.

Much of Freud's late paper on anxiety is an attempt to link defensive trauma to a libidinal theory of the Oedipal Complex and can be seen as an answer not just to Rank's (1924) thesis of traumatic birth, but also the First World War physicians, who declared that war neurosis was a consequence of a fear of death, not castration. Of course these fears are never really distinct for Freud, but he stumbles in trying to make traumatic anxiety and danger fit with his libidinal model. Freud (1926) no longer sees anxiety as transformed libido, but he does argue for it as a 'surplus of unutilized libido'. Anxiety is being described here as dammed-up affect, exactly the kind of blocked-off affect that is reminiscent of the hysteric.

Key to Freud's economic theories in his later work is the theme of primal repression, an affectual, physiological tie to the mother where distinctions between ego and object remain indistinct. Repression enters into this equation not as wish fulfilment, but as flight or defence associated with anxiety. This harks back to Freud's earlier phenomenological accounts of hysteria in association with Breuer, where repression is associated with dissociation and psychical splitting off of unwanted affects.

Freud's classical theory of the Oedipal Complex asserts repression of sexual wishes as ideas, ideas that become converted through hysteria into bodily symptoms. This differs from his very early work where hysteria is seen as a defence against past traumatic experience. It also differs from his later economic theories where repetition of binding and unbinding in relation to the early instinctual tie takes precedence. Here, it is not unacknowledged desires, but a more primal, symbiotic relation with the other that is asserted.

I suggest that Freud's early, Oedipal, and later texts on anxiety and hysteria can all be connected if we frame them within a more immanent model. Primal repression and Oedipal anxieties are thus both a mimetic and defensive doubling, where the imaginary and real, and life and death have become divided. Freud separates anxiety into a primal fear of separation and a later protective signal. Nevertheless, one could argue that the real meaning of castration is the fear of, and defence against, death. In this case anxiety, whether 'primal' or 'Oedipal', is simply a matter of degree. Trauma and separation from the early mother lead to a defensive hysterical and Oedipal mimesis where the other is situated as the bodily ground for a fixed self-state.

In order for this thesis to work we have to abandon a psychoanalytic model that places a pre-Oedipal dissolution of self and other as a primordial immature state, succeeded by a separated ego and object – the

Oedipal subject of representation. Instead, there would be a mimesis or doubling between self and other which is narcissistic and defensive, and alternatively a mimesis between self and other where affects and virtual fantasies are actualised within a lived duration of the body. Such a creative mimesis or dissociation of the *élan vital* would be able to move between different self-states. Like Benjamin's and Proust's notion of embodied memory this vital force would reimagine and constantly remake these self-states in relation to the object.

Dissociation of a libidinal energy, here, is reminiscent of Jung's early ideas and again raises the question of how different are ego and object love. Do we have to distinguish so radically between an ego and a sexual libido? Indeed, it is in Freud's life-long struggle with the concept of hypnosis that we see questions of the libido, as narcissistic or object related, or questions of the psyche as repressed or dissociated, continually return. Hypnosis and the symbiotic bond with the other remain at the origins of Freud's career, and reappear in the last stages. As Borch-Jacobsen and Leys have noted, this theory of mimetic identification steadily undoes Freud's more Oedipal interpretations, positing cannibalistic identification with the other where desire easily switches from love into exterminating hatred. In his text 'Group Psychology and the Analysis of the Ego', Freud (1921) follows le Bon's description of the group mind and argues for it as a primitive, primeval horde bound together through libidinous identifications. When Freud came to analyse the libidinous identification that lies behind group ties, we find his theory of the Oedipus Complex seriously unravelled. Here bisexual identifications and group hysteria lead Freud to a theorisation of narcissism, the increasing split between ego and ego ideal, and suggestive hypnosis, as the key components of the group mind.

Although the Oedipal economy in Freud's work emphasises the repression of libidinal desire, there is a primary identification at work in Freud's texts which disrupts this notion of subjective desire for an object. Emotional identification or binding with the object is an earlier expression of love and is expressed in Freud's texts in relation to numerous ideas of imitation, sympathy and mental contagion. Texts such as 'Mourning and Melancholia' (1917) and 'Group Psychology and the Analysis of the Ego' (1921) posit the ambivalence of this primary emotional identification. In 'Mourning and Melancholia', he states that identification is 'a preliminary stage of object choice', where we narcissistically identify with the other, and where the ego wants to devour the object or other, cannibalistically taking it into itself (Freud 1917). Melancholic mimesis involves loss, hate and love of the other, which is indistinguishable from the loss, hate and love one feels for oneself.

But all this leads us to question the status of desire in Freud's text. If desire as it stands in Freud's trajectory seems to start and finish with the hypnotic bond, a bond that is sadomasochistic, narcissistic and ultimately death embracing, then what does this mean for the analytic cure? More pertinently, what does it mean for an understanding of psychoanalysis through a model of hysterical mimesis?

Ruth Leys (2000) structures her analysis of the mimetic principle through an opposition between mimesis and anti-mimesis. So, in Freud's body of work, the Oedipal theory of the subject and representation is the anti-mimetic principle, one that his writings on mimetic identification steadily undo. However, Leys is not writing from a clinical point of view and this leads her to neglect the importance, in her distinction between mimesis and anti-mimesis, of the transference. If the transference is mimetic, hypnotic and indissolvable, then there is no resolution of the analytic transference through Oedipal representation or conscious anti-mimesis. As Leys so admirably shows, the opposition between mimesis and anti-mimesis which she analyses in numerous critical authors on trauma is one that is always being undone. But she does not, as she is not an analyst, discuss what consequences this might have for the analytical cure. If, as Roustang (1996) and Borch-Jacobsen's (1992) early work has shown so clearly, hypnosis cannot be separated from either the practice or theory of psychoanalysis; and if psychoanalysis is in one sense simply long-drawn-out suggestion, then how is the hypnosis that cures distinct from the hypnosis of mimetic identification: the repetitive mimetic desire which Freud tells us ends in death?

Following on from this, if Oedipal representation does not resolve the transference and if representation is part and parcel of the neurotic suffering of the hysteric – the illness and not the cure – then what understanding of mimetic affect can release us from this ill, Oedipal storytelling? We suffer, then, from representation in analysis, as hysterics suffer in a way that is of course enjoyable and addictive. But what does it mean to leave Oedipus behind as a melodrama that fixates us in the past and within a certain trajectory of time and language?

I want to explore the idea that the Oedipal Complex is a defensive hysterical mimesis that defends against death. I also want to understand this complex as a more creative doubling that can continuously remake the object as it becomes actualised, again and again within lived time. Let us first consider the Oedipal Complex as hysterical defence. 'Inhibitions, Symptoms and Anxiety' is an important text because it links primal repression, and the repetition compulsion of the death drive, with an earlier emphasis on repression as a hysterical defence or flight. Why is this important? I think it is important in two ways. First, because it changes the way we understand the Oedipal Complex; second, because it introduces a link between hysteria and time. Freud changed his mind over his career as to the meaning of the Oedipal Complex. Whereas in his earlier essays on sexuality the Oedipal Complex and castration anxiety were the consequence of infantile pleasure colliding with reality and the castrating threat of the father, thus provoking repression, his later texts on anxiety linked repression with the early pre-Oedipal mother. In 'Inhibitions, Symptoms and Anxiety', Freud suggests that repression arises from the ego, shutting out the 'idea which is the vehicle of the reprehensible impulse from becoming conscious'. Repression, then, from the ego means that 'the excitary process in the id does not occur at all'. Freud goes on to say that 'if this is so the problem of "transformation of affect" under repression disappears' (Freud 1926: 91). It disappears presumably because access to the affectual id is blocked and repression becomes located within the neurotic mental conflict of the ego.

Returning to the hysterical phobia of Little Hans, Freud (1926: 125) suggests that, in contrast to his earlier ideas, it was anxiety that produced repression and not repression which produced anxiety. He is clearly here trying to interweave his theory of castration with that of traumatic anxiety and the death drive. But if we understand repression in a sense as a flight or defence against anxiety, then we have to ask where the flight of the hysteric is too. In Freud and Jung's early thoughts the adult hysteric flees into his or her past and takes refuge there to avoid the unpleasant reality of the present. For Hans, his flight is into a phobia about a horse biting him, a defence against his castration anxiety and his repressed hostility towards his father.

Repression of death, manifested as hysteria and the Oedipal Complex, is a flight into the past, but as we have seen in Chapter 3, this is not so much a flight into past reality, but a past of fixed ideas, virtual fantasy and romantic nostalgia; in fact all the family romances displayed by Freud and Breuer's hysterics. For children, separation from the mother faces them with the anxiety of losing their loving union with world. Separation threatens death to the affirmation of life so central to childhood. Children's neurotic solution to this is to substitute activity for passivity, replacing the emotional bond with the mother with a narcissistic inflation of the self. In other words children replace dependence on the mother with a narcissistic solution of becoming their own world or parent to themselves. This mastery, that is also a flight from death, separates affirmation of life from its natural counterpart – an acceptance of death.

A mimesis with the mother and world that affirms life *and* death is then an ability to live within the present. It is a repetition in Nietzsche's sense that returns always to the same moment, except that that moment is always lived differently as a new 'attention to life'. The Oedipal Complex is a defensive retreat from this life force, a narcissistic and hysterical retreat into a virtual world of fantasy. Here, mimetic identification and rivalry with the Oedipal parents is all about mastery and becoming a parent – to yourself. Aggression, which should be a natural component of life, is thus split off, externalised and projected onto the other.

The Oedipal Complex is a defensive hysterical mimesis, but it is also an uncanny doubling in Bergson's sense, where a virtual or fantasy past haunts the real action of the present. Such hysterical doubling is thus regressive fantasy that can become a creative return to narcissism and childhood. As such it can offer possible future identifications to be mobilised actively in terms of consciousness. In Freud's late essay 'The Dissolution of the Oedipal Complex' (1924), he acknowledges that the Oedipus Complex is both destroyed and retained. He qualifies this by saying that if the complex is only repressed, rather than abolished, it surfaces later as a 'pathogenic effect' (Freud 1924: 319). In order to be actualised in an attention to life, the Oedipal scenario has to lose its repressive flight from death; it has to be destroyed and remade into the possible affirmations that can expand our conscious world.

For the male heterosexual, this might mean exploring his repressed homosexuality or femininity. For a lesbian it might mean exploring her repressed heterosexuality. For the depressed heterosexual woman, in an abusive relationship, her fantasies of active male aggression would have to be removed from her partner and owned as part of herself. Repetition compulsion as the traumatic compulsion of adult relationships is thus a hysterical mimesis. If we understand the case of Little Hans in terms of hysterical mimesis, then he faces not a triangular situation in relation to his mother, but a libidinal and rivalrous identification of love and hate towards his father. His narcissistic need is to father himself in the face of instinctual ambivalence towards the mother. The Oedipal scenario of having to choose between identification and desire is in a sense a defence against a more primal anxiety and fear of death, or separation, in relation to the mother. Repression here is not simply about a wish or desire for the prohibited mother, but for a whole scene of affectual identification which involves the father not as a third term but as an extension of that early mimetic relation with the mother.

In 'Group Psychology and the Analysis of the Ego' (1921) and 'Moses and Monotheism' (1937) Freud postulates a primal father who castrates his sons, but if we see this primal father mimetically (Borch-Jacobsen 1988) then not only does the whole concept of the repressive Oedipal father and castration collapse back into a model of mimetic devouring identification, but also it becomes impossible to distinguish the mimetic relation with the early father from the anxiety and ambivalence to the primal mother. Freud acknowledges this hysterical Oedipal conflict in 'The Ego and the Id' (1923), when he suggests that all the ambivalence to the father, which kick-starts the super-ego, is in fact also found in the child's relation to the mother.

If the Oedipal Complex collapses back into an ambivalent relation of mimesis to the primal mother, it is also simultaneously a defence against it – a doubling which refuses to recognise death as an integral component of life. Freud discovers two things in his late texts on the death drive and anxiety: first, a primal relation of mimetic affect, and second, repression as a defence against this. This repression is not a transformation of Oedipal libido in the face of a castrating reality principle, but an anxiety that is linked to a dangerous (anticipated) or a traumatic loss of the mother. We can also see the relationship to the Oedipal father as a mimesis of love, rivalry and devouring identification that mirrors the mimetic death drive to the early mother. Loss of this father or mother is traumatic, helpless and automatic in all the ways that Freud states because the child's ego is undifferentiated from the mother/father object. Repression in Freud's early work is the external reality principle, represented by the castrating father. However, in Freud's later work repression becomes immanent, part of the early relationship between mother and child, something the child represses in his or her mimetic relationship with the other. But if this repression is not in response to a castrating father figure, then what exactly is this anxiety and consequent repression that Freud talks about in his late texts?

In 'Beyond the Pleasure Principle' (1920), Freud talks about a dualism of the life and death instincts: 'Our views have from the very first been *dualistic*' (Freud 1920: 53). He criticises Jung's libido theory for being *monistic*. However, if we look closely at Freud's description of these drives, we see this duality constantly unravelling. Earlier on, Freud made a distinction between the drives of sexuality and self-preservation, or between libido and ego, but his concepts of narcissism undermined this duality. In 'Beyond the Pleasure Principle' Freud argues for an ambivalence, between love and hate, life and death, and again this supposed duality does not hold up. Freud identifies the death drive with a Nirvana principle which becomes modified in the person to become a pleasure principle: death becomes transformed into life. He also identifies the early ambivalence towards the mother as a sadomasochistic complex where primary masochism becomes transferred, projected onto others, as sadism.

Aggression towards others is then a flight from feelings of masochist death within the self. We can therefore argue that this flight from death is a repression of our relation to death, a repression in the sense that the life and death instincts cannot be separated; they are a monistic force, to quote Jung. Of course this militates against Freud's speculative view that the death drive is a primary, non-organic entity. Death, as Nietzsche reminds us, is an integral part of life. Repression of our relation to death, therefore, is also a repression or flight from the affectual and life-driving mimesis in relation to the (m)other. When Freud states that 'every thing living dies for *internal* reasons' and that 'the aim of life is death', he is arguing that the human being has a drive back to the pre-organic existence that preceded it (Freud 1920: 38). Death instincts assure us not only that we follow our own path to death but also that the human organism 'wishes to die only in its own fashion' (Freud 1920: 39). However, if we understand this dying not in opposition, but as part of the whole we call life, then the meaning of the death drive changes.

Note that Freud states the human organism's need to acknowledge and accept death 'in its own fashion'. This is not death at the hands of another, or death that is fought and defended against. A sense, then, of one's own death, not as anti-life but more creatively as a part of what makes existence alive and meaningful. Heidegger's (1967) notion of *Dasein* comes to mind, here, the notion that our dwelling is dependent on an awareness and acceptance of death and mortality.

Freud's death drive can be seen to introduce issues of being and time, most notable in terms of the death drive as repetition compulsion. Linking his ideas to war neuroses, Freud considers how a trauma is associated with a repetition of past events, where the unpleasant traumatic event is repeated time and again. Referring to dreams, Freud notes that in traumatic neurosis the dream repeats the scene of the trauma, a scene where the patient 'wakes up in another fright' (Freud 1920: 13). Linking this to his early ideas of hysterics who suffer from reminiscences, Freud also argues that this traumatic repetition is a fixation on the past. As we have seen, this traumatic repetition, whether it occurs in war victims or the reminiscences of hysterics, is a retreat to a virtual world of the double. The past is repeated as though it was continually present and not past and movement into the future becomes impossible.

Now Freud also talks in this paper about the repetition of childhood play, his famous account of the Fort Da game where the child plays at conquering the absence of the mother. This imitative behaviour is pleasurable and can master unpleasant experiences through taking an active as well as a passive role. The creativity of this mimesis or doubling is that activity does not replace passivity: both components are still in motion. Repetition compulsion in children is pleasurable: it is how the child learns and plays; but in adults repetition compulsion exceeds the pleasure principle to become lost in a defensive traumatic anxiety over death.

The difference between these two models of mimesis and repetition can be seen as structured in relation to time. Whereas child's play is a lived and eternal time of the psychic body, the adult's traumatic repetition has entered conventional, abstract time and has become subject to repression. A conflict between pleasure and repetition is not found in children, who live in a world of mimesis where affectual being is relatively unaffected by goal-seeking aims, towards the future, which in adults is linked to linear and conventional clock time, or the progress of history. I want to suggest that this timeless repetition of the child can also be seen as a lived time of the present, where being takes precedence over a subjection to the time that is designated by conventions of society. Implicit in this child-like repetition or mimesis is, in Nietzsche's sense, an affirmation of life; it is a return to the same eternal present, as a discovery of the new. And like Bergson's affirmation of life, this repetition is not a doubling that is split in relation to a virtual past, so weakening attention to the present. It is an exploration of fantasy that is also always in the process of unconsciously selecting those possible parts of being, and actualising them in an embodied way in terms of the world.

Thus in my reading of Freud's death drive, traumatic repetition in adults is a hysterical flight into virtual past fantasy, or a fixation within conscious perception where intellectual registers and psychosomatic existence become separated. It is a repetition that has undergone repression. This is where the force of life and a mimesis of lived time have been exchanged for a hysterical mimesis as a flight and defence against a sense of one's own death. Such hysterical repetition is inherent in the Oedipal Complex. In this narrative the Oedipal Complex becomes the hysterical flight from death, which is also a defence against the ambivalent affectual tie with the early mother. We can see from this argument how a dualism and conflict between the life and death drives arises from repression of this early affectual bond. The Oedipal Complex is a dualism: the splitting into masculinity and femininity, activity and passivity that arises from the flight of the child or person in defence against death.

I have argued in the preceding chapters that we can see Oedipal repression as a dissociation that is both defensive and creative. Freud's concepts of signal anxiety and a more primal anxiety are both in differing degrees a defence against death. However, anxiety in life or the symptoms we meet up with in the therapy room are not just defensive. They also hold the key to accessing the life force of the body. Roustang suggests that anxiety is an expression of the pure psychic state 'in relation to consciousness' (Roustang 1996: 98). Because consciousness attempts to master the living bodily psyche, then the psyche has to leave its pure state and enter into a representation that is external to it, thus manifesting as anxiety. Such anxiety becomes solidified in consciousness, as symptoms that have become cut off from their psychic source. Tracing symptoms back to the root anxiety is how therapy forces the symptom 'out of its isolation and reinvigorates it'. We can think of symptoms as vitalities that have been split off from a more lived duration and have become abstracted. Affects and vitalities turn into anxiety and symptoms when they are abstracted and represented within consciousness. Our suffering can be alleviated only by returning anxiety to the psychic flows that animate the body. I will choose an example to illustrate this.

A young man I saw suffered great anxiety, to the point of obsession, with thoughts and fantasies that he desired much younger girls. He did not actually feel desire for these children, but was constantly terrified that he might. This fear was linked to the part of him that had felt abused as a child by a very mad father. It was only when this young man could acknowledge and get over his raging grudge against his father that his anxiety disappeared and he could move forward into independent adulthood.

In 'Beyond the Pleasure Principle' Freud writes of traumatic repetition compulsion in terms of dream. He wonders about the fact that dreams which are meant to be based on wishes continually put the patient back into the scene of trauma. He remarks, 'This astonishes people far too little' (Freud 1920: 13). Our repetitive anxiety in dreams, as in life, is a suffering that has become externalised and separated from the immanent flows of psychic life. For Freud, either the function of dreaming has become perverted or 'we may be driven to reflect on the mysterious masochistic trends of the ego' (Freud 1920: 14). Masochism, we are led to understand by Freud, is an instinct whose function is to follow its own journey towards death, 'to ward off possible ways of returning to inorganic existence other than those which are immanent in the organism itself' (Freud 1920: 39).

Masochism, like anxiety, is a suffering cut off from lived time and needs to be returned to a psychic immanence. Although Roustang and Henry would understand this as a pure self-immanence of the body, I understand the lived psychic body to be immanent in relation to the other. Winnicott best describes this state of being in relation to an 'other' as the child's capacity to be alone in the presence of the mother. Another example would be the primary maternal preoccupation of the woman in pregnancy. When masochism cannot be returned to an immanence of lived time, it becomes extraverted as aggression and sadism. It is in the splitting off of the death instinct from the organic, loving tie to the mother that the terror of unprepared death experience occurs. This is because death is projected onto the undifferentiated other who is then experienced as persecutory. Melanie Klein's work has mapped this early relation of projected hate, but it is important to note that this automatic experience of trauma, however early, is also a defence against an organic mimesis where death can be accepted as part of what grounds life.

This brings us again to a discussion of the transference. We can see how hysterical mimesis in the Oedipal Complex is a repetitive doubling that is both a mastery and defence against death. As the transference this hysterical mimesis is a hypnotic bond to an all-powerful other. Setting up the parent, analyst or lover as the all-powerful other is investing them as our world. It is an identification that makes us feel safe. For the child (or the adult) it is how they can form a sense of belonging that is in their control and defends against the terror and chaos of the world beyond that powerful other. As Ernst Becker (1973) suggests, in this scenario it is not the world that is terrifying, only our parents. Transferring hypnotic wonder and fear of the world into a person is a defence against helplessness and isolation.

> This is the logical fate for the utterly helpless person: the more you fear death and the emptier you are, the more you people your world with omnipotent father figures, extra magical helpers.
>
> (Becker 1973: 147)

Transference, then, is not primarily about sex, but about the existential terror of the human condition. This, as Becker (1973) points out, is the real meaning of the castration complex. But transference onto the other is not just about a hysterical fear of life and death, it is also an expansive identification onto the other, one which, as Otto Rank (1958) reminds us, is creative because it enables us to move beyond ourselves and into the world as a life force.

Like Jung, Rank (1958) saw this heroic expansion of the self as a spiritual dimension, life longing that expands beyond the personal realm to an idea of God. Unlike Freud, Rank saw a hunger for God as the love ideology of Agape, as opposed to the power ideology of Eros. Whereas Eros can only enhance the narcissistic ego, Agape can create a bigger world:

> In a word, the truly creative type is bigger than his tasks and accomplishments, and never finds or even seeks fulfilment in the world of reality but only in the true spiritual world of creation.
>
> (Rank 1958: 195)

For Rank a necessary dualism exists between the soul and the body. Personal relationships cannot carry the weight of the expansive transference or life force, only an identification moving beyond the individual can achieve this. Becker (1973) puts it succinctly: for him guilt is not a problem of infantile fantasy but of self-conscious adult reality. Thus it is existential. As children we repress the overwhelming nature of the world: 'Repression fulfils the vital function of allowing the child to act without anxiety, to take experience in hand and develop dependable responses to it' (Rank 1958: 262).

Although Nietzsche was as much a mentor to Rank as Freud, Rank refused the cynicism of both these father figures when it came to Christian morality. Of Nietzsche he said, 'he overlooked the deep need in the human being for just that kind of morality' (Becker 1973: 174). Rank (1958) and more recently Becker (1973) see regression to Eros and the body as a backward step that sets up an unrepressed narcissistic drive – modern man's new terrorism. Within their dualism (which is typically Freudian) the body is an unconscious infantile and erotic force that has to be transcended through repression. Sublimation of the body is through a creative and spiritual life force.

I want to suggest, however, that an alternative to hysterical mimesis does not lie in such creative spiritual transcendence. Rank's spiritual solution seems in many ways to replace the Oedipal Complex with God. In this scenario we are left with a pre-Oedipal, Oedipal binary: repression or the body, civilisation or the discontented narcissist, as Freud would say. In Chapter 3 we saw how the hysteric's dilemma is not a regression to bodily symptoms because he or she cannot Oedipally represent or sublimate desire.

On the contrary, hysterics suffer too much from the representation of themselves to the other. Hysterics are lost in a continual need to tell their stories and immerse themselves in narcissistic self-consciousness. If this continual representation of the hysteric, which is also Oedipal repetition, is a refusal to acknowledge death, then what kind of mimesis or repetition, what form of identification can move to embrace life *and* death? The difference between the Oedipal adult death drive and a childhood mimesis, of repetition, is the relation to time. Whereas the adult lives a life of dualisms in order to master time, the child's mimesis repeats but creatively discovers time as a repetition of the new.

Winnicott discusses how this creative mimesis of being and affect structures the transitional object. The child, in optimum conditions, not only discovers reality again and again, but also makes it up through fantasy and discovers it anew. In Nietzsche's view this is an eternal return, a timeless doubling, where we always return to this life, this same experience, differently. The creativity of this eternal mimesis or doubling is that we can acknowledge this present experience as the same, but also as something unique and different. Affirmation of the present, and of our vital force, as lived time, is also what Bergson and Janet call an attention to life.

So to sum up the argument so far, the Oedipal Complex figures both as a hysterical defence against death and a more lived immanence in relation to the body and the early mother. Hysterical doubling can move, as Freud described, between a more protective signal anxiety and primal trauma. However, dissociation is not just defensive; it is also creative of a more lived multiplicity and bodily duration. Hypnosis and self-hypnosis is one way of de-linking from our cut-off conscious symptoms and suffering, allowing our anxiety to return to psychic lived flows that move between virtual and actual.

For Bergson lived time is the movement between virtual to the actual. Time is not the abstract representation of our suffering in space. In fact representation, as the hysteric lives the symptoms, is a false solidified self in denial of time. Lived time is the constant movement of time – and it is only in this active duration that the past can be acknowledged in the present. This is also Freud's realisation that the hysteric does not fly back into an actual past, but to a virtual one of fantasy and reminiscences. Those fantasies, archetypal complexes for Jung, and fixed ideas for Janet, are unconscious representations that have to be moved away from – either forgotten or actualised within bodily perception. The mimetic double has, therefore, two temporalities or propensities, hysteria and life.

In his work on the narcissistic double, Rank (1989) links the legend of Narcissus with the theme of the double. In the myth Narcissus, a young man, is emotionally cold to both men and women; he falls in love with his own reflection, in a pool, and subsequently commits suicide. Freud's (1914) essay on 'Narcissism' tries to distinguish between primary narcissism and object choice, but fails miserably. This failed distinction is also the dualism upon which the Oedipal Complex is founded. Heterosexual object choice versus homosexual identification breaks down as Freud eventually acknowledges the hysterical ambivalence and mimesis that refuses any distinction between ego and object:

> You remember the choice of the object according to the anaclitic (attachment) type, which psychoanalysis talks of? The libido there follows the paths of narcissistic needs and attaches itself to the objects which ensure the satisfaction of those needs. In this way the mother, who satisfies the child's hunger, becomes its first love object and certainly its first protection against all the undefined dangers which threaten it in the external world, its first protection against anxiety, we may say. In the function of the father (of protection) the mother is soon replaced by the stronger father, who retains that position for the rest of childhood. But the child's attitude to its father is coloured by a peculiar ambivalence. The father himself constitutes a danger to the child, perhaps because of its earlier relation to its mother.
>
> (Freud 1927: 24)

This movement of narcissistic identification between ego and object choice explains how, in depressive melancholia and in self-critical activities of the super-ego, we give up the object only when we replace it with an identification. So there is active identification with the loved object and a passive refashioning of the self as we incorporate the lost object and identify with it. We can see how narcissism forms the basis of these active and passive identifications. Hysteria is the mimetic identification or Oedipal ambivalence that illustrates a defence against death and the lost object. As such it entails a passive incorporation of the lost object as we model ourselves upon it. The hysterical and the narcissistic double are, therefore, indistinguishable. Otto Rank (1989) describes the narcissistic, hysterical double in relation to Oscar Wilde's *Picture of Dorian Gray* (1890).

Dorian, who is directly modelled on Narcissus, is the beautiful boy in love with his own image. Rank shows how Dorian, as a literary double, represents Freud's thesis on primary narcissism. Dorian, unable to love, is fixated on his own image of himself mirrored back by Basil Hallward's beautiful painting of him. In the story, Dorian's fear of growing old and dying hits him when he gazes at his own loveliness in the picture. He declares: 'When I find that I am growing old, I shall kill myself.' Locked in a room, the picture of Dorian ages and becomes evil, whereas in life Dorian remains youthful and unblemished despite his cold character and ruthless activities. For Dorian seeks only self-gratification, surrounded by men and women who love him, he remains like Bergson's hysterical double, someone who can only watch himself – on a stage or in a play.

Dorian is certainly narcissistic and his double in the picture is a literal defence against death; his double is also hysterical and Oedipal. Basil Hallward is in love with Dorian; he is the rivalrous father figure, infatuated with Dorian's youth. He is also the ageing and needy man that Dorian won't become. As a father–son relationship, Basil and Dorian represent Oedipal and hysterical ambivalence. Dorian is the sadistic, narcissistic boy who won't grow up, incapable of active love. Basil is his double, a father who ages and shrivels, masochistic and self-hating; he is as incapable as Dorian of acknowledging life and death.

Dissolution into rivalrous sexual love, Basil's love for Dorian, or Dorian's love for himself, is an Oedipal and hysterical ambivalence which become characterised through the double. This narcissistic double, indistinguishable from primary narcissism, is a defence against death; it is a dualism which sets up the ego in rivalry and opposition to itself and the world. As such it is essentially a passive, hysterical mimesis that can't transfer active love for the mother onto the world. Early ambivalence towards the mother and father is defended against by Dorian and Basil through a narcissism that sets up life and death as antagonistic, an antagonism reminiscent of Freud's death drive.

One of the problems for clinical work about Freud's Oedipal theory is not just that it sets up the father (even if only in name) as the law, but it posits self-knowledge as the cure. As Rank acknowledges, in Freud's favourite myth, Oedipus discovers his history and gains self-knowledge but this provokes death, not recovery. Knowledge and theory are not what heals in therapy or life. Ferenczi and Rank challenged Freud's emphasis on recollection and self-truth as the goals of therapy when they published *The Development of Psychoanalysis* (1925). Here, they argued for the importance of repetition of past neurotic fixation in the analytic session, and the present experience in relation to the analyst. Therapy at its best elicited something new, a relational experience which had never been conscious. For Rank the therapist was a midwife, not a symbolic father, and psychological rebirth was centred on the creative emergence of the individual from his neurosis as an artist. Although Rank has been acknowledged as the first object-relations psychoanalyst, his thesis on the trauma and separation from the early mother in *The Trauma of Birth* (1924) has been criticised for being too literal, an emphasis on this trauma as a real event. A large part of this critique lies with Rank's refusal to separate psychology from biology. He argues for the inimitable 'biologically tangible substrate of the psychical' (Rank 1993: 23). This is seen as detracting from the precious emphasis on the unconscious; in other words, Rank is seen as too ready to substitute psychical reality with the reality of conscious experience.

Another way to read Rank's *Trauma of Birth* is to read it through Bergson's notion of the unconscious. Rank suggests that the significance of *The Trauma of Birth* lies in its attempt 'to substitute so-called primal fantasies with real, individual experiences' (Rudnytsky 2002: 104). Peter Rudnytsky uses this as more evidence of Rank's literal approach, reiterating that analytic work can take place only through the projection backwards of fantasy and the excavation of the psychic reality of our past. However, if we read Rank alongside Bergson, we can see the importance of being able to embody fantasies, allowing them to flow together with real experiences. Therapy work involves the exploration of fantasy, and without neurosis the doubling of our fantasy world is not possible. Within the neurotic lie the seeds of the artist. In order for the neurotic to move into the future and access his creative function, he has to learn how to transform 'primal fantasy' into real experience. And this brings Rank to a consideration of the double. For the double is not just the narcissistic, neurotic double illustrated so well by Dorian Gray, whose Oedipal rivalry defends against death and a more active, organic love for the mother. The double is also the key to a more creative, plural self. As our mimetic other it haunts us but remains deathly only if we split it off and set it up in a sadomasochistic relationship.

Acknowledgment of our mimetic double and our dependency, in relation to the mother or the world, means recognising not just that death is part of life, but that, as Bergson reminds us, we are always other. Rank recognises the psychology of what he calls the self lies within the other, whether that other is another individual, another country, another ideology. The tragic outcome of this dependency is that an active sense of self is garnered by setting ourselves up in opposition to the other. Real creative activity and the healing goals of therapy are gained not through this false distinction into self and other, but through the acceptance of the double as one fantasy amongst many. The double is me and it is you, but I can live this bond creatively only if I understand this doubling as a constant movement of lived time between fantasy and real experience, a movement that opens the mimesis of our desires to our present and future, a mimesis which can perhaps only recognise that past by distinguishing it from the evolving experience we have created anew. Perhaps the metaphors of Oedipal father or pre-Oedipal mother confuse the role of the therapist, because they suggest the analyst's function as *either* knowledgeable law or as a regressive imaginary (m)other. Maybe the role of double, in all its many manifestations, is a more apt definition; the double as Oedipal and hysterical – but always creatively on the move.

She entered the therapy room and I was immediately aware of her powerful presence. A woman looking much younger than her forty years, dressed in eccentric beautiful clothes with long blonde Rasta locks and heavy black boots. She worked as a top executive in the National Health Service (NHS).

She said, 'I don't like my job much. Working for an institution it's so faceless and conventional. My clothes make me feel alive.'

I said, 'What do they remind you of?'

'They remind me that I am still me. I used to work much more directly with people, sex workers, the homeless, with drug addicts, crisis work. I left because I got burnt out. Now I get paid lots and hate what I do, it's so meaningless. I'm paid to do a job I can't do because no one will give me the resources.'

This woman's powerful status at work was contrasted with her experience of being powerless in her personal relationships with men. These sadomasochistic relationships were all characterised by an initial intense romance, followed by a scenario where she would become increasingly bullied, physically and mentally, to a point where she risked her life.

I listened to her current account of being tortured by her partner and asked her why he was so important to her.

> I don't know, we were so in love and somehow I feel responsible, there must be something in me which makes him behave like that. He's a baby really and he is always so sorry afterwards that I forgive him. It never used to be like this between us. Now everything I do seems to provoke him. I can't seem to get angry with him, just paralysed. I am so angry at work, so frightened at home. I can't seem to leave him and I can't decide whether or not I want a baby. He just gets enraged at the thought.

'What about you, do you want a baby?'

'I don't know. I'm scared of not being able to cope. Most of all I'm scared of what being pregnant will do to my body. The thought of my body changing is terrifying.'

We talked about growing up in her family. She remembered retreating into her bedroom as a child and being content to read and draw for hours. As she grew older, battles between her and her mother developed, with her mother accusing her of withdrawing. Her mother would say:

'I don't know what's changed you. We used to be so close.'

This woman experienced her mother in a competition which became more intense as she entered adolescence. Everything she wanted to do, and be, her mother disapproved of. Every time her mother said no, her father said yes. He was the seductive parent and her Oedipal guilt around these parents was that she had indeed won the father. He loved and preferred her, not her mother. He was the one who championed her to go to art school. Her parents split up and she embarked on a relationship with an older man who progressively became more and more possessive and abusive.

Talking about this relationship, the woman said, 'It's made me feel damaged about my sexuality. Sexuality is really important to me, it's part of what I have done with my life, working in the field of sexual health, helping other women.'

I said, 'I wonder why you swapped being an artist for working with women who walk an edge between sexual danger and trauma?'

'I don't know, but sexuality is something creative for me. It's about dressing up and being someone different.'

This woman was very powerful sexually and very seductive to men. A big part of her personal and social life was spent dressing up seductively as a kind of game to promote sexual health or just simply to have fun. But this powerful seductive femininity and being irresistible to men caused jealousy with women. We talked about the links between her Oedipal family arrangements and the current triangles she became caught up in. I wondered aloud about her anger with women. She said, 'I find women difficult to really trust.'

I said, 'You always seem to have to be the strong one, it's like you can't ever really depend on a woman.'

We talked about her fear and desire of pregnancy and one day I said, 'Maybe you are so frightened of becoming a mother because your mother never really managed to hold you.'

'Yeah, my mother has always been just collapsed really, so unable to live her life.'

'That must make you very angry.'

> I guess so, but these days she is such a victim. It's hard to get angry with someone who is so passive. We used to fight when I was a teenager, but it was always a competition. We never really made up. These days she never gets in touch with me and when we do meet she is never direct about anything. It's as if she is scared of me or something.

The abusive behaviour towards this woman from her partner continued to the point that she was physically at risk. She managed to leave him and in the subsequent months talked about why she seemed to repeat these relationships.

'I don't understand why I pick these men,' she said, one day. 'Sometimes I worry that I was sexually abused, but my relationship with my Dad was the most loving.'

I said, 'Maybe you start replaying your relationship with your Dad with these men. At the beginning you are the powerful seductive woman making other women jealous. But maybe you end up replaying your relationship with your mother. You play your mother and the abusive man is your anger.'

'What do you mean?' she said, interested.

'It must provoke terrible rage in a child to have a mother as collapsed as yours,' I continued. 'Maybe these men are acting out some of that rage for you?'

The woman got very upset. There followed a period in the therapy where she became very regressed, found it impossible to go to work and would come to therapy and just cry. Work was another arena where this woman was superwoman, but there always came a point where she needed the support of a more experienced female manager and this manager always turned into another version of her mother. I saw this woman's depression and her rage, at the collapsed female managers at work, as a positive sign. She started to plan her escape from her job and started to take more seriously her work as an artist. Bringing her artwork to therapy, we talked about the images of powerful female sexuality intertwined with motherhood that she painted. As time went on she brought more abstract, aggressive images of masculinity. The woman swung between being collapsed around work and inhabiting a sort of ideal play space where she would practise her art and display it on the local festival circuit. These festival spaces were where she would also play at dressing up and enacted familiar scenarios involving infatuated men and jealous women.

We talked about how her play world of dressing up and her role as an artist took her back to the child who had retreated to daydream and draw. She wanted to retreat into her ideal world of seductive performance – I stuck up for the collapsed side of her in relation to her job.

'I hate my job, it's killing me. I'm permanently off sick. My boss is so useless. I have responsibility for bringing sexual health to the community and no one seems to care that it isn't happening. I can't do it on my own. But neither can I leave my job, without feeling like a failure.'

'Maybe it's time to take responsibility for yourself, rather than the traumatised women you want to help in the community? Perhaps being an artist for real is taking your collapsed side more seriously.'

'What do you mean?' she said.

'Well, I wonder how you imagine yourself – as an older woman?'

'You know, when I am dressing up, I never think of being 40, I feel more like 20.'

'Perhaps your seductive all-powerful performance is a defence against becoming an artist in your real life.'

'I don't agree, they go together. It's work I can't stand. I just go there and cry all day.'

'Dressing up is fun and it's a neat way to wrap up your aggression, but maybe there is more of a connection between that and the part of you that can't trust your mother?'

'I'm so angry my mother was never there. Even now, I can't have it out with her. And my Dad, he tries to rescue me, but he makes promises he can't keep.'

'Maybe you are too old to have a mother,' I said, feeling rather brutal.

'You mean I have to accept what I have never had?' she asked.

Over time this woman took steps to leave her job and set herself up as an artist. This was a period in therapy where she became very vulnerable and needed me intensely. She found a new romance with an ideal young man who seemed more fantasy than reality. After a while, when her disappointment at his vanishing acts turned into anger, we discussed how he was a kind of accomplice to her ideal self. She began to realise that her father could not live up to being a romantic hero who rescued her, and anyway being rescued by a fantasy prince always carried a price. She also began to understand that acknowledging the real limitations of her mother, and other people, meant that she could acknowledge dependency and the resourcefulness garnered through the actualisation of her artistic desires. As this woman's fantasy world and her real one became less split off from each other she managed to turn her dreams into the reality of becoming an artist in the world. About this time, she brought a particularly vivid dream to therapy.

She was in a house with many rooms, but could not figure out whether the house was hers or belonged to her girlfriend. She returned with some mates one night to find a party going on. The party seemed to get bigger and bigger, filling with people she did not know. She went into one room after another, feeling more and more panicked because these people ignored her. Going to the police station, she met a female police officer who refused to help. She went back to the house and came to a big central room and in the middle was a big fat Sumo wrestler with big breasts, brandishing a scimitar and scowling. As she watched, the wrestler swelled up and split down the middle, an aggressive-looking man stepped out with a machine gun and fired at her. She turned round to see her friends lying on the floor, heads together. Gradually the heads turned blue and became angels. She realised they were dead.

We talked about the dream, and I asked her who the female police officer was. She mused about it for a while and said, 'The police officer is like the NHS and it represents my mother who is supposed to help but doesn't.'

I asked if the police officer was also me. She thought about this and said, 'No, because I trust you and because the police officer is a kind of ideal of responsibility I don't want any more.'

I said, 'Like looking after damaged women, rather than being an artist for yourself?'

'Yes, being an artist is my desire, but I don't understand who the wrestler is. Do you think it represents the aggressive men in my past?'

'Maybe, but I also think it's you. I think the dream is partly about owning your aggression.'

Chapter 5

Trauma

In Chapter 4 I discussed the relation between death, life and doubling in Freud's texts. Whereas in his early work Freud theorised the Oedipal Complex in terms of libidinal desires that had to be repressed in relation to the reality principle and the threat of the castrating father, in his later theory repression becomes an internal and mimetic anxiety in relation to the early mother. I have argued for the Oedipal Complex as a mimetic identification and doubling, which is both a defence against, and repetition of, the earlier primal bond with the mother. The Oedipal Complex is thus a defensive mastery of identification with the early mother, manifest at a symbolic level as a splitting into active and passive, masculine and feminine, language and the body. But the Oedipal is also imaginary fantasy, thus not differentiated from pre-Oedipal fantasy, and as such can be repeated to create new and immanent selves of a lived duration.

Otto Rank (1924) situates his argument of anxiety in terms of the early maternal bond as the *event* of birth trauma. We can also see it, following Freud's late texts on death and anxiety, as a trauma integral to the mimetic bond. In 'Beyond the Pleasure Principle', psychical processes of binding protect the infant from unpleasure and the unbinding of external excitation. When the ego is unprepared and subject to unexpected quantities of stimulation, then the ego's protective shield is breached traumatically. Now, Freud's late texts on anxiety were a response to the First World War and to the analysts and doctors who challenged his theory, by arguing that war neurosis was a response to death, not castration. Freud stated that anxiety to actual danger also harks back to an earlier fear of castration. The self-preserving ego is not separate from libidinal concerns, as his theory of narcissism proves.

But if Freud tries to link war anxiety to castration, his very texts on anxiety, death, group psychology and mourning all point to an earlier emotional and mimetic identification to the mother. As Borch-Jacobsen and Leys have discussed, this emphasis on an early emotional and hypnotic tie disrupts Freud's Oedipal thesis of the representative subject. For Freud, Oedipal theory marks out psychoanalysis from earlier thinking on hypnosis

by situating the unconscious as an arena of repressed infantile representations that can be recollected with the analyst in therapy. The early and
late emphasis on hypnosis and suggestion in Freud's career is distinct in
that it privileges a hypnotic mimesis of identification that precedes the split
between subject and object. Charcot originally made the link between
hysteria and trauma by suggesting that the hysterical outbreak was a repeat
of an earlier traumatic scene and hypnosis was a kind of mirror to this.
Trauma was the absence from the self, or dissociation, where the victim
would identify with the aggressor in a hypnotic trance. Thus trauma was
not just external stimulus but an immanent force – hypnotic imitation or
mimesis. This description is more complicated because the hypnotic trance
was also understood as the scene of healing between patient and doctor. I
will come back to this point presently.

For Freud the early hypnotic mimesis, the unconscious tie to the mother,
is before division into ego and object; it is an arena of binding and unbinding, of love and hate, with the other. When the ego's protective shield is
breached traumatically, there is a mimetic dissolution of the ego, which
lapses into unconsciousness. At the same time, life and death drives become
uncoupled and the death drive becomes radically unbound. Examples of this
traumatic splitting and unbinding can be seen as the traumatic loss of a
loving protective figure such as the mother or the group leader. As Freud's
texts on the death drive reveal, the instinctual life and death drives are not
separate: binding and unbinding are inseparable opposites. Borch-Jacobsen
(1992) spells this out in describing how in Freud's analysis of the group, the
loss of the loving tie with the leader results in a panic which constitutes a
traumatic unbinding but also a binding with other individuals. Narcissism,
in other words, is the centre of the mimetic relation to the other, where
loving identification is always subtended by rivalry and hate. Panic, as
Borch-Jacobsen points out, is 'the uncontrollable breaching by the ego
by (the affects of) others' (Borch-Jacobsen 1992: 9). Death and love are
inseparable. We might love our father and hate our siblings, but we also love
because we identify with our siblings, and hate because we love – our father.

Freud calls the early anxiety associated with the mimetic tie, primal
repression. Trauma is, therefore, an unconscious identification with this
primary scene. Now, according to Freud, this early stage is governed by a
narcissism which is supposedly mediated by a developmentally more mature
stage of object choice within an Oedipal scenario. In Lacanian theory, the
Oedipal scenario is where the constituted 'subject' can represent themselves
in a specular relation to the other. This formation of the Oedipal subject is
also the moment where internal and external become situated and trauma is
located as an external event or cause that breaches the ego's defences,
rather than an implicit mimetic identification.

I want to consider both these moments, the early identification with the
mother *and* the later Oedipal scenario of 'subject representation' in terms of

mimetic identification. If we understand our relation to the mother and the world as mimetic – our very sense of being as mimetic – then the idea of separation from the other is a myth. If we are brought into being through hypnotic suggestion, then we are part of each other and we also take part in the objects of the world in which we live. The idea that we develop and move away from a world of primitive unconscious pre-Oedipal affects to a more conscious world of the representative Oedipal subject (where we are somehow more distanced and separate) is erroneous. It is the myth of Enlightenment rationality and modernity that we *progress* towards a reflexive mental self and repress our more 'primitive' affects and instincts.

Trauma can be understood as the mimetic splitting and radical unbinding of the death drive, an anxiety in terms of loss and separation of the early mother. This is a birth trauma, not as the literal event that Otto Rank often seems to suggest, but as a metaphor for the trauma of the human condition. To exist, and live, means dependence on the other. Identification is traumatic because we both love and hate the other. The hypnotic mimetic tie that Freud describes is not something that we ever give up. But I want to argue that this hypnotic tie is not simply traumatic, it is also creative. Hypnosis did not just mirror the early traumas of hysterical patients, it also cured them.

Leys and Borch-Jacobsen describe the mimetic paradigm in Freud's work as a trauma that is unavailable to recollection and representation because it belongs to a hypnotic rapport before the constitution of the subject. It cannot be remembered, but can be repeated only in the transference. Leys contrasts this mimetic theory of trauma with the theory associated with the modern definition of post-traumatic stress disorder (PTSD). This latter disorder is mimetic in Leys' view, because it posits the unrepresentable nature of trauma, but it is also anti-mimetic because it demarcates between a constituted subject and object or between the victim and the external event. Thus trauma as PTSD is understood as the literal imprint of an external event that becomes walled off in the brain and is then unavailable for subsequent integration or recollection.

I have several problems with the way Leys distinguishes so abruptly between models of mimetic affect and so-called anti-mimesis or representation. Although she argues that the mimetic paradigm in her work is indebted to Borch-Jacobsen, his notion of mimesis is not anti-representational as such, for it is derived from Derridean deconstruction. I am also unhappy with the opposition, set up by Leys in relation to Freud's work, between a representational and conscious Oedipal subject and a mimesis of unconscious identification and affect. Of course, this division is one I have drawn on in this book and does to some extent mark the difference between say Roustang's and Henry's emphasis on the self-immanence of the unconscious, and Lacan's thesis of representation. Such a division also neatly distinguishes between a Freud of Enlightenment rationality, where the unconscious is the repository of knowledge and memory, and an anti-Cartesian narrative where the unconscious is seen as living affect.

However, as I will argue in this chapter, trauma cannot be located as somehow outside of representation, any more than being situated completely within it. We don't, I will argue, have to choose between an unconscious based on representation and one that is premised as living affect. In the same way we don't have to choose between memory and the body – in fact Freud never did. It is perhaps this refusal to see the unconscious as either a purely mental phenomenon or a biological one that singles Freud out as an anti-Cartesian thinker. In order to hang on to the notion of the unconscious as something that is simultaneously psychological and physiological, we have to carry a double understanding of memory as recollection and knowledge, and memory as the living psychic body. With this vital distinction in mind, one that is so crucial within Freud and Bergson's writings, my argument on trauma will proceed.

I want to leave aside the question of external trauma for a moment and concentrate on the idea of trauma as a mimetic, hypnotic trance which constitutes the early unconscious tie with the mother. Now, Freud saw this early scene as subject to an automatic anxiety in relation to the potential loss of the mother. We can see in his theory of the life and death drives, that anxiety and the threat of maternal loss would unleash a radical unbinding of the death drive. However, I think it is important to make a distinction between an early scene of hypnotic trance where life and death drives become separated and set up in opposition, and a creative hypnotic tie where life and death are integrated and there is acceptance of mimetic dependence.

In Freud's Oedipal theory such acceptance would be achievable only through a specular distance and mental self-representation of the more mature 'subject'. But I suggest that this Oedipal scenario is in fact a defensive repeat and mimicry of the earlier primal tie with the mother, defensive in the sense that life and death drives are organised and fixed into the familiar dualisms of masculinity, femininity, activity and passivity. This hysterical and Oedipal doubling is a mimicry and mastery of earlier infantile dependence. At the same time, the Oedipal Complex is not only a defence, but also a repeat of the earlier tie with the mother as creative fantasy. How can the emotional mimetic tie be traumatic and creative? To understand this we have to go back to Bergson's theory of the unconscious and his ideas of memory and time. Bergson starts not with the conscious subject, but with unconscious being. For him, being is a flow of time and the unconscious is a virtual world of fantasy and memory, which we subtract from and actualise through perception. Memory is virtual. Like a bank, or computer, it stores whatever has happened to us. It is also inseparable from fantasy. Memory is a constant mirror image or double that is unconscious and normally we are not aware of it. We constantly subtract from this unconscious world as we actualise these memory fantasies in a constant flux of becoming. Only in states of hysteria or trauma do we become too aware of this unconscious world; observing two temporalities we take up a specular distance and watch ourselves as if we are on a stage or in a play.

Notice that Bergson's idea of specular distance and self-representation seems opposite to Lacan's representational 'subject', although I propose that there are many similarities between Bergson's moving mirror of mis-recognition and Lacan's famous mirror stage. Lacan himself says that the specular distance the subject takes up with regard to the other is a fantasy of misrecognition, which is why language becomes so important in rescuing the individual from subsidence within imaginary identifications. For Lacan internal division is the necessary cut or lack enabling us to move from the imaginary to the linguistic symbolic. Bergson's view is more holistic because, although we inhabit two streams or vitalities, the virtual and perceptual, these streams in health are indistinguishable and harmonious. It is only when we become too aware of having two temporalities – when uncanny doubling appears to us as memory – that we feel split between virtual and actual worlds. Hysterics inhabit this split, being too absent from themselves in a virtual fantasy land, but at the same time they are too present, too full of a conscious over-intellectual vitality. Here, affects become fixed within representations and symptoms, blocked off from the flow of psychic life and duration. So hysterics are too intellectually abstract and they are also too literal in their body. Their symptoms and body speak because they lack translation into more imaginative psychic flows of time.

The hysteric's split where imaginary and real vitalities conflict rather than flow together is described by Janet and Jung as fixed ideas or complexes. Indeed, Jung always perceived archetypal complexes and ideas as both pathological and a key to a more creative and plural self. Bergson sees the hysterical fantasy world of the double as a misrecognition and evidence of a weaker hold on life. But the therapeutic cure, as Janet, Breuer, Freud and Rank all discovered, involved *repeating* this unconscious doubling within the therapy. We can see how the transference is precisely the repeat of this hypnotic trance in relation to the therapist. The transference repeats this hysterical, mimetic trance but the aim of therapy is to make the trance less fixed and more creative.

The hysteric or traumatised patient swings between a shadowy virtual world and a conscious intellectual vitality that is fixed in terms of certain representations and symptoms. This mimesis, in relation to an all-powerful imaginary other, is the same old Oedipal play again and again. As therapists we often come across this melodramatic monologue, where patients are stuck for example in playing the victim to their father or being unable to separate from their mother. The aim of therapy is to enable the hysteric to actualise fantasy within a more embodied perception, or to put it another way, to enable a flow between psyche and consciousness. This bodily flow of memory consists of actualising multiplicities through a creative dissociation that translates memory into perception. Although this is something in health we do all the time, we are unaware of it because we are creatively and actively being and becoming, rather than meditating on our fantasy representations. If we can mobilise our fantasy world in an active way, we choose different fantasies and lose the ones that are not helpful. Because hysterics can't transform their fantasies in relation to experience they remain stuck in a fantasy world that becomes a defensive mimicry.

Freud understood that hysterics suffered from having affects severed from their proper representations; hence his search in therapy for the 'right' repressed Oedipal interpretations. But as Roustang has so acutely realised, hysterics who suffer from representations need to be released from the scene of representation in relation to the other. They need to be able to leave their narcissistic representation of suffering in relation to the other behind and return to their affectual state of being, a life force which for Roustang lies below or beyond more complex relating and abstraction.

I discussed in Chapter 3 whether or not the modification of the transference at the end of a successful therapy is due to affects being returned to an auto-affection or self-immanence, or whether affects are produced in a more affective immanence in relation to the other. Is the origin of affects located, as Henry (1993) thinks, in self-immanence? Or are affects situated in a mimesis to the other, as Borch-Jacobsen proposes? I contend that affects and feelings are brought into being through the suggestive and creative force of the psyche and, as Bergson says, this primary dissociation means we are always mimetically other. One of the problems with Borch-Jacobsen's thesis is that there does not seem to be an alternative to the hysterical mimetic tie, or an alternative to the envious death drive to mimetically displace your rival. This is an ultimately negative view of origin which gives no hope for the future and makes the therapeutic cure rather pointless. Perhaps another way of seeing this is to suggest quite simply that babies also have a good time with their mothers. Mimesis is traumatic in the sense of a death drive unleashed, but there must also be an original mimesis with the mother that is positive and life-enhancing. Maybe this positive mimesis is more in tune with Henry's notion of self-immanence – an affectual unconscious immanent tie with the other which is indistinguishable from the self.

This bond is hard to talk about because the moment we try to think of it symbolically we are abstracting it intellectually from its lived duration. Examples of such pre-reflective experience are captured in bodily and aesthetic ways. Breast-feeding and 'good' sex characterise the former sense of organic engagement, with poetry and music illustrating the latter. I don't want to suggest, like Henry and Roustang, that in these experiences we somehow leave the order of representation, because that presupposes some kind of unmediated reality which in my view is impossible. But we can move between images which are more or less directed towards representation or the body.

In distinction to this positive mimesis is the hysterical tie to the mother – the anxious trance. This is a traumatic tie of emotional identification where virtual and actual worlds have become defensively fixed and we can link this to the splitting apart of the life and death drives. Unification of this split entails connecting fantasy with the real of the body, actualising virtual memory within perception, and so making fantasy and lived existence into a mobile and fluid encounter.

It is not a case of choosing between affect and representation, but understanding how we need to keep losing our representations and liberating the psychic body into a more active force that produces new experiences. As Freud and Breuer both noted, changing a patient's representations is useless unless it is accompanied by abreaction of affect. Abreaction of affect in a Bergsonian model would occur only when fantasy representations become transformed by the body into conscious action and perception.

So Roustang is right to liken the unconscious to the force of the imagination, but a creative imagination is not simply self-immanent; it is an imagination that is constantly mobile in transforming fantasies in relation to actualisation and lived existence in the world. Immanence, here, is always in relation to an 'other'. Mimesis is hypnosis and we do not simply have to understand mimesis in terms of envious and deathly rivalry with the other. Our affectual identification extends beyond the breast. It is the breast, but it also always the breast in becoming and the breast elsewhere. Hypnosis is a mimetic trance, but its characteristics are fixing *and* delinking, concentration *and* dissociation. Hypnosis is at the basis of our identifications but it is also instrumental in changing them. As the suggestive movement of our psychic bodily memory, hypnosis brings our conscious reality into being, but it can also mirror our neurotic transference and representation of suffering to the other.

In order to understand how hypnosis is both a model analogous to hysteria and a therapeutic cure, we need to return to the debates on trauma and hypnosis that were resurrected in relation to psychoanalysis directly after the First World War. The hypnotic cure was a subject of hot dispute between three psychotherapists who had each worked with hypnosis in relation to soldiers suffering from war neurosis. William Brown (1920) worked extensively with shell-shocked soldiers suffering from extreme hysterical symptoms such as convulsions, loss of sight and hearing, anaesthesia, trembling limbs and repetitive hallucinations and nightmares. According to Brown (1920), soldiers confronted with the stress and horror of war repressed their emotions, converting them into physical symptoms. Hypnosis cured these soldiers and restored forgotten memories through an abreaction of the traumatic event. Catharsis of the emotions was central to this cure; it was the relived feelings rather than the actual recovered memory at stake that enabled the men to achieve relief and recovery.

William McDougall and Charles S. Myers, the two other physicians, disagreed with Brown, arguing that it was the cognitive ability of the soldiers that mattered and the therapeutic overcoming of the dissociated memory. McDougall (1920) notes that those amongst his patients who are made to relive their trauma under hypnosis show an increase rather than a decrease in symptoms. He is dismissive of Brown's thesis, because it entails the notion that 'packets' of energy become attached to and then detached from ideas. In McDougall's view affects and emotions cannot be dissociated. Such splitting off occurs only through cognitive channels:

> Dissociation, we must believe, though it may occur at various levels of the nervous system, as Dr. Brown suggests, never involves an emotional centre or affective disposition as such. It affects rather the various channels through which our intellectual or cognitive processes play upon each other and upon the affective disposition.
>
> (McDougall 1920: 26)

Jung enters this debate agreeing with McDougall that abreaction of affect is not by itself a cure and can make patients worse. For Jung, McDougall lays 'his finger on the right spot' when he suggests that the crux of things is the dissociation of the psyche not the high level of affect (Jung 1921: 15). Jung discusses the importance of integrating the dissociated psychic complex – within the therapy. It is not just the abreaction but its activity in the presence of the therapist that counts. This is of course the transference, but Jung neatly gets rid of the problem of hypnosis by arguing that the transference is a false relationship of projections, rooted in the past. The aim of therapy is to replace the transference projection with a real, psychological relationship in the present.

Jung seems to be saying we can end the transference or the hypnotic mimesis between patient and therapist, substituting it for a more individual psychological relationship. However, I suggest, along with Roustang, that the transference is never resolved; it can be modified only beyond the therapist, to be transformed into an active mimesis of the world that is productive of difference. Dissociation is not simply a dissociation of cognitive processes but a traumatic splitting off of affect, where affects have become fixed in terms of certain representations. The Oedipal Complex is a case in point here. On one level the Oedipal Complex can be seen as a defensive hysterical mimesis, a mimesis that splits identification and desire, the narcissist's refusal to enter live time and acknowledge death and the organic bond with the mother. However, on another level an Oedipal Complex that is always being remade can be seen as a creative bed of the imaginary providing new fantasies, which can be transformed into the affectual life of our futures.

Dissociation (or the hypnotic trance) is not just traumatic, but also creative. In dissociation we can retreat into a defensive world where fantasy and fixed representations lead to our affects and feelings becoming split off and not experienced. However, we also dissociate in relation to dreams or creative imagining, associating with new fantasies which we then transform into productive, different experiences. In trauma the psyche splits and we retreat into a dissociation of fixed representation – a virtual world of fantasies. This dissociation becomes creative when it can select or link with certain fantasy representations and lose others.

Again, if we use the Oedipal Complex as an example, we can say that we remake the Oedipal Complex and our relationship with our parents over and over again throughout our life, with the opportunity of making it new and different each time. We keep certain representations and lose others, mobilising different desires and identifications in the process. Heterosexuality is hysterical in the sense that it is the Oedipal Complex fixed in one dominant representation, rather than an imaginary gallery of different fantasies that can be creatively gained and lost as we move forward in life. But what does this mean in terms of deciding whether abreaction of emotion or cognitive dissociation is the central factor?

William Brown (1920) actually acknowledged that the intellectual processes are part of the therapeutic effect and that emotional abreaction goes hand in hand with adjustment of ideas. Both affect and intellect are involved in moving from a state of traumatic dissociation to one of mental and physical harmony.

For McDougall and Myers it was the recollection or memory at stake that was important not the emotional catharsis. Their stance mirrored that of Freud in the sense that Freud too saw the recovery of repressed representations to be the main issue. Like Freud, McDougall and Myers took a rather authoritarian approach to the transference, in the sense that they were the analysts-cum-hypnotists supposed to know or discover and the patient's participation was largely not invited. Hypnosis for Brown, on the other hand, was all about eliciting the patient's collaboration. His emphasis on emotional catharsis or abreaction within the session mirrored the more active stance taken by Ferenczi and Rank, who critiqued Freud's more intellectual interpretations. As I have discussed, they argued for the necessary repeating or acting out of emotional experience on the part of the patient.

Now the First World War therapists are interesting because they resurrected the hypnosis that Freud had so energetically tried and failed to expel from psychoanalysis. It was the influence of the psychotherapist Paul-Charles Dubois (a pupil of Bernheim) in the early twentieth century, whose emphasis on hypnosis as a dangerous manipulation of the patient's childish effeminacy did much to quell the use of hypnosis in the pre-war years. But Dubois's notion of the hypnotist as an all-powerful magician and manipulator was an extreme example connecting with the notion, prevalent at the turn of the century, of hypnosis as blind obedience and mimesis.

Nowadays, it is commonly recognised that hypnosis is always self-hypnosis and it is impossible to hypnotise someone who is not willing. Ruth Leys notes that in order for hypnosis to be brought back as a therapeutic agent during the First World War, it had to re-emerge as a more participatory model (Leys 2000: 89). This more participatory model was William Brown's position in using hypnosis, not as direct suggestion, but as a tool with which to recover in cathartic mode emotional memories which could then be reintegrated and worked through. So, it is not emotional abreaction on its own that cures the patient, but one which reconnects the patient in a less defensive way with the object.

The First World War psychotherapists saw hysteria linked to the terror and threat of death, rather than to sexual conflict. Hysteria in this later sense was not understood as a repression of a wish, but as a more primary splitting and dissociation of the ego. These ideas of repression went back to Breuer's early emphasis on hypnoid splitting, but it is useful to think of these mechanisms in terms of the difference between ideas and affects. An idea can be repressed but an affect or emotion can only be dissociated. In this sense Brown's idea that we have emotional memories is incorrect. Freud himself insisted on this in his paper on the unconscious (1915b) when he argues that when ideas become repressed, affects cannot find their 'proper representative' and thus become connected with other ideas and misconstrued. Ideas then can be repressed, but there is no such thing as unconscious affects.

If affects are not remembered, then they repeat as a direct manifestation of the drive. Borch-Jacobsen hammers the point home: affect 'may well [be] "suppressed" ("inhibited", "blocked", reduced to the state of a "rudiment"), but it can by no means be repressed' (Borch-Jacobsen 1993: 139). Interestingly, this is also an argument put forward by William James and Henri Bergson in different ways. James (1901) suggests that when we think we are having a past feeling, it is not a memory of the feeling, but a new feeling in the present. We might feel the grief of a dead mother, but that grief is not a memory but a new emotion each time, experienced in the present. Bergson, in a similar vein, discusses how memory passes into something else by becoming actual.

> When we dwell on the memory of a sensation, it is a weak virtual thing and impossible to distinguish between sensation and imagination. But as we dwell on it more it becomes more actual – it is 'the sensation beginning to be'.
>
> (Bergson 1912: 174)

The present is what Bergson calls sensori-motor consciousness of the immediate future and the realm of action. When memory becomes actualised in the present image, it is transformed from a virtual imagination to an actual perception. We are conscious of the past only through the present. It is only when virtual (or what Bergson calls pure) memory materialises into a present image that it transmutes into affectual sensations. Only in this present state of perception can the past be distinguished as something that has gone before (Bergson 1912: 179).

So feelings coincide with the actualisation of virtual or pure memory within consciousness. Affects are not ever repressed but dissociated and, as Freud says, displaced, solidified within representations that have become blocked off from psychic time. McDougall (1920) and Jung (1921) are right to say that emotional catharsis on its own would not have helped the shell-shocked soldiers; only an abreaction which allowed the movement of fantasy to materialise into a different experience in relation to the world and the object. But Brown's (1920) emphasis on participatory hypnosis is also vital, and can be linked to Ferenczi and Rank's (1925) active technique. This active method challenges the classical interpretative stance of the therapist/hypnotist, who focuses only on retrieval of the past. Emphasis on the hypnotic transference as a participatory bond, in the present, enables the transformation of virtual fantasy into new emotional experiences. Transference and hypnosis, here, bring about something different, a new, experiential relationship to the object in the present which is embodied.

The proposal, by James and Bergson, that emotions and affects are not past but exist as an actualisation in the present, was taken up in 1911 by the Swiss psychologist Edouard Claparède. He suggested that projections into the past bring up a scene of the double that is psychologically distinct from the present. Moreover, this past self is the arena of a 'phantom self' where we are distinct from any self-experience or emotion – we objectify ourselves. He writes:

> One cannot be a spectator of one's feelings; one feels them, or one does not feel them; one cannot imagine them (image them, represent them) without stripping them of their affective essence.
>
> (Claparède 1911: 368)

This description is very close to Bergson's account of weak or false recognition. Leys (2000) notes how Claparède's theory of phenomenological affect breaks with the dominant theories of representation leading back to Descartes, where the conscious Cogito can represent himself to an other through a specular distance between ego and object. For Leys, Claparède's ideas, together with Freud's emphasis on the irreducibility of affect, take us back to a mimetic theory of affect; a hypnotic tie preceding 'the distinction between "self" and "other" on which the possibility of self-representation and hence recollection depended' (Leys 2000: 100). Such a theory of affect thus displaces a Cartesian model of psychoanalysis, indebted to Enlightenment ideology, where the unconscious is the seat of repressed memories and therapy is aimed at the retrieval of knowledge and meaning.

This is a persuasive reading but Leys (2000) polarises models of affect and representation, mimesis and anti-mimesis. Such polarisation gives to memory purely a role of conscious recollection and knowledge, ignoring the emphasis, made by Freud and Bergson, that unconscious memory is a force linked to affect that becomes transformed into something *different* when it becomes part of the perceptual/conscious system. Reading Freud through Bergson allows us to see how virtual memories are affectual vitalities that become actualised in relation to perception to produce different experiences. Rather than dividing psychoanalysis into a theory of memory or a theory of affect, I want to propose it as a theory of corporeal time – a lived psychic time of the body.

For Leys the model of mimetic affect endorsed by Freud and Claparède means that we cannot remember a trauma that preceded the representative ego. Such trauma cannot be recovered and brought into conscious representation within therapy, because 'that trauma was never "in" the unconscious in the form of repressed or dissociated representations' (Leys 2000: 103). As we can see, this model of mimetic affect makes it very difficult to ascertain the origin or the truth of a reconstructed event.

We can't recollect a trauma that was never conscious and therefore never repressed. However, if memory is transformed into something different to become recollection, then there is no recollection that can be said to bear actual witness to the true event. When trauma is repeated as flashbacks or hallucinations, it is accompanied by virtual images. Freud said these affectual images or reminiscences, and the repeat of these fantasies, in say the deliriums of Anna O, were because they remained neither past nor present. The past is only ever distinctly defined when it has become actualised within present perception.

I have described how, in states of hysteria, we become split between, on the one hand, a virtual world of fantasy and doubling which is passive and unable to translate into a lived attention to life. And how, on the other hand, the hysteric is also rigidly fixed in conscious representations that are blocked off from movement in relation to a psychic time of the body. I want to consider whether the trauma victim can also be seen to inhabit this split world, one that is both absent and overly present.

Bergson makes a clear distinction between memory and perception. He insists, 'to picture is not to remember' (Bergson 1912: 173). As a memory becomes an actual perception it comes to live in the image, but the image itself is a virtual memory, and the recollection, the effort or intellectual act. Memory is thus a process of materialisation and once the virtual image is made actual it is transformed into something else. Another way of putting this is to say that when we remember we also forget the memory traces that brought that actualisation into being.

Freud agrees with Bergson that memory and conscious perception are different things: 'consciousness arises instead of a memory-trace' (Freud

1920: 25). Once a memory has entered consciousness it ceases to be a memory. Freud discusses this in 'Beyond the Pleasure Principle' (1920) and in 'A Note upon the "Mystic Writing Pad"' (1925a). He argues that the perceptual system can't hold on to traces of memory whilst at the same time receiving and generating new excitements and affects. His description of the mystic writing pad illustrates this. The writing pad is a brown slab of resin or wax covered with a sheet of wax paper and cellophane, secured at one end, so that they can be lifted away from the wax. When written on, the pad shows the marks of the dark wax through the two outer layers, but once the cellophane and wax paper have been lifted away from the wax and laid back down again, the writing mysteriously disappears.

The wax slab represents the unconscious and the two upper pieces of wax and cellophane paper represent the perceptual conscious system. Freud likens these papers to the ego's protective shield against external stimuli, mentioned in 'Beyond the Pleasure Principle'. The mystic pad then explains the relation between conscious and unconscious systems, with the conscious being kept clear of memory traces and wiped clean to receive new impressions. The pad also shows how trauma breaches the ego's shield to become inscribed as a memory trace on the wax, unconscious slab below.

But Freud also notes how the most enduring memory trace is 'one which never entered consciousness' (Freud 1925a: 177). External trauma can breach the ego's shield to such a degree that it goes straight through or bypasses the conscious system to become inscribed as unconscious memory traces. But trauma as unconscious memory traces can also be inscribed from within, a death drive in relation to the primal mother. Walter Benjamin (1973) takes up Freud's claim of a memory that has never entered consciousness to put forward his idea of involuntary memory or *mémoire involontaire*. Benjamin explains this through Proust's famous story of involuntary memory, where Proust tells of a visit to his mother and the eating of a Madeleine cake. For Proust, it is the sensual experience of eating a Madeleine cake that opens up an image sphere where he free-associates about his childhood in Combray, elaborating on an important bit of his past. Proust thus reveals how the past is located beyond the realm of the intellect and discovered accidentally in external material objects.

Now, Benjamin's (1973) notion of involuntary memory is indebted to Freud and he uses the example of Proust to make an immanent critique of Bergson. According to Benjamin, Proust's description of his involuntary memory is dependent on the accidental finding of an object, and this is a critique of Bergson's view that we can always exercise free will and active consciousness. Very cleverly, Benjamin realises that there is a distinction in Freud's thinking between conscious remembering and unconscious memory (linked to affects) and it is the latter which constitutes involuntary memory.

But there is, I suggest, also a similar distinction between voluntary and involuntary memory in Bergson's work. Bergson separates conscious representative memory from his concept of duration that is unconscious and voluntary. Duration is a threshold that produces a conscious attention to life, but it is, in its movement or actualisation, a bodily and involuntary process. So, we can say that Bergson *and* Freud see memory traces as located in a bodily unconscious. When these traces become conscious they become transformed into recollection, which is simultaneously forgetting. For Freud this coincides with the abreaction of unwanted affects. Recollection entails the translation of bodily affects into mental representation. Bergson, however, gives much more to the creative power of the unconscious and so for him what is at stake is the production of virtual and actual vitalities and the ability to move between imaginary and real forces. Using Bergson's model we can see that the ability to lose certain fixed representations is also linked to the restoration of an affectual power, but images and ideas also have the power to produce new affects.

For Freud the unconscious is essentially negative and has to be translated into conscious representation, whereas in Bergson's account the bodily memory of the unconscious is positive and creates differences. This is not a celebration of conscious representation or our desiring body of affects. Instead, duration is privileged, a memory and movement of time and the body where affects come to life through the use and materialisation of objects. This usage, as Winnicott reminds us, is the destruction of certain representations and the refinding of new ones. We don't just discover our mother or the various objects that people our world, we also always refind them and make them up. Surely, this is also Proust's memory – a refinding of his childhood in the Madeleine cake? What is necessary is the fluid relationship between imaginary and real, where virtual images are always being translated into conscious activity and where representations are always being forgotten and lost as we return to the immanent psychic force of the body.

To sum this up, we can see that in Freud's model the relation between the conscious and unconscious is more hierarchical. Freud sees the unconscious as timeless, whereas for Bergson unconscious memory is time and heterogeneous movement. Recollection for Freud and Bergson occurs when unconscious memory traces are translated into conscious perception and recollection is dependent on forgetting. But whereas for Freud this recollection is synonymous with mental representation and the loss of unwanted affects, for Bergson translation of unconscious memory is a selective perception and forgetting, where affects are always in a state of becoming. It is this affectual life and vitality which enables a more conscious attention to life. We can perhaps use the example of hysteria to clarify this difference. For Freud the hysteric's free association enables the hysteric to transform memory traces into mental representations and to lose unwanted affects through a motor discharge. In a Bergsonian model, the method of hypnosis enables free association so that memory traces can move again and become translated into affectual differences. The emphasis in this account is not on the loss of affects and establishing mental representation of the memory trace. Rather, affects are brought to life as the hysteric's memory traces are put back into movement with the psychic body and transformed in relation to an external object. The external object is not just discovered here but it is in Winnicott's sense also created.

If we return this debate to a discussion of trauma, we can see that the trauma victim's inability to remember is also matched by an inability to forget certain fixed representations. Split off from the psychic flows and corporeal time of the body, the trauma victim is both detached from life and fixated within a neurotic suffering and representation in relation to a dominant other. In health, translation of virtual fantasies into a lived actualisation means that some fantasies are selected and transformed, whilst others are forgotten. Pierre Janet, Bergson's colleague, devoted much of his work to the study of hysteria and trauma. Janet has attracted the attention of many contemporary trauma theorists such as Judith Herman and Bessel A. van der Kolk. Both these writers utilise Janet's distinction between traumatic memory and narrative memory to account for the necessary therapeutic approach to trauma. In their view, trauma is an overwhelming experience that cannot be integrated into the memory system, remaining in the psyche as a literal and repetitive event, one that repeats over and over again, because it cannot be spoken or represented. Thus the traumatic event remains unassimilated as a story in someone's life. Cathy Caruth (1996) argues that because this literal event cannot be integrated at the time, it literally possesses the trauma victim in a belated fashion. Recovery for the trauma victim is dependent on putting this repetitive, dissociated, trauma into words. This narrative will reconstruct the walled-off experience, integrating it into mental organisation and representation.

Van der Kolk and van der Hart (1995) explicitly use Janet's famous case history of Irène to explain their case. Irène was a young woman who suffered amnesia after the traumatic death of her mother and was subject to somnambulistic re-enactments. These repetitions were labelled 'traumatic memory' by Janet because they were timeless and would be performed over hours as a literal replay of the scene. Janet treated Irène with hypnosis and she recovered her memory, bringing it into a conscious narrative where she could tell the story of her mother's death in a few minutes and express grief. Whereas Irène's traumatic memory was solitary, inflexible and dissociated, her recovery of narrative memory as a life story was a social and symbolic act enabling her to reconnect with others and her present.

This emphasis on Janet's narrative memory by trauma theorists completely ignores, as Leys (2000) points out, the ways in which Janet often used to get his patients to forget their traumas as well as remember them. The best known illustration of this is the case of the 19-year-old girl Marie. This hysterical woman's symptoms coincided with a menstrual bleed of only 24 hours every month. Through hypnosis Janet retrieved the traumatic memory or event which related to her first menstruation at the age of 13 years. Terrified of the onset of puberty, this girl had jumped into a bucket of icy water and successfully stopped her bleeding for the following five years. When her periods returned, so appeared her first hysterical symptoms. Janet suggested to Marie under hypnosis that she had had a normal period at that time and that her subsequent periods had been regular. He therefore replaced her traumatic story by suggesting another one. The suggestion worked and Marie was cured. Now what are we to make of this case history? It seems to fly in the face of the emphasis of narrative memory that trauma theorists are so keen on.

I don't think we can really make sense of Janet's method of making his patients remember and forget, unless we link his work to the model of memory put forward by Henri Bergson. Van der Kolk pays lip service to Janet's debt to Bergson but is much keener to align Janet's theory to the cognitive psychology of Piaget. This developmental model understands the child's development to move from sensori-motor action to perceptual representation, and then to symbolic and linguistic modes of mental function. Van der Kolk uses this mental map to suggest that traumatised individuals become trapped in an automatic memory level akin to the one described by Janet. But this traumatic memory is fixed at an iconic and perceptual level. The flashbacks, perceptual hallucinations and bodily sensations experienced by trauma victims are dissociated from linguistic, symbolic functioning. This is why, in van der Kolk's view, talking therapy might not work as a therapeutic intervention. He suggests, as an alternative, the methods employed by art psychotherapy where the production of iconic images through painting are thought to be more successful in healing the dissociation.

The problem with this argument is not the recommendation of art psychotherapy, advocating the production of painterly images which so creatively mirror our images in dreams. Iconic images can be more powerful than linguistic representations in therapy simply because they have not become fixed within abstract representations and therefore have a greater ability to move in time and produce new experiences and affects. The difficulty with van der Kolk's position is his valuation of linguistic, symbolic representation over iconic images and sensori-motor action. The general idea here is that in trauma the person regresses from mental representation and narrative memory to bodily perception.

If we link Janet's model of the mind as memory to Bergson, and there is plenty of evidence that they were influenced by each other's ideas, both as students and professional colleagues, then we have to revise the notion that the trauma victim regresses from mental, cognitive memory to perceptual affects. In Bergson's work what we think of as narrative memory, the ability to distinguish and link past, present and future, is achieved only when we are able to transform virtual memories and fantasies into an actualisation of the perceptual, conscious image. If we take Bergson's model of memory as a framework to understand Janet's clinical work, then we can see that what happens to his traumatised hysterics is not that they get invaded by the overwhelming literal event, or the real, which is ultimately not capable of being represented. On the contrary, Janet's patients retreat into what he called a subconscious world of virtual fantasy and fixed ideas. Jung later took this notion of fixed ideas as the basis for his understanding of unconscious archetypal complexes.

These subconscious or fixed ideas are the fantasies that Janet uncovers through hypnosis. With the help of the hypnotic rapport and suggestion, the patient is enabled to lose and liquidate the fantasy or idea and to transform it into a new actualised perception that is accompanied by sensori-motor action and emotions. The important thing, as Bergson and Janet note, is that the traumatic cure entails an attention to life. We can call that narrative memory, but then the confusion sets in, as we have seen with the trauma theorists, who insist on reading Janet's narrative memory in terms of an argument about representation or non-representation. The cure for the hysteric or the trauma victim is not primarily an issue of representation, although part of the therapeutic process is to make unconscious representations more visible. Van der Kolk and van der Hart (1995) argue that the perceptual and iconic images that repeat with trauma victims are not symbolic. Leys is dismissive of this, saying that 'to treat pictures and visual images as if they were inherently non-symbolic is . . . absurd' (Leys 2000: 249).

Leys (2000) wants to argue for iconic images as a part of representation, whereas van der Kolk and van der Hart (1995) want to align them with ideas of literal repetition and the thinking espoused by other trauma experts, who see trauma as leaving a literal, non-representable wound in the mind. However, I want to go back to Bergson's distinction when he says 'to picture is not to remember' and that the perceptual image materialises out of the virtual image (Bergson 1912: 173). For Bergson is also saying that in vital health the movement between streams of perception and memory unifies them; only in weakened mental states do we perceive them as separate. In trauma, as in hysteria, we remain split between conscious perception and unconscious or virtual fantasy. Here, conscious representations are fixed, literal and repetitive. Likewise, we occupy a world of shadowy fantasies that cannot penetrate into reality. Time, for the trauma victim, is stopped, but this is not because trauma is non-representable. On the contrary, victims of trauma are often too conscious of what they have endured and are still suffering. What they cannot do is either to lose the fixed representations of their suffering, or to translate fantasy into new creative realities.

Perhaps we can see the trauma victim's recurring flashbacks and iconic perceptual images, on the one hand, as virtual pictures or fantasies that are trapped (by the trauma victim's retreat from active reality), awaiting trans-formation into a present perception and recollection. But we can also see them as fixed ideas that are continually representing and mimetically reproducing themselves in relation to another. In this latter sense the trauma sufferer cannot allow his or her anxiety to turn away from representation and return to the psychic immanence of the lived body.

Van der Kolk and Caruth both advance the argument currently fashionable with many trauma theorists that the visual pictures inherent in the traumatic flashback are literal repetitions, as opposed to representations, which are created by a wound in the mind. This wound or structural weakness means that the sufferer reverts to a childhood state where experience can only be processed on a sensori-motor or iconic level. These sensory images are dissociated from the necessary symbolic sublimation and linguistic retrieval. Trauma victims, often cases of childhood sexual abuse, have only fragmentary memories and intuitive feelings. A narrative of the trauma for these people is something that is only developed over time (Leys 2000: 251).

Surely, it is impossible to regress to a childhood state? We always pull into those early memories the subsequent symbolic representations and we can't as it were simply revert to a state before language was available. Now it is true that we can dissociate, occupying an intense mentally self-reflexive state for example where we objectify our bodily emotions rather than subjectively experience them. And conversely we can occupy intense feeling states where self-reflection seems absent. In schizophrenia these two states become extremely split so the feeling self and the reflective self are parallel but distinct; this is a scenario where total objectification of the experiential self takes place: the person is psychically disembodied. In hysteria, and I suggest in trauma, this splitting is less extreme and the person will swing from one pole to the another, occupying what seems like a very literal and conscious perception on the one hand, and being lost in a shadowy land of fantasies that cannot penetrate reality on the other.

Trauma theorists suggest that dissociation rather than repression is the main psychic defence at work in trauma. In this I agree with them, but they argue that it is a literal event that somehow repeats as a structural wound or blank in the mind; a sense then that the traumatic event bypasses consciousness to become lodged as an unconscious absence. For Caruth this means the traumatic event is not experienced at the time and is done so only belatedly, returning to possess the subject. Van der Kolk insists that the trauma victim is stuck in a non-verbal, literal re-enactment of the event where fragmentary images and feelings take the place of more symbolic functioning.

Now it is strange that van der Kolk insists so strongly on the literal nature of trauma, a reading he derives from Janet. But he does not attempt to square this with Janet's notion that trauma is linked to fixed ideas or representations. Van der Kolk explicitly mentions how trauma and a lack of the integrated experience leads to dissociation and subconscious fixed ideas, which in extreme form develop into multiple identities. If this is so, then why should the repetitive images and flashbacks associated with trauma have to be attributed to the literal event, returning over and over again as a form of possession? Why can't they instead be seen as repetitive fixed ideas and fantasies that repeat because they are symptomatic of a fixed dissociation or splitting between actual and virtual flows of time?

In his brilliant book *Rewriting the Soul*, Ian Hacking (1995) declares that the hallucinations or flashbacks that trauma victims report should not be treated as somehow more real than what is understood as a more conventional, continuous memory. Indeed, Hacking does not see why we have to describe memory as narrative at all. If we see memory as the recall of scenes and episodes then flashbacks and more continuous recall can be seen as the same thing. I agree with Hacking (1995) that flashbacks and more continuous memory are both memories and one is no more 'real' than the other. How would we think of flashbacks in terms of Bergson's and Janet's ideas? In Janet's work flashbacks would be part of what he called 'traumatic memory', the unconscious fixed ideas that repeat, but have not become translated into conscious perception of the present. Janet writes:

It is only for convenience that we speak of it as a 'traumatic memory'. The subject is often incapable of making with regard to the event the recital which we speak of as memory; and yet he remains confronted by a difficult situation in which he has not been able to play a satisfactory part, one to which his adaptation has been imperfect.

(Janet 1919: 663)

Remember that Bergson and Freud also state that memory changes into something else when it becomes conscious perception. The flashbacks and the iconic images that repeat in trauma are when the person retreats into a weakened attention to life, what Bergson (1908b) calls misrecognition. These images are memories as fixed ideas that have once perhaps been more conscious; it also possible that these painful ideas never had much awareness attached to them. Such images, nevertheless, can also be virtual fantasies: reminiscences that repeat because they cannot become seeded and transformed within a more lived reality. What is the difference between what Freud called hysterical reminiscences and what he defines as a screen memory? Both of these images are memory/fantasies that refer us to a virtual past. I suggest the difference between them is that the screen memory, unlike the hysterical fixed idea, is one that can be elaborated on and transformed into a new reality.

Virtual fantasies and actual perceptions are a mixture of imaginary and real and so we can agree with Hacking (1995) that traumatic flashbacks are no more real that what is called narrative memory. Regression to iconic bodily perceptions, as a response to trauma, cannot be said to be returning to the literal event, as van der Kolk and Caruth suggest. However, these bodily perceptions, because they are fixed ideas/representations *and* virtual fantasy, can be used to transform memory into a different lived time and experience. Simply put, trauma patients have lost the ability to reimagine their suffering. The iconic perceptions and images that repeat in trauma are ones that we have to lose in order to release our affects in a return to the bodily psyche. This enables memory and the body to move so that fantasy can actively penetrate into reality.

What Janet calls narrative memory is an ability to adapt and interact with life, and he sees it as a necessary redescription, forgetting and translation of the traumatic memory or fixed idea. Now, van der Kolk also understands narrative memory as a necessary distortion of the original memory, and in this I completely agree with him. Nevertheless, where my reading differs is that I don't see traumatic memory or flashbacks as somehow more literal or true. Neither do I see Janet's definition of narrative memory as implying a linguistic, mental representation of bodily perception. I take Janet's definition of narrative memory as an ability to reimagine our reality and to actualise an attention to life or lived force. Attention to life is not dependent on a person forming linguistic representations, any more than mental recollections and meaning are the true goal of psychoanalytic therapy.

It is interesting, here, to consider the difference between a conscious and an unconscious idea. If the unconscious idea is just an idea elsewhere, then we don't have to distinguish or polarise conscious representation and fantasy. Both conscious and unconscious ideas can fix and alienate us in our suffering. They repeat because they cannot be transformed into different productive vitalities which make us alive and present in relation to the world. Therapy is about bringing subconscious fixed ideas into view, but it is also about changing them and releasing life forces of affects and imagination. Images are important because, as Bergson says, they lie halfway between representations and things. Thus images are the vehicles of sensual affects and a productive mental imagination. If our life force is about moving between real and imaginary worlds through images which endure and produce multiple differences, then in trauma, or hysteria, this movement becomes stultified and we are unable to forget, translate or redescribe the fixed representations that keep us within our neurotic suffering.

Whether they are subconscious fantasies or more obsessively conscious ideas, these representations prevent us from experiencing a more lived time. Now Janet did call the ability to transform these fixed ideas into lived time 'narrative memory'. But narrative memory for Janet was less the linguistic symbolic representation it seems to denote for van der Kolk and more an ability to make fantasy and memory move again in a more flexible way. If, as I have suggested, hysteria is the symptom of our paralysed bodily memory, we can see the hysteric as neurotically stuck between conscious perceptions of fixed representations he cannot lose, and a virtual fantasy world that cannot seed itself within his experiential reality. Janet described how bringing subconscious ideas to consciousness was only the first part of the therapy work, the second being the ability to liquidate or change them. In Bergson's terms this would entail a return to the translation of virtual and actual in relation to each other.

Mitchell argues that in trauma the victim has regressed from 'memory to perception' (Mitchell 2000: 281). She argues that Caruth (1996) is wrong to suggest that in trauma the Lacanian real invades the victim. Instead, Mitchell argues there is a regression away from memory to a perceptual iconic image that repeats. In Mitchell's view, 'there is too much conscious-ness' in the traumatised child and the hysteric. Too shocked to protect themselves with memory, hysterics in Mitchell's view regress to repeating the original perception of trauma over and over again (Mitchell 2000: 292).

Mitchell (2000) uses the example of Freud's mystic writing pad to point out how memory and perception are incompatible. In hysteria and trauma there is a primal repression or anxiety where the person's protective shield (the cellophane and wax paper of the writing pad) are breached and the trauma makes 'permanent marks below'. According to Mitchell, hysterics respond to this shock, 'not with memory or thinking, but, as it were, with a repeat of the original perception' (Mitchell 2000: 291). Hysterics remember their shock as a child and repeat it as a perception of the original trauma that seems completely real. I know what Mitchell means by saying that the hysteric is too conscious but I don't think this is because the child has regressed to some original perceptive experience.

Her argument seems to confuse Freud's two definitions of memory and psychoanalysis. In the first reading the unconscious is about the recollection of mental meaning as representation. It is the translation of unconscious memory into conscious meaning. This is Freud dedicated to Enlightenment rationality – a scenario where mental representation and recollection is the goal of therapy. Mitchell (2000: 281) tells us that traumatic shock 'eradi-cates the victim's capacity for memory as representation', and in its place we are left with the perception or the presenting experience.

Here, Mitchell refers to the incompatibility between perception and memory that Freud alludes to in the mystic writing pad. When memory traces become conscious they transform into something else – perception. Memories, Freud tells us, are wiped clean from the perceptual unconscious system because when they become conscious they become retranslated, thus 'memory is present not once but several times over' (Mitchell 2000: 288). This means that the act of becoming 'conscious and leaving behind a memory trace are processes incompatible with each other within one and the same system' (Freud 1920: 25).

Mitchell reads this retranscribed unconscious memory *as ideas*. The trauma victim, in her view, regresses to a perceptual consciousness that is wiped clean of memory, ideas, representation and history:

> Memories, then, are 'ideas' that flow over and over again along the same trace marks. Consciousness is the state that is without such traces, memory and consciousness are thus alternative (they cannot happen at the same time). This notion of consciousness became defined as a system known as 'perception-consciousness.' It is to this perception-consciousness and not to 'history' that I believe trauma returns its victim when her memory is shattered.
>
> (Mitchell 2000: 288)

But this is a reading of unconscious memory as mental representation; it thus ignores an alternative reading of the unconscious as virtual affects or psychic body. Of course ideas can be unconscious (strictly speaking subconscious); however, the real creative work of the unconscious is not primarily about retrieving mental representations but about releasing fixed representations (whether conscious or subconscious). Losing fixed ideas allows the return to a more affectual psychic memory of the body. This more permeable relation with the psychic body enables the actualisation of fantasy and the creation of new experiences and ideas.

So, Mitchell is right to say that in hysteria or trauma there is a kind of fixation within perceptual consciousness, but this is not an opposition between a perception that is bodily and memory that is mental representation. I read the mystic writing pad as offering a model of memory much more similar to Bergson. In trauma and hysteria the person becomes fixed in a perceptual consciousness which has become detached from unconscious memory. Freud (1925a) says that although perception and memory are separate they are also interrelated. This permeable relation, and the writing on the mystic pad, disappears when these two forces become separated. The meeting and breaking between these two systems is determined by internal and external stimulation or shocks, and this discontinuous function 'lies at the bottom of the origin of the concept of time' (Freud 1925a: 180). Discontinuous movement between perception and memory is a dissociation that is both creative and defensive. In trauma and hysteria the dissociation leads to a defensive detachment where the 'hysteric' is too full of consciousness but also too lost in a virtual world of disembodied fantasy.

The bodily perception of iconic images, which Mitchell describes as repeating in the trauma victim, is akin to the early hysterical reminiscences recounted by Freud and Breuer. But rather than seeing these images as either conscious perceptions or unconscious fantasies, we can perhaps see them as both. These are fantasies and representations that become fixed and strangulated in relation to affect, because they cannot become transformed or move in relation to each other. To read memory in terms of mental representation, as Mitchell does, is to forget the important distinction that Freud and Bergson both made between remembrance and unconscious memory. It ignores the fact that the most powerful tool of the unconscious is its role as a psychic imaginative body which can refigure experience. Whereas Mitchell opposes history and the thinking of memory to the bodily presentation of perception, Janet places an opposition between hysterical fixed ideas (both subconscious and conscious) and a memory that is flexible and permeable in relation to conscious perception. This latter memory is, for him, what makes history liveable.

An Enlightenment model of psychoanalysis makes mental representation and knowledge the key aim of the therapeutic encounter. But surely the successful therapy is one in which we change and redescribe ourselves in relation to the world in which we live. Such change is not primarily dependent on mental representation, but on the ability to open up a more affectual immanence with our psychic world of bodily memory. Hypnosis, as Janet realised, could mirror the hysterical trance of fixed representations as an anxious trance, but it was primarily a tool for opening up the relation to the psychic body and for enabling it to move more effectively in relation to our conscious perceptions. Hypnosis is at work in the dissociation between the wax slab and the outer layers of cellophane and wax paper on Freud's mystic writing pad. It can keep the conscious and unconscious defensively apart as a response to trauma. Or, it can enable the writing to appear and disappear as these two systems work in harmony with each other, creating multiple differences, or self-states, that are permeable in relation to each other.

Memory as representation in Bergson's and Janet's thinking is not the key to a more vital life or a cure for mental illness. Quite the opposite: it is something that has to be continually forgotten and reinvented. This definition of memory as life and vitality is very different from the Lacanian subject of linguistic representation. What is interesting about the double consciousness model that Bergson and Janet both ascribed to (a model that was widespread at the end of the nineteenth century) is that a Cartesian rationality, placing mental representation over the body, is being continually displaced. For Bergson and Janet mental representations have to be made fluid in relation to the psychic body; they have to live and move between the imaginary and real.

Lacan, on the contrary, splits symbolic and imaginary, conscious and unconscious, making them oppositional through his notion of the Oedipal phallus. But I suggest that we have to rethink the binary implicit in psychoanalysis and dominant theories of representation where the Oedipal representative subject is placed in a hierarchy over the so-called affectual pre-Oedipal body. This idea that we developmentally move away from a bodily perception towards a more linguistic mode of mental operation is implicit in van der Kolk's approach. In a different way it is also intrinsic to Mitchell's thinking. My argument is that in states of hysteria and trauma we don't regress to a childhood state of pre-Oedipal affects, but to a defensive symbiosis or mimesis, where affects are split off, as we inhabit a world of fixed ideas and fantasies that cannot move creatively with a lived time of the body.

Trauma theory has made a forceful argument, especially in relation to the traumatic legacy of Holocaust victims, arguing that the literal historical event has invaded them. This literal event is not ultimately available for conscious comprehension; it cannot be grasped or integrated. Van der Kolk makes the point that narrative reconstruction of the traumatic event is always a distortion and that 'in therapy, memory paradoxically needs to become an act of creation rather than the static recording of events' (van der Kolk et al. 1996: 19).

This has led him to consider further whether or not it is 'a sacrilege of the traumatic experience' to distort the past (van der Kolk and van der Hart 1995: 179). Leys (2000) sums up the consequences of this argument, that witness or testimony to trauma is impossible as narration always implies distortion. So, all we can do is simply repeat and relive the traumatic experience again and again (Leys 2000: 252). But maybe the truth about trauma is not that the repetitive images or perceptions are any sort of literal recall of the 'event'. As psychoanalytical therapists know, it is quite impossible to distinguish hysterical re-enactments from traumatic flash-backs. Maybe what trauma tells us is the impossibility of ever witnessing anything in a completely veridical way, which is not to say that we cannot agree on shared meanings of events. Obviously, with something like the Holocaust and in the light of historical denials, it is vitally important to give witness. But there is no literal transmission of history and, as the trauma therapists and theorists so rightly note, narrative integration of the traumatic event always involves a translation. Unfortunately, for under-standable reasons they see it as a transformation from literal to narrative, whereas I argue that it is a translation from fixed or impoverished rep-resentations to a more flexible memory or duration of the bodily psyche.

There can be no idealisation of so-called traumatic perceptions or flash-backs; there is nothing absolutely sacred or true or real about these images. However, I suggest that these petrifying hallucinations can be also seen as potential screen memories. The difference with the latter is that they repeat differently because they are able to move creatively between virtual and actual reality. Witnessing and the simultaneous apprehension of life and history is always something worked out between at least two. For the victim of trauma what is important in terms of the cure, whether that is the horrors of the concentration camp, world war, or sexual abuse, is that the victim can transform the nightmare fantasy into actualised, emotional experience in relation to an 'other'. It is only when someone can have this creative experience and translation between fantasy and reality, that they can truly own the trauma as happening to them. The past arrives and can be distinguished from our present only when we can actualise its virtual nature through this affectual movement of becoming.

One of the horrors of trauma is that it prevents a realisation of the past at the same time as halting our movement into a future. For therapists to become hung up on proving the factual veridical nature of the event is to risk losing the creative movement of redescription, integral to living time. It confuses the issues to call this movement narrative, as trauma theorists have done, even though in so doing they are remaining faithful to Janet's ter-minology. But we only have to study the role of hypnosis in Janet's work to realise how problematic it is to equate psychic cure with some notion of linguistic retrieval or symbolisation.

I want to end the theoretical part of this chapter with a consideration of Sandor Ferenczi's work on trauma. His understanding of simulation and its inherent place within relations of origin and trauma is important because of the way he struggles with whether his case histories of trauma and hysteria are encounters based on fantasy or reality. Ferenczi divided his approach into broadly two modes of memory. Following Freud, these modes followed Oedipal logic with a primary memory based on the id and located in the body, followed by a more developed memory associated with the ego. For Ferenczi, the difference between these modes of memory was based on the degree of their object relatedness. However, he also saw these two memories as mixed up with each other, dialogical voices continually intertwined.

Ferenczi (1933) valued the id-based memory as linking to a 'language of tenderness' and the uncorrupted child. Ego memory was linked to the adaptation of the child to the family environment through the regulatory super-ego producing anxiety and guilt. This ego or Oedipal constellation was thus a 'language of passion'. Problems arise when the super-ego, with its derivatives of anxiety and guilt, come into conflict with the id-based bodily memories. Another way of putting this is to say that the symbolic goes to war with the real, resulting in hysterical symptoms. Now, Ferenczi's solution to this conflict between the two systems was not located in the traditional Freudian method of remembering prohibited Oedipal desires, but centred on a positive regression of the patient to an id-based 'language of tenderness'.

Ferenczi places mimesis and an identification between ego and object as central to both models of memory. And in both models of memory he attributes a defensive mimicry at work in splitting ego and object. As the forerunner of object relations theory, Ferenczi underlines the importance of not only internal fantasy but also the relationship to the external object. He explains that in early childhood a splitting or defensive mimicry takes place between ego and object where the 'wise baby' facing an aggressor will yield and adapt to the object – imitating it. Meanwhile, the wise part of the baby splits off in self-protection, objectifying and looking down on the part of the psyche that has yielded to the other. In adults this same model of identification and splitting seems to operate, with the suffering part of the self being dissociated from representation of the scene, so that feelings and affects become cut from objective representation.

Ferenczi describes one of his patients, whose 'emotional life vanishes into unconsciousness and regresses to pure body-sensations' (Ferenczi 1988: 203). However, her intelligence, detached from all emotions, takes flight in progressive identifications devoid of emotion. The 'wise baby' takes over as emotions become dissociated from thoughts and representation to become lost in the unconscious. This defensive form of mimicry can be seen, then, to operate in a range of traumas relating to experiences of childhood abuse, shellshock and concentration camp horror. I want to compare this with the portrayal of hysteria and trauma outlined above, where the hysteric becomes fixated within representations that have become cut off from the lived psychic body.

Healing of trauma, for Ferenczi, occurs through accessing a 'language of tenderness': a positive regression where splits between affects and represen-tations can be healed. A dilemma arises here, for Ferenczi, because verbal recollection of the event only recovers a conscious representation devoid of emotion. But putting his patient into a cathartic trance doesn't work either: 'he feels the suffering in the trance, but still does not know what is going on'. So when he awakes, 'the trauma will only be grasped from the outside, by reconstruction, without any feeling of conviction' (Ferenczi 1988: 39).

This, of course, was Freud's reason for swapping hypnosis for his famous method of free association, on the grounds that because the patient could never remember what happened under hypnosis the results did not last. Unlike Freud, Ferenczi did not abandon the hypnotic method; he adapted it along with Otto Rank into an active technique. Here, active lived experience is chosen over the interpretive knowledge of the analyst. The patient repeats 'a large part of his process of development, but also as experience has shown, it is a matter of just those portions which cannot really be experienced from memory' (Ferenczi and Rank 1925: 3). The analyst embodies a role

> He is invited to take by the patient, but he is not just taking the role, he is 'really carrying out those roles which the unconscious of the patient and his tendency to flight prescribe'.
>
> (Ferenczi and Rank 1925: 43–44)

This is a very important point and leads us straight to an understanding of the healing potential of transference. What makes a difference is not just putting patients in a trance and trying to get them to relive the experience under hypnosis or remember it when they wake up. In the participatory model reminiscent of William Brown, Ferenczi would elicit the participation of the patient, but he went further in allowing himself as the analyst to be drawn into the hypnotic regression. This was not an artificial transference as substitution, where intervention relied on the analyst not being a participant, a view that both Freud and Jung agreed on. Instead, Ferenczi and Rank (1925) proposed a reintroduction of hypnosis into their active model, a method that did not so much repeat an old developmental experience as live a new one.

Acknowledging that Freud gave up hypnosis for free association because it obscured 'vital psychic motives', Ferenczi and Rank go on to state that

> Hypnosis owes its undeniable successes to the complete elimination of the intellectual (ethical, aesthetic, etc) resistances . . . If one could, for example, combine the inestimable advantage of the technique of hypnosis with the advantage of the analytic ability to free the hypnotic affect situation, a tremendous advance in our therapeutic ability would be achieved . . . The final goal of psycho-analysis is to substitute, by means of the technique, affective factors of experience for intellectual processes. It is well known that this is just what is achieved in an extreme way in hypnosis, in which conscious material is called forth or eliminated according to need.
>
> (Ferenczi and Rank 1925: 61–62)

Ferenczi and Rank (1925) then proposed using together the two techniques that had been tried by Freud, one after the other, combining hypnosis with interpretation and working through. Now, this double technique makes sense only if we see the liberation of affect to be achieved by connecting the hypnotic trance to a real conscious experience of the object relation. In other words, healing the split between representation and affects is not achieved, as Ferenczi realised, by recourse to either simple hypnosis or intellectual representation. Cure is managed only through the creation of a different experience in relation to the other or object.

Hypnosis does not simply liberate unconscious affects; it liberates fantasies of virtual affect and representation into actual affective experiences in relation to another. However, I also think that Ferenczi struggled with what hypnosis meant. He knew it worked but also wanted to distance himself from its association with suggestion and persuasion on the part of an all-powerful analyst/parent. From my own experience and knowledge of hypnosis I think we need to recognise that hypnosis can be used in a collusive way in relation to a powerful therapist. This is the hypnotic bond that is in some ways naturally put into place by the neurotic transference and it is idealistic. It simply, as Lacan says, repeats transference onto the suggestive other as the one who knows. This is the transference of the hysteric and I argue it is just as likely to come about through an absent, analytic stance of the therapist as through one who is more obviously suggestive. But hypnosis, as Milton Erickson reminds us, is ultimately self-hypnosis and it can provide lasting healing only if it brings about self-change for the person.

In trance we open ourselves to a range of different states of consciousness and there is a movement between the hidden observer who stays aware of the external environment and another part of us that goes travelling in relation to subconscious states of mind that are more open to the immanence of the psychic body. You are aware of suggestions from the other in trance, but you are also aware of having a choice, of being able to leave some ideas behind and choose others. Hypnosis can be said to have two functions in therapy. To begin with it mirrors the hysteric mimesis as a transference onto an all-powerful other of all our fixed and neurotic representations. This hypnotic trance and transference are full of suffering and alienated or dammed-up affects: symptoms and stories the person cannot stop repeating as fixed melodramas onto the other. But hypnosis can also free itself from this neurotic trance, where representations and affects are split off from each other, and allow a release from suffering into a more lived relation to time and the body.

Because we are always so attached to our suffering, the hypnosis that we recognise most immediately, indeed as the positive transference, is where we fall in love with the therapist as our 'Other'. As Roustang says, it is only when analysts can implicate themselves as more relative, when they cease to enact the law that the hysteric can fantasise without guilt. Not acting out the fantasy means the hysteric has made a choice between a fantasy analyst and a real person. But perhaps the hysteric has also created an experience which is new, the transformation of old representations and fantasies into a new reality. In trauma we need to leave behind not the literal event so much as a neurotic suffering of fixed ideas and fantasies of the other which *is our history*, albeit not one which we can creatively live.

He walks in, a middle-aged man, strong and athletic. He sits and starts to talk to me as if the problem is a purely practical one. As he talks it is clear that this man is self-sufficient and not used to talking about himself. He has come about two things, the problems in his marriage and his anger. He says his anger leaves him feeling helpless and done in and it is affecting his role as a manager at work.

I ask him to describe his marriage and he tells me of an essentially abusive relationship with his wife, who consistently attacks him, putting him down verbally or playing the child-cum-victim when he legitimately loses his temper with her.

At one point early on I say, 'Maybe you are scared that you want to leave your wife,' and he replies, 'I'm scared of losing my children. I don't want the family to break up.'

This man came across as perceptive and rational but very detached. He described fights with his wife where he would be reduced to a quivering heap of rage and yet the rest of the time he was extremely detached with her, his work colleagues and with me. Retreating into an objective detached very responsible self, this man was rather like Ferenczi's (1923) 'wise baby' who looked down on the mad suffering self, who was a victim to his wife, as though it was nothing to do with him. This man would fly into rages over small things, like not being able to find a particular thing he needed on the shelves in a supermarket. Rather than risk a repeat of this frustration the following week, the man went all the way across town to another supermarket rather than risk the possibility that the item would be missing for two weeks running. I likened the missing stock to his relationship with his wife. I suggested that there were lots of options in the face of his disappointment, from tackling the manager to blowing up the supermarket. Rather than face his rage it was better to arrange things so he avoided being disappointed. Maybe having a wife who could not give him anything he wanted was preferable to a wife who might give him something, but then disappoint him.

He merely said: 'I don't really have any desires, or things I want for myself. I want to be happy, but longing is not an emotion I can ever remember feeling.'

This man had never been in therapy and had never thought to connect his past with his present. With encouragement the man began remembering his childhood. Growing up in his family was rather like being in a mental hospital. His father was a veteran of the Second World War and had suffered severe shell shock and trauma when all his comrades were blown up in front of him. After hospitalisation he was unfit to fight, so the army made him carry on working as a gravedigger for his comrades. On his final discharge after the war ended, he married but never recovered. He used to tell his son a repetitive story about his discharge from the army. He was given a brown paper bag with his clothes, a pot of jam and money for a couple of weeks. This memory seemed to sum up all the cruelty and injustice with which he had been treated. As a father he had flown into terrible rages all the time and my client had been forced to walk the streets with his sister until the father had calmed down. The mother was either at work or sick and she became progressively in need of her son, but oblivious to his needs as he grew older. The man excused his parents, saying:

It wasn't their fault; they were both bullied by my maternal, Catholic grandmother. She never accepted my father, as he was Protestant. I remember her always telling me I was illegitimate and worthless. I was forced to stay with her as a child and can still recall the feeling of how much I hated her.

The man remembered how the grandmother continually put him down in front of his favoured Catholic cousin. He also remembered being made to sit in the corner at school because he couldn't learn and sometimes having to wear a dunce's hat on his head.

We discussed the links between his father's rage and his. He reminded me of a soldier who had survived the traumas of an unparented childhood. When he eventually decided to leave home and go travelling as a young man, his mother became furious and told him not to come back. She told everyone he knew that he was dead.

This man's traumatic childhood had led to a splitting off of his vulnerable feelings of rage and neediness so embodied by his parents and returned again in the figure of his wife. Ferenczi famously said that the cure was arrived at not through free association, but through the patient's ability to free-associate. The therapy for this man consisted in an exploration of his ability to free-associate about his fantasies and desires and to translate his fantasy/memories of his childhood, especially his father's rage, into a more affectual response to his present life. His father had lived in a world of his own, apparently quite submissive, when he was not angry. My client remembered him always agreeing with the grandmother to the point of mimicking her words, a parody that had always infuriated the old woman. This defensive mimicry would then also become manifest in the frightening fits of rage where the father's face would twitch and contort, but there seemed to be no real or live object to the release of emotion.

The object of his father's rage was the split-off feeling of rage to the repetitive and fixed representations of his past. Like Ferenczi's (1921) account of the *ticquer*, this father had regressed to a narcissistic state of ironic and mad mimicry where his tic-like movements were a result of dammed-up excitation. Regressed to a narcissism where no relation to present reality or objects existed, the father's rage was an attempt to abreact emotion and to master past trauma. But this father failed to translate what Ferenczi called auto-symbolisations or fantasies into an emotional relationship with another, within lived time. The result was the rage and tic as a damming-up of these virtual fantasies or symbols in the body. The whole family seemed coloured by an inability to change or resist the behaviour of the people they interacted with. Bullying by the grandmother, the hysterical fits of the father, or the illness of the mother were accepted as though they were unalterable facts of life.

One day as we were exploring his desires the man said: 'I would like a boat, maybe just for a day, maybe for ever.'

He explored this fantasy of the boat as escape, freedom from responsibility and also because a boat, which could rock on the waves or be still according to the weather, was something he could both desire and leave. He could be excited in the boat and at peace within it. He said, 'I have an image of a boat, a wooden painted boat, it's a memory of my father giving me a present when I was young.' Unlike the repetitive traumatic memories from his past, this image seemed a more creative screen memory.

The man started crying and he cried for a long time:

> I feel really angry about what the army did to my father and I realise that my wife will never disappoint me, because she hasn't got anything I really want. She is like my mother and my grandmother. I don't want to be bullied any longer; neither do I want her as my child. I want a relationship with someone who can be equal.

I said:

> Maybe your constant reparation to your wife is because you are unconsciously destroying her so much all the time with your rage. Maybe it's like a child being angry with their parents, killing them off and making them better – and yet the child can't leave home and start his life until they are okay.

He replied:

> I've been having fantasies about the kind of woman I could desire. At the moment she is still a fantasy. I don't know how real I want her to be. I guess I know now that if I leave my wife, my children will still be there. I won't disappear for them, but I need some time to think and be interested in what it is I might want.

My role in the therapy was about being able to help this man dream of the things in life he could want, and have, but also leave. Therapy became a repository for him of possibility; it was a place in which he could dream and perhaps mourn, but it also had to be somewhere that didn't claim him. Eventually the man stopped putting up with his mother's demanding behaviour and one day turned up for a session telling me of his latest visit home.

> We were in the kitchen and I was looking out into the garden and suddenly I saw myself as a 10-year-old boy in the same kitchen. It was uncanny, a sort of *déjà vu* experience where I was seeing myself. I had this profound feeling that this boy, who was me, could actually be anything he wanted to be. I don't know but that experience has changed me: it's made me realise that understanding my past is important because I don't have to carry on repeating it.

This man did not just remember mental representations; he forgot fixed ideas and recreated new feeling experiences. He discovered that leaving home didn't have to be deathly or traumatic. In fact when he left therapy he had not left his wife, he had simply stopped putting up with her role as a victim and her bullying behaviour. He had stopped acquiescing in the story of suffering that had seemed such an inescapable part of his past. As a result his wife's behaviour started to improve dramatically. Free association, and what I would call self-hypnosis, led this man to a place where in place of old fixed ideas about himself and his past, he could begin to access emotions and dreams about his future. His association of his fantasies within the session was also the translation of his past into a more emotional experience within the present. He achieved, in short, the translation of trauma into lived time that had been so sadly unavailable to either of his parents.

Chapter 6

Psychoanalysis and the time of life

In an age of globalisation

> Pure duration is the form which the succession of our conscious states assumes when our ego lets itself live, when it refrains from separating its present state from its former states. For this purpose it need not be entirely absorbed in the passing sensation or idea; for, then, on the contrary, it would no longer *endure*. Nor need it forget its former states; it is enough that, in recalling these states,it does not set them alongside its actual state as one point alongside another, but forms both the past and the present states into an organic whole, as happens when we recall the notes of a tune, melting, so to speak, into one another.
>
> (Bergson 1960 [1889]: 60)

I want the reader to consider the above quote by Bergson as a model for psychoanalysis where the temporalities of conscious and unconscious are not distinct. They are not divided into spatially discrete topographic modalities, but intrinsically connected. Past and present leak into, and penetrate each other, in a continuous state of becoming and duration. However, Bergson warns, if one note is concentrated on more than another, then we abstract lived time and extend it into space, thereby positing a before and an after, a line of succession where the parts of our lived being are no longer connected. When this happens a qualitative change occurs in the musical phrase. We can liken this to the dilemma of the hysteric who can be described as living a defensive dissociation, split between virtual and actual worlds, either retreating into a past state of fantasy, or alternatively being far too full of consciousness. Consequently, the hysteric lives an intellectual vitality that is cut off from affectual sensation, and at the same time she literally experiences the body as physiological symptoms which cannot be connected to her mental fantasy life. The hysteric, as I have described elsewhere, performs the body, but remains psychically disembodied (Campbell 2005). She remains fixed and unable to enter into lived time. For Bergson, lived duration is the flow of images and perceptions that are in a state of becoming between virtual and actual.

Now dissociation for Bergson is the creative way we move from one flow of images or perceptions to another. He argues that matter is an 'aggregate of images':

> Matter, in our view, is an aggregate of 'images'. And by 'image' we mean a certain existence which is more than that which the idealist calls a representation, but less than that which the realist calls a thing – an existence placed halfway between the 'thing' and the 'representation'.
>
> (Bergson 1912: vii)

The hysteric is compromised in relation to images, because for the hysteric images don't endure or live, they become stuck within the transcendental realm of representation or the real world of the thing. Dissociation has ceased to be a creative movement of the psyche, where images can flow between imaginary and real, creating lived time and difference. The inability to produce this creative exchange leads to the imaginary and real as split and at war, a death drive, or as Luce Irigaray describes, a one-way mirror, where realms of the carnal and transcendental remain disconnected.

Bergson's work is interesting for psychoanalysis because it enables us to think of the unconscious and conscious mind not as an internal hierarchy, but as a creative flux of flows and images where ideas and affects are vitalities that move between virtual and actual in a state of becoming. The proliferation of post-classical psychoanalysis with all its differing schools of Freudian, Kleinian, Object relations, Lacanian, as well as the more American brands of interpersonal and self-psychology, has meant that there is no longer any clear agreement about what fantasy and reality mean. The boundaries between psychic reality and external reality, or indeed the difference between what happens in the mind and what happens between people has been moved to the point where we need to reconsider what we mean by a structure of conscious and unconscious. Freud's classical model posed a positivist, unitary concept of the mind, but nowadays a complex network of related and dissociated states is acknowledged by many analysts as a more workable description.

Every analyst knows the clinical paradox that clients present to the therapist as the beginning of therapy. Clients arrive wanting to change and then make it obvious that nothing in the world is going to shift them from their particular mode of suffering in the world. The analyst has to work with this paradox, going along with the delusory hope that change can take place and everything can still stay the same. This is important because people's defences and their self-meaning matter and the client needs to feel a continuity and a going on being of self-states, at the same time as being able to generate new meaning and self-states. These new vitalities are created in relation to the other, inside and outside, in relation to both the fantasy other and the real object and, as I have said, this is a very permeable threshold.

Bergson's concept of affectual and ideational vitalities is then an interesting way to think of our minds as creative networks of different intensities and flows. These vitalities in neurotic and pathological conditions become excessively dissociated and split off. Deleuze and Guattari (1984) have taken Bergson's emphasis on affectual vitalities and intensities to argue for the productive flows of desire, which predate and outstrip being and identity. These schizoid flows of desire or lines of flight are virtual in the sense that they always in a state of becoming. As such they are a 'deterritorialisation' of any original territory or subject. Such free-floating desires characteristic of the schizoid are incorporeal and virtual, the fantasies of becoming which dissolve Freud's bounded ego. This emphasis on virtual fantasy is what leads Deleuze and Guattari (1984) to reclaim Melanie Klein's emphasis on a fantasy world comprising part-objects. They argue that Klein's

> Partial objects unquestionably have a sufficient charge in and of themselves to blow up all of Oedipus and totally demolish its ridiculous claim to represent the unconscious.
>
> (Deleuze and Guattari 1984: 44)

According to Deleuze and Guattari's groundbreaking *Anti-Oedipus* (1984), Melanie Klein's work holds the seeds of a more radical construction of desire. For them these part objects signify an energetic and fluid libido that traverses and exceeds persons, which is non-human, social and collective – a body without organs which precedes and can outlive the Oedipal Complex. However, for Klein and object relations theory in general, part objects are merely roles which lead to the integration of the ego within an object relation, the continuity of experience over time and a stable, unified identity.

We can agree with Deleuze and Guattari (1984) that Klein refuses the radical virtual fantasy that is implicit in her theory. Instead of shattering Oedipus, Klein merely refinds it earlier on, as her famous analysis of little Dick illustrates. Their withering and funny critique of this analysis shows how, for Deleuze and Guattari, desire cannot be reduced to desire between persons, or Mummy and Daddy:

> As his analysis progressed . . . Dick had also discovered the mother's body, and he displayed an extraordinary dread of being wetted with water. 'Say that it's Oedipus or you'll get a slap in the face.' The psychoanalyst no longer says to the patient: 'Tell me a little bit about your desiring-machines, won't you?' Instead he screams: 'Answer daddy-and-mommy when I speak to you!' Even Melanie Klein. So the entire process of desiring production is trampled underfoot and reduced to (*rabattu sur*) parental images, laid out step by step in accordance with

supposed pre-oedipal stages, totalized in Oedipus, and the logic of part
objects is reduced to nothing.

(Deleuze and Guattari 1984: 45)

Deleuze and Guattari suggest that the incest taboo and the first primary
bond between mother and child are cultural fictions which personalise
desire as Oedipal, thus removing it from its proper collective and political
function.

I think that we can acknowledge that desire is immanent, proceeding
through and moving beyond the subject, without having to refuse the
significance of Oedipus, although, as I have discussed within this book, this
significance is both a defensive and creative phenomenon in relation to time
and the body. If we think of Hamlet, maybe his tragedy is his inability to
recreate his relation to life and the maternal object, his incapacity to move
between being and doing. As a result he becomes stuck in an Oedipal
Complex that has, as Winnicott says, no alternative to being, and no
alternative to doing. Literal and virtual are permanently estranged; we can
actually sleep with our parents, or we are stuck within the fantasy of incest
as prohibited, leading us back to a passive compliance with the object.

If Freud saw incest in quite literal terms, then Jung and Lacan argued, in
different ways, for its symbolic meaning. However, it is perhaps Winnicott
with his unerring sense of the necessary movement of psychic life who
understood how the Oedipal Complex is really no different from the dilemma we are faced with in relation to the maternal object. Like Hamlet's
unfathomable dilemma where being and doing are split, and where incest is
both literal and an everlasting fantasy, we are confronted with the need to
join our fantasies with reality. Desiring and being the mother is just like the
desire and being integral to the Oedipal Complex: in order to live these
relationships we have to constantly destroy and recreate them. Adam
Phillips (2000) shows how this very destruction and creation of the object is
indeed displayed through Winnicott's (1971b) rereading of Freud and
Jones, through the play of *Hamlet*.

Castration, as Luce Irigaray has said, is a one-way street or mirror,
because it sets up destruction and separation from the mother's body as
somehow distinct from a loving identification and union. We are alive in
the symbolic and she is vanquished. Or, we are symbiotically fused and
unactualised as distinct human beings. But if the origin story of psychoanalysis is just how we recreate our imaginary and real worlds in relation to
each other; if it is nothing more or less than the creative screen memory, the
worked-on dream or the dreamed object, then Hamlet's Oedipus conflict
becomes the object we need to dream more, or the dream that needs remaking
a bit more in terms of reality. Incest or Oedipus is not the truth narrative of
psychoanalysis because the only true self, in an unconscious sense, is a
fantasy or reality that has already been changed into something else.

We can think of part-objects as the implicit dreams that are waiting to be created in reality. Kleinian theory, with its polarisation of good versus bad object, has often become too locked within the notion of a reparative Self, as a kind of unified humanist identity, fixed for all time. Most psychoanalysts these days, however, recognise (with or without recourse to Lacanian theory) that the unified self is an illusion. The part-objects of Klein's theory are arguably situated as the multiple selves and others which we locate either subjectively or in other people. These objects are transformational – in the sense that they elaborate our unconscious worlds, translating into a lived duration. Or, they are fixed, in all the defensive and paranoid ways that Klein suggested. However, as analysts we can posit the existence of vital, internal objects and flows and also acknowledge the importance of environmental objects in the world, like Winnicott's good-enough mother – objects which meet our unconscious durational selves and help materialise them as imaginary and real, made-up and discovered.

It is precisely this materialisation of affective flows as creative differences that leads to an integration of the ego with the imaginary and a continuity of being over time. Disintegration and splitting result when these real and imaginary worlds become dissociated, when, like Oedipus or the hysteric, we are forced to adopt certain meanings that divide intellect from living in the body.

I have argued for the Oedipal Complex as hysterical mimesis, a defensive doubling against time and death. But this Oedipal doubling is also creative in a Bergsonian sense, in its ability to produce new affectual vitalities. One of the problems with Deleuze and Guattari's (1984) schizoid flows lies with their status as always only virtual or possible, a becoming which dissolves the ego, preceding and transcending any notion of being and identity. These virtual desires go beyond the human to the inhuman; detached from any actual or original territory they designate a non-corporeal sense, an affect detached from any 'individual State of things' (Deleuze and Guattari 1984: 61).

Now, I want to argue that Deleuze and Guattari's (1984) emphasis on the virtual differs from Bergson. In Bergson's thinking, especially in his essay 'Memory of the Present and False Recognition' (1908b), he argues that a retreat into a virtual, dream world and a turning away from conscious perception means that we have a weakened attention to life. So, for Bergson, the virtual has to be connected to an actual becoming in terms of the perceptual object. Here, becoming and the duration of time signify a constant movement between virtual and actual, but also a means of corporeal actualisation. Difference here is not just virtual becoming, but remakes the image or object again and again in an actualisation which is grounded in time and space.

Remember that Bergson understands false recognition as a self-reflective dreaming where we are too aware of our virtual and actual forces as separate temporalities. It is only when we translate virtual into actual that we live time. So although living time is real, it is also an unaware or unconscious dreaming. We can link this to Freud's thinking on dreaming. Or, to be more accurate, the dreaming described by Bollas (1993). Psycho-analysis divides the dream into the complex dreamer who watches, thinks and represents, and the simple dreamer who experiences. Freud says that although the complex dreamer dramatises his or her wishes and memories in theatrical form, the simple self-experiences and lives the dream uncon-sciously. This unconsciousness is necessary for self-experience to be realised within the dream space. Bollas likens this dream-work between simple and complex self to the way we also live everyday life, moving between reflective and immersive engagements with objects (Bollas 1993).

The simple experiencing self, Bollas tells us, is a form of being that elaborates our personal idiom, through transformational objects we uncon-sciously select, as we walk and dream through life. This transformational self is near to what Winnicott calls the 'true self' of object usage. Now, Bergson's false recognition is a passive dream state of self-reflection that is quite opposite to Freud's, and Bollas's evocation of the simple, experi-encing self. It is in fact, part of the split world of the hysteric whose dream and real worlds become so divided.

The unconscious being of the self that Bollas describes is much nearer to Bergson's notion of a lived duration or 'attention to life' where our two temporal streams of virtual and actual are irremediably intertwined. This has consequences for the way we think of Deleuze and Guattari's (1984) schizoid flows. The schizophrenic is withdrawn within a virtual self-reflective dreaming and does not yield to the transformations in relation to the object that characterise the simple experiencing self that Bollas describes – a self that can immerse himself in the duration of lived time. Thus, the schizophrenic is immersed in a reflexive virtual world, a space where hyper-consciousness and virtual dreaming go hand in hand. This is simply a more extreme form of hysteria. As long as schizoid flows remain incapable of transformation in relation to the Oedipal object, they remain virtual, autistic and cut off from reality.

The virtual lines of flight that Deleuze and Guattari (1984) describe are certainly part of the free association embarked on in different ways by the therapist and client in therapy. These schizoid fantasies are multiple objects that in the case of the neurotic can be used and made real. For the psychotic these objects cannot be entered into, in any generative sense; they remain lifeless, trapped within a virtual world of detached self-reflection. We can see the root of the Oedipal Complex and schizophrenic fantasy to be in a doubling or splitting which in pathological conditions makes fantasy and reality, masculinity and femininity, activity and passivity extreme opposi-tions which are mutually exclusive. This defensive doubling is a division between doing and being, desire and identification which, as Hamlet shows us, descends into a spiralling madness. The psychotic inhabits narcissistic fantasy as a retreat from the reality of the world, only to find that world returned as an overwhelming nightmare of the real. Dissociation is the way in health in which we can move creatively between affectual vitalities of virtual and actual; it is how we move between unconscious and conscious worlds. In pathological states this dissociation becomes rigid Oedipal splitting taken to extremes. Deleuze and Guattari argue that the schizo-phrenic suffers from not too little of Oedipus but too much. They cite Gregory Bateson's famous schizophrenic double bind as 'oedipalizing par excellence' (Deleuze and Guattari 1984: 79). Perhaps it would be more true to say that the schizophrenic suffers from living within an Oedipal Complex which has become rigidly fixed against moving in the time. The difference between the schizophrenic and the neurotic is that the former opts for a world of passive dreaming and the latter becomes locked within a com-pulsive, objective reality.

As Freud himself acknowledged, everything points to moving beyond the father, but that movement is always prohibited by the incest taboo. But we forget that prohibition exists because what is taboo is always possible. Incest is possible and actual, and moving away from the family might feel impossible, but is something that has to become actualised in order for the individual to recreate him or herself. Dissociation is a more flexible term than repression because it enables us to think of the psyche as something that either is fixed or can move within time. Repression, as a term, enables us to think of how our mental contents are pushed away, but it does not encompass an understanding of how the structure of the psyche functions.

In discussing the hysterical case of the young woman Katharina, whom he had encountered on a holiday in the Alps, Freud (1895c) described her dissociation of attempted sexual abuse by her father, which was brought to light only by her subsequent memory of the events in talking to him. He makes it clear here that for him there is really no difference between dissociation and repression:

> Moreover, I should like at this point to express a doubt as to whether a splitting of consciousness due to ignorance is really different from one due to conscious rejection.

> (Freud 1895c: 200)

Bergson places suggestion, hypnosis and dissociation as the founding pro-cess of the psyche, as our construction of our world, whether that reality is aesthetic or natural. In their book *A Critique of Psychoanalytic Reason*, Léon Chertok and Isabelle Stengers (1992) argue passionately for a recon-sideration of the importance of hypnosis for psychoanalysis. Freud did not break with hypnosis in their view; he merely found new ways of practising it. As a practising analytical therapist who is also trained in the skills of hypnotism, I agree with them. We all practise hypnosis, I suggest, when we work as analysts, but because of the taboo that has been set up around terms such as suggestion and hypnotism the profession has followed Freud in distancing itself from a conscious use of hypnosis in the analytic setting.

There are many good reasons for this, not least for the unregulated nature of hypnotherapy training. Literally anybody in Britain can set up in practice: training and indeed learning the skills of hypnosis is pretty simple. How you would integrate those skills in analytic therapy is much less straightforward. One of the main problems these days is that whilst hypno-therapists are equipped to help you stop smoking and lose weight, they are often not properly trained as therapists to deal with deep-seated psychological issues. Regulation, however, is not the only reason why psychoanalysts eschew hypnosis. A much less admitted motive is that hypnosis is simply too close to the bone and that although analysts are well aware that suggestion remains a central part of the therapeutic cure, they prefer not to link this to what seem the mysterious and perhaps uncontrollable powers associated with the roles of hypnotiser and hypnotised.

Freud originally distinguished between the curative artificial transference manufactured inside the therapy session, and the real and neurotic transferences situated in childhood. He did not maintain this position and the resolution of the hypnotic transference and the whole nature of therapeutic cure has become one of the legacies of Freudian psychoanalysis that still raise urgent questions as to what our goals are as therapists.

Freud's original separation between the artificial transference and real neurosis was a technique where analytic interpretation of meaning and knowledge were supposed to free the patient from illness. Ferenczi's active technique, as I have discussed, challenged this interpretative model and argued for the analytical transference in the here and now as something new and therefore not ideal, but real in its own right. The use of active repetition in the therapy, of affects directed towards the analyst, made Ferenczi realise that he had to go beyond free association of thoughts to encourage sensations, images and emotions that freely arose in the patient when he was in a relaxed state. Ferenczi then asks himself how far his method 'may be called hypnosis and suggestion' (Ferenczi 1931: 133). His response is to say that suggestion is legitimate provided it is confined to 'general encouragement rather than special direction'.

He then goes on to discuss that free association in his active technique leads directly to trance states. When a patient is called upon to go deeper in the direction of free association:

> It sometimes happens – with me, let me frankly confess, very frequently – that a more profound abstraction develops. Where this takes a quasi-hallucinatory form, people can call it auto-hypnosis if they like; my patients often call it a trance state.
>
> (Ferenczi 1931: 134)

Hypnosis is at root self-hypnosis and, as Milton Erickson has taught us, is more effective for being indirect. Ferenzci and more recently analysts such as Léon Chertok and François Roustang are analysts who all realise that in analysis we are dealing with the modification of affectual powers, and that hypnosis is the phenomenon in which we deal with that opening and crossroads between mental and physiological processes. Ferenczi is especially interesting because he reveals how he elicits suggestions from the patient and then reciprocally puts them back in a more comprehensible way to the patient. This is not didactic hypnosis; it is not the hypnotic effect that Freud tells us emanates from the leader of the group or the primal father. Rather, it is hypnosis and suggestion in the service of producing a new relationship between analyst and patient. Ferenczi's student, Michael Balint, developed Ferenczi's understanding of the mother–child relationship in his analysis of the 'basic fault' or trauma arising in the separation from the primary object; such trauma may be either environmental or congenital. Balint (1968) follows Ferenczi's techniques in emphasising the importance of holding and empathic understanding especially when states of strong emotion or regression are present in the therapy. Acknowledging how language is often not enough in these strong regressions, and how interpretation is often, especially in the beginning, inappropriate, Balint suggests that sometimes analysts might resort to simple gestures like holding hands.

Balint (1968) recommends physical contact only in the context of benign regression; that is, regression in the service of self-recognition and growth of the ego. He distinguishes benign regression from what he sees as malignant regression, the latter being an aggressive overwhelming state where the client seeks instinctual gratification from the analyst. This emphasis on a holding environment within the session is very much a characteristic of the tradition of object relations psychoanalysis and indeed Winnicott was known for his acceptance of physical holding in the analytic situation. For the independent object relations tradition, empathy and holding are often seen as important for more borderline patients as a preliminary stage where mutuality can be established. But of course this sets up a hierarchy where mental interpretation of conflict is the main meat for healthy neurotics, whereas patients with more primitive defences need a more bodily holding.

It is very true that very borderline or psychotic patients cannot bear much interpretative work, and that this is because there is no shared meaning or experience between client and analyst. However, the idea that interpretative work and mental representation is the high goal of psychoanalysis and that affectual relating, through bodily empathy, is a sort of subsidiary, makes the affectual tie secondary to mental interpretation. In this sense for psychoanalysis nowadays, Freud has won out over Ferenczi and we still, as analysts, privilege knowledge and interpretation as the main principles of therapy, over and above the affective tie.

Merton Gill and Margaret Brenman, authors of *Hypnosis and Related States: Psychoanalytic Studies in Regression* (1961), interpret the hypnotic relation in therapy as transference. They suggest that the hypnotic state is 'a regression in the service of the ego'. This is also Balint's definition of benign regression. According to Gill and Brenman (1961) hypnosis has the benefits of lowering defences and liberating affect. Contrary to the myths surrounding hypnosis, the client is not taken over by the hypnotist. Rather the ego of the client sits in the background and allows the hypnotist to take control over certain bits of him or her that relate particularly to the external environment. So, hypnotism does not produce for the patient an essentially different environment from that of psychoanalysis. However, Gill and Brenman do suggest that this raises conflicts for analysts, who will be faced with the power of their role – their so-called analytical neutrality gets called into question. Moreover, the temptation to become the omnipotent parent, identifying with the regressed childlike aspects of the patient, is also an anxiety for analysts who practise hypnotism.

I want to consider this for a moment because I don't think there is much difference between the role of the classical blank screen analyst, whom Roustang (1996) calls 'Nobody', and the omnipotent parent as hypnotiser. In both cases the client will transfer their unconscious histories onto the role of this all-powerful Other. What modifies the affective powers in the analysis is the necessity of the analyst changing his position. Direct hypnotism then raises the issue of the analyst's power and confronts him with his desire, and, as Gill and Brenman (1961) argue, this clearly raises issues for analysts who have their professional respectability at stake and want to distinguish their practice. Freud wanted to differentiate analysis as scientific, as the recovery of meaning and knowledge, whereas Ferenczi challenged this in his emphasis on the primary role of affect. What is often ignored in the contemporary return to Ferenczi is that he practised indirect hypnosis. There is no need for hypnosis to be named and deliberately induced for it to occur in the therapeutic setting.

What really is the difference between the trance states evoked in hypnotherapy and the trance states that are conjured up and worked with in the analytic session? In hypnosis there is a deliberate induction technique with the hypnotiser proceeding through eye fixation, imaginative relaxation scripts and post-hypnotic suggestions. In psychoanalysis patients are asked to come repeatedly and lie on the couch and are then encouraged to free-associate on their dreams and images. In response to this elaboration of suggestive material, the analyst makes associations, interpretations and suggestions.

We know the problems that Ferenczi ran into in his therapy sessions, through experimenting with his active technique, and there is no doubt that at times the affective tie Ferenczi initiated with his clients got out of hand. However, this does not mean that hypnosis per se is dangerous, as long as it is practised by experienced therapists. Hypnosis, I suggest, is simply a tool which provides access to a threshold phenomenon between mental and physiological processes. It is a proven, holistic, therapeutic technique to heal physiological ailments in much the same way as other alternative health approaches. However, because of its power to deeply relax and liberate affectual processes it can also be used in more psychological therapy which would then involve conflict and issues of power between therapist and patient.

Harold Stewart is one psychoanalyst well known for his use of hypnosis. His rejection of it as a collusive practice is a prime example of why today hypnosis is shunned by the psychoanalytic profession. Stewart (1992) argues that the hypnotic state is based on a collusive deception between the subject and the hypnotist. This deception is the pretence that the analyst/ hypnotist is all-powerful. The subject projects his omnipotence and super-ego onto the analyst and feels because of this that he is in control. Meanwhile the analyst uncritically accepts the projections and feels magically powerful and elated. The hypnotic state is thus an expression and denial of the subject's aggressive and hostile instincts. Stewart cites as evidence the observations of the subject after a session who says 'I feel marvellous' (Stewart 1992: 13). According to Stewart this is indicative of a manic and triumphant euphoria. The headaches that often appear are likewise a somatisation of unconscious guilt for the attack.

Physically feeling good and having headaches are also common characteristics of how we feel after having a massage, and are more commonly associated with the release of toxins. Hypnosis is undoubtedly cathartic, but whether this means it is *always* a collusion obscuring the patient's aggressive feelings is highly debatable. What is the difference between the trance induced by Winnicott, holding his patient's head, and the affective trance elicited by Ferenczi? For Stewart (1992), the difference between Winnicott's regression to dependence and the earlier cathartic abreactions based on hypnosis is quite obvious. He writes:

> The essential difference between regression in hypnosis and psycho-analysis is that the former results from a collusive relationship between patient and hypnotiser, which must necessarily be unacknowledged and unexamined if the hypnotherapy is to continue as such. The latter, however, is a naturally occurring, spontaneous event, which is acknowledged, scrutinised, and examined to the maximum in the patient–analyst relationship. The difference is the authenticity of the phenomenon.
>
> (Stewart 1992: 107)

Or we might say, for Stewart, affective regression is made safe, tamed and trammelled into meaningful interpretation that keeps Freud's original

Enlightenment project alive and on track. But what if interpretation and suggestion are not so very different; what if the abreactive trance and regression in psychoanalysis are exactly the same thing? Adam Phillips acknowledges that suggestion 'has always been a dirty word in psycho-analysis' (Phillips 1998: 63). He goes on to discuss how we can distinguish orders from hints, and how the interpretations that Klein made were normally the former, whereas Winnicott excelled at playing or hinting. Whether or not you make orders or hints as a psychoanalyst, they are both suggestions, it is just that one poses as knowledge and the other is more easily usable. Hints are ambiguous and deconstructive, like dream-work. Klein's suggestion, Phillips notes, arouses such hostility because she makes clear the nature of analysis. The unconscious is made up by Klein, or resides in her descriptions of what the client is pointing to. Her orders create the unconscious; as Phillip says, 'No interpretation, no unconscious' (Phillips 1998: 83). Hints are equally productive as Winnicott shows through his squiggle game. Suggestion, then, produces knowledge and dream-work.

I am not saying that Stewart is wrong to label hypnosis collusive. Of course it can be, and we all know of the cults and New Age therapies, where people for a short time experience exaltation and a sort of religious liberation and transcendence of the self. This exaltation does not last and can leave the person feeling disappointed and depleted. Perhaps this is also Freud's realisation of the short-term benefits of hypnosis and the reason he tried to abandon it. Such hypnosis is merely a mirror to the hysteric's escape, but this does not mean that hypnosis and psychoanalytic regression are different things. Regression, as Balint (1968) tells us, can be malignant or benign, and the trance states we inhabit can lead to exalted transcen-dence or they can be much more Buddhist, a more meditative acceptance and letting go of suffering.

As long as the two definitions of hypnotic trance and psychoanalytic regression are kept distinct, then psychoanalysis can continue on its happy career with its principles of interpretation and mental meaning firmly intact. However, if the trance and psychoanalytic regression are synonymous, then we have to begin, as Roustang has done, to examine how the hypnotic trance, as psychoanalysis, functions. Hypnosis confronts Freud's original project, the Enlightenment project of knowledge and reason. Chertok and Stengers (1992) not only argue that psychoanalysis is simply another way of practising suggestion and hypnosis, but also *suggest* that this practice raises a wounding truth or narcissistic wound to the tradition of scientific reason, a tradition that Freud so badly wanted psychoanalysis to belong to. Hypnosis and suggestion abolish the distinction between heart and reason or fantasy and reality, a distinction that the history of rational science has been indebted to. Psychoanalysis, as Freud unhappily discovered, does not deliver rational truth; it uncovers how knowledge and reality are a product of hypnotic suggestion.

Hypnosis has, in the popular imagination anyway, been seen as something that suggests a dream-world as a substitute for a lived reality. I want to argue for hypnosis as a method of transport; it is how we move in time between real and imaginary worlds and as such it can lead us into escape fantasies, but it can also enable us to confront new realities. This is where hypnosis and psychoanalysis as clinical practices really would benefit from each other. Take, for example, a woman I saw who came to see me because she had a phobia about sick, in particular her little girl being sick. This sick phobia kept this woman attached to her child, her husband and her mother, but it also protected her from the feelings of abandonment and loss, which stemmed from her early adoption and a career that had been sacrificed to marry a man she did not love. A hypnotist would merely have got rid of the phobia, leaving the client far too free to embrace the reality of her depressive feelings, whereas, as a therapist, my role was to refuse this quick fix, in the knowledge that she needed this phobia. Uncovering her depression through suggestive hints allowed this woman to find her own way of substituting the phobia for a more creative life. I don't practise what is formally recognised as hypnotic skills, I don't induce a formal trance, and yet I am alive to the different trance phenomena that are an integral part of the analytic session.

Daniel Stern has been central to the argument put forward in this book for his thesis of an intrinsic phenomenology of the unconscious. A phenomenological view of the mind understands mental activity as embodied in relation to both the individual's sensori-motor activity and his or her physical environment. The mind is then brought into being with its interaction with other minds and objects in the world. In his latest book Stern (2004) distinguishes between a verbal register that is in essence Freud's intra-psychic model, and a phenomenal conscious that is the here-and-now experience of the person. This experience is implicitly known, not verbal, and is non-conscious, i.e. what we are unaware of. Stern, as I have discussed in Chapter 2, links this phenomenal consciousness to Bollas's concept of the 'unthought known' where experience is pre-reflective and potentially symbolic. Distinct from this phenomenal consciousness is reflective, verbal introspection attached to symbolic systems and the realm of the dynamically repressed unconscious. What Stern calls the intersubjective consciousness is a socially based interaction where each person co-creates experience using their phenomenal consciousness, whilst still retaining their sense of self-consciousness.

The distinction Stern makes between phenomenal and verbal registers mirrors the distinction in psychoanalysis between the maternal pre-Oedipal order and an Oedipal domain of symbolic representation. Although Stern does not make these domains developmental, for him both verbal and phenomenal modalities operate and interact with each other. The problem with a phenomenological account of consciousness, as I have argued elsewhere, is that it evacuates the role of memory, and of course psychoanalysis provides this emphasis. Stern's description of the verbal self accords with the classical psychoanalytic account of the repressed subject. This introspective consciousness reflects on and interacts with the more here-and-now phenomenological experience, although for Stern these are two different models demanding different explanations (Stern 2004: 227).

Stern is hazy about how phenomenological consciousness relates to psychoanalysis. At one point he says that 'the psychoanalytic unconscious, at its most simple, is consciousness masked by repression' (Stern 2004: 143). I don't think we have to separate, as Stern does, consciousness into differing registers of phenomenal, introspective or social (and thus intersubjective). Rather, we can see them as affective vitalities that are not set out in space as separate units but as states that are permeable. Stern does talk about psychic states as intermingling but he also classifies them into different units. In *Time and Free Will* (1889), Bergson discusses how a false phenomenology of mental states results if we think of them in spatial terms. Human experience does not perceive real life as a succession of demarcated conscious states, progressing along some imaginary line, but rather as a continuous flow. Objects and events should not be seen as a succession, but time should be understood as duration, something that flows and cannot be cut up into abstract bits. For Bergson, real or lived time is experienced as duration and apprehended by intuition, not through separate operations of instinct and the intellect.

We can, I argue, understand Stern's three registers of consciousness as different experiences that become abstractly divided when we apprehend them in space. But as he would himself admit they are also part of a much more heterogeneous multiplicity, in terms of the becoming of our different selves or self–other relationships. Bergson emphasises how consciousness is a multiple becoming that is organised through dissociation and suggestion. In Stern's earlier and famous work *The Interpersonal World of the Infant* (1985), he rereads psychoanalysis. Instead of reading child development in Freudian stages, which have to mastered, he sees different experiences coexisting and interacting throughout life.

In this book, Stern designates four different experiences of the emerging, core subjective self and verbal self. These different orders are events that are organised between mother and child, for example through 'attunement' and suggestion. The mother suggests affective vitalities and experiences to her infant, but this is also in response to the suggestion of the infant. These events are then always in a state of becoming. Attunement is also something the therapist and client engage in; behaving towards each other in terms of suggestion that brings different experiences into being. But as Stern emphasises, this attunement is selective although not always at a verbal and conscious level.

We can see that Stern does not predicate a move from the pleasure principle to the reality principle in the same way as Freud. For him the baby apprehends reality from the start, but by the same token, if reality is brought into being through suggestion, then fantasy is also at the heart of this reality. Stern (1985) argues that fantasies of oneness or splitting can occur only after a verbal sense has come into being, and there is also no possibility of regressing back to before this event as an adult. In terms of psychoanalysis this would mean that the conflict between fantasy and reality would be ushered in only after language – the Oedipal stage. However, this can no longer be seen as a 'mature' stage that has been reached or not reached.

Reading Stern, through Bergson, allows us to add an immanence to his phenomenology of consciousness; it also allows us to understand how so-called dynamic Oedipal repression and the implicit knowledge of non-reflexive experience can be brought together under a more general organising principle of suggestion and dissociation. We can see, for example, how the different experiences that Stern describes are affectual vitalities that move suggestively between self and other. But, as Bergson points out, these vitalities can become fixated, ideas that are abstracted in space, and when this happens movement between virtual and real becomes compromised. This is the dilemma of the hysteric, and hypnosis is fascinating because, as Charcot realised over a hundred years ago, although hypnosis models hysterical dissociation as a defensive mode, hypnosis as dissociation is also involved in the creative and psychic production of new realities. Chertok and Stengers (1992) outline how hypnosis challenges the opposition we set up between heart and reason, suggestion and rationality. In a similar vein, Bergson also argues how the events of lived time are brought into being through a suggestive intuition that also confronts any distinction between materialist or idealist philosophies.

How do we relate this reading of psychoanalysis, as immanent time, to our current global world? Michael Rustin (2001) and Anthony Giddens's (1991) work represents a modernist and a postmodern account of psychoanalysis and the self within present-day global society. Rustin adheres to a traditional modernist reading of psychoanalysis exemplified by a meta-psychology of reason and unreason. Psychoanalysis can be measured empirically and rationally: Oedipus as our scientific project of progress.

Giddens (1991) utilises a phenomenological reading of the reflexive self which eschews this modernist depth model. And yet the new global self that Giddens envisages in our society of calculated 'risks' and 'brands' is just as certain and self-knowing as Rustin's (2001) more Enlightenment Oedipus.

Giddens argues that it is positive that people in our current society have such choice over their own self-trajectories and lifestyles. When we can be reflexive and transform ourselves on an individual level, then we can celebrate a sort of privatised consumption within the couple, to replace older structures of tradition and community. The true self, here, is the pure relationship, an ideal reflexivity, between two which can also incorporate others, but which necessarily moves beyond traditional roles of family and social bonds. This individualised 'pure relationship' provides territory for a future relational and reflexive identity. Instead of society we have the mutually explorative and interdependent couple.

Rustin (2001) is cynical about such upbeat individualism in our present-day global world that promises, in Blairite fashion, a freedom based on the responsibilities/reflexivity of the 'self'. Rustin emphasises the necessary constraints that society imposes on individuals. We can't have autonomous reflexivity outside social institutions such as the family. In Rustin's post-Kleinian mind view, reality is always beyond our senses. Grounded in the established rules of traditional institutions, like the British Institute of Psychoanalysis, this reality is a loving reason, personified in the right Oedipal analyst. This analyst, who acts as the knowing parental mind, detoxifies the irrational omnipotence and projections of his patients, leading them away from narcissism and paranoia, towards the emotional pain and truth of the depressive position.

In Rustin's view the global, postmodern state of mind that floats free of reason has become so enthralled to the dominant ideology, it cannot recognise it for what it is. There is no feasible alternative, except, it seems, the traditions of the modern, like the British psychoanalytic movement with its 'conservative' insistence on limits and its 'refusal to step outside its distinctive sphere of competence and interests' (Rustin 2001: 26).

Rustin is a self-acknowledged follower of Enlightenment Freud, a psychoanalysis of reason and self-knowledge. However, Giddens also subscribes to a version of psychoanalysis, where self-knowledge as self-transformation takes centre stage. Therapy, here, is a self-help programme, advocating a disciplinary process where as individuals we gain reflexive control and autonomy, watching what we eat, listening to our body. If this sounds frighteningly like a modern-day anorexic, don't worry, it is, except that, for the anorexic, body regulation has turned into compulsive mastery and has got way out of hand.

Psychoanalysis does not work in my opinion by swapping narcissistic fantasy for Oedipal laws of reason, whether these are invoked by the father, god or Tony Blair, or even the conservative limits of the British psychoanalytic institution. These laws are merely imaginary bodies that have been made into symbolic truths or ideologies and their self-certainty, like Hamlet's false self, cannot be or move in time and so disintegrate into progressive sadomasochism.

But neither does therapy work through directing clients to a range of consumer lifestyle trajectories, or body-step programmes to personal reflexive self-identities. Therapy, at its best, acknowledges the life and immanence intrinsic to our desires but also the pain and helplessness involved when those desires are not met through our social environment. Entering into a more lived time of the body has to be connected to the cultural clearing in which we live; engaging with the possibilities of one means moving the horizons of the other. One of the biggest problems with therapy historically is that it sets itself up as a privatised dreaming which substitutes for more social and political concerns. The danger for therapists is when they delude themselves that the cure lies on the couch when in fact it is always elsewhere, beyond the privatised lines of the consulting room.

Giddens is not convincing in his valuing of a reflexive self, which fashions, re-forms and performs the body. How different is this self from the narcissistic, anorexic and hysterical body that psychoanalysis seeks to cure? Lifestyle planning cannot enable the embodiment or the articulation within lived time needed by the dissociated hysteric. The reflexive project that Giddens (1991) sets out is explicitly phenomenological in that it urges the individual to be aware and reflexive over her or his embodied presence in the world. We are advised to open up a dialogue with time and the future, to be mindful of death, although the similarities between Giddens's reflexive project and Heidegger's concept of dwelling end here. Self-therapy and lifestyle politics are ways of controlling and taking charge of time and the future. We can even master death, or our fear of it, by organisational self-narratives that track development from past to anticipated future. 'Self-actualisation implies the control of time' – only through the constant self-surveillance and reflexivity of our time and our bodies can we organise, project and plan for the future taking calculated risks (Giddens 1991: 77).

I suggest that a lot of what we do as therapists is the very opposite to what Giddens advocates as the control and monitoring of time through self-reflexivity. If I were to choose another metaphor for therapeutic healing and self-help in our society, it would be to live in time. Now we can call this hypnosis, but I don't mean hysterical hypnosis as transference onto an all-powerful other, but hypnosis as a suggestion that brings new experiences into being between self and other, hypnosis as a creative dissociation we can use to de-link from the more defensive and dominant hysterical identities we enact, and to actively produce new vitalities.

Frederic Jameson (2000) is critical of celebrations of globalisation but he is equally suspicious of a political resistance that becomes informed by the philosophy and politics of modernity. Indeed, he sarcastically remarks that modernity is often invoked to veil the loss of socialist ideals that have been destroyed by the advent of late capitalism. He writes that modernity is often used

To cover up the absence of any great collective social hope, of telos, after the discrediting of socialism. For capitalism itself has no social goals. To brandish the word 'modernity' in place of 'capitalism' allows politicians, governments and political scientists to pretend that it does, and so to paper over the terrifying absence.

(Jameson 2000: 62)

We have to be deeply critical of global capital and the world it has delivered to us. Recognising that global culture offers no really social horizons any more makes it all the more important to try and change not just ourselves but the cultural space in which we exist. Heidegger calls the cultural geography in which we each live, a clearing, as in a forest. This clearing contains the possible and the dismissed potentialities of our being in the world. In Toni Morrison's acclaimed novel *Beloved* (1987), the grandmother Baby Suggs represents the relation to the ancestor and the community for African-American people emerging out of slavery. Baby Suggs's sunlit dance in the clearing in the woods is a call to her community to love their bodies and themselves; it is a reimagination of the clearing so new possibilities can be landscaped.

As I have said at the beginning of this book, the work of therapy is not just about opening the immanence of the body to a more lived time; it is also paying attention to cultural context. In global culture our identities and desires get sucked up and commodified; they become fetish selves and wishes. Siegfried Kracauer (1995) describes how under capitalism we become part of a hysterical mass ornament, a kind of formulaic masquerade where the self we show, the feelings we emanate and the objects we consume, are all part of a distracted existence. In this clearing we are involved in a kind of abstract self-objectification where we are dissociated in a defensive way from actually living and experiencing time. So many of the desires we are taught to want in our capitalist clearing such as money, education, romance, passion, careers and family end up being something we narcissistically invest in. These desires create fixed identities dissociated from each other and from those moments of being and time, where the ego can be forgotten in favour of more transitory energies; where what we individually have can melt into or connect with a more imaginative embodied community.

A disturbed young woman in therapy won't go back to university because she realises, quite rightly, that it is a mix between her mother's narcissistic investment and the reproduction of the right identity brands or portfolios getting her ready for the market. Luckily, universities can also be cultural clearings where this sort of thing gets discussed! A gay woman I see can't access any desire and is very depressed because she identifies with and romantically loves women but feels sexual desire only for men. The straight woman who seduces men and competes with women is terrified that motherhood and passion, caring and excitement are mutually exclusive things. Sadomasochism and parenting are two currently popular ways we choose to have relationships and, in both, one party carries all the ruthlessness or power that is relegated by the other.

Such dissociation where power and strength are unequally allocated is the hysterical melodrama that characterises so many of our current social arrangements. Reality is not something in global capitalism that we can, or arguably should, emotionally come to terms with – raging melancholia rather than the depressive position seems a more apt response. However, reality as virtual and future possibilities that we can reimagine in a bodily and social context offers us more real or alive desires. Maybe what is troubling about Rustin's (2001) realist model is that it seems to eschew fantasy and the more desiring productions that Klein's part objects invite. In his valorisation of the depressive position Rustin offers us a sane model of society, but one where desire and fantasy seem strangely lacking. Rustin talks forcibly about the role emotion plays in reason, but not of the role of fantasy. Unlike Rustin, Susan Isaacs (1952), a famous Kleinian, followed Freud's later writings in insisting that reality thinking is based on unconscious phantasy. We can also bear in mind Adam Phillips' (2005) words when he reminds us that the sane person is someone who can remain kind without losing their appetites – their capacity for excitement.

Fantasy changes reality and the way we think; it also fundamentally alters our bodies and the way we desire. Deleuze and Guattari (1984) hold up Kleinian part objects as lines of desiring production that have in their view the power to explode representative Oedipus. Now, undoubtedly they idealise the possibilities of virtual desire, just as the realism of Rustin's modern psychoanalysis seems to negate fantasy (Rustin talks constantly about how our earliest 'objects' are charged with feelings, without acknowledging that he is actually talking about fantasies).

The Oedipal Complex is, on one level, the institutionalisation of heterosexuality and the family as social and real roles. It is also dissociation or doubling, frozen within the symbolic, as a defence against death and a more organic relationship with the other. In this hysterical mimesis self-knowledge is set up as the cure. However, as I have argued, the Oedipal Complex is also imaginary fantasy (it is always infused with so-called pre-Oedipal desires) and as such it contains the creative possibility of being remade again and again as virtual fantasy transforms actual reality.

Bergson enables us to understand dissociation as the creative way our psychic multiplicities are formed; it is a way we move between virtual and actual to produce lived time. Dissociation can also become a pathological defence where virtual and actual worlds become hysterically split and the person becomes disarticulated from a more embodied temporality. Deleuze and Guattari (1984) base their concept of desiring production partially on Bergson, arguing that desiring flows of production can deterritorialise Oedipus and capitalist, global society. However, we need to bear in mind that these flows, if not actualised within a lived duration, cannot remake the objects in our world; consequently our temporal flows and the objects attached to them become divided and defensively split off from each other.

Michael Hardt and Antonio Negri, the authors of *Empire* (2000), theorise our new world order in terms of a positive notion of productive networks. Utilising Deleuze and Guattari's (1984) ideas of affectual vitalities they argue for the transformative force of the multitude within global capitalism. This utopian take on the uprising of the globally disenfranchised masses misses how changing horizons, for clearings and communities, relies on a specific cultural context. We need a specific community and cultural objects that we can creatively use, in Winnicott's sense, so that dreams don't just remain passive, unselected and virtual as they do for the schizophrenic. Without imaginative grounding in the body of the community, the mass networked flows so valorised by Hardt and Negri (2000) are much more likely to operate defensively as a hysterical dissociation and splitting. We can also link this argument on immanent flows to the analytic session. In order for our bodies to endure in time they have to move or flow between virtual and actual, fantasy and reality. Thus the immanent desire we explore and hopefully set into motion within therapy must have, as I have discussed, a cultural context or clearing to be imagined within. And this is why psychoanalysis has to understand a double dwelling – our phenomeno-logical being in the world, as well as our psychic immanence.

Production or transformation of the self in relation to others (in the self and other) is an ability to live time by moving between imaginary and real worlds. For some people, living time will mean getting off the career ladder and dreaming in the garden, or perhaps learning to care for those with dependent needs. For other people, who have retreated into too much fantasy or privacy, for example through mental illness or mothering, then acting in the world is part of awakening and legitimating more aggressive competitive parts of themselves. A certain self-reflexivity or rationality is like the consumption of lifestyle politics. It makes us simultaneously too self-sufficient and too helpless. Self-sufficient in a narcissism where how we look, what we own, and our private relationships substitute for something less known and therefore less possible to master. The mystery of how we are always other is not entered into in this narcissistic relating. Bergson tells us that the world always exceeds our subjective psychology. Living time means being able to transform our virtual psychic selves in relation to an attention to life. Living time also means acknowledging the pain of what we can't have or know because life exceeds our power; it is always other to our subjective centre. Life and its limit is Freud's interpretation of the death drive, but we have to make dying a part of what we live, not something we master, but as a limit without which there would be no life or duration. The danger of Giddens's reflexive 'self' and the ideal 'pure' relationship is that within such individualist bonds the other person just becomes a kind of accomplice to our narcissistic story, however self-reflexive, of who we are. Rustin's child of Enlightenment reason is not really any better, for here a return to the tradition of psychoanalysis and the modern only reveals the hysterical transference onto an institution that cannot remake its ideas or practice in relation to the culture in which it lives. Rustin seems to idealise the British Psychoanalytic Society for its

> Intellectual transmission, its 'craft practice', its sense of its own tradition, its loyalty to its great individual pioneers (there has been no 'death of the author' here).
>
> (Rustin 2001: 27)

But of course, as other analysts have pointed out, another way of seeing this canonical establishment is to acknowledge its status as a kind of hypnotic cult; one which remains frozen in time precisely because its reason cannot be moved by different suggestions.

Giddens makes much of Winnicott's notion of basic trust: it is basic trust together with the self-reflexive project and therapy which can become a 'phenomenon of control' with which to sustain ontological security and fight personal meaninglessness (Giddens 1991: 202). But Winnicott did not see basic trust as a self-reflexive control. He saw it as the possibilities that opened up for the child or adult when they were able to explore contingency of being. Like Proust, stumbling upon his past through eating a Madeleine cake, the objects we explore and bump into in the world are linked to our basic trust in being able to open ourselves up to unknown possibilities and contingencies. This is also the trust and contingency at stake in acknowledging our shared relations with others. It is less about control than about our ability to be surprised by ourselves and others. If the surprise is too great we call it a trauma; nonetheless this contingent self, our involuntary unconscious, is integral to allow the different suggestions of who we are to come into being.

Present-day global society might well be a place where the cultural reflexive body is increasingly planned and grown. However, this is arguably a hysterical masquerade that is performed as a defensive dissociation. The intensely reflective self is often accompanied by dissociated bodily affects, the alienated symptoms of our confined suffering within the fixed representations of who we are. Maybe the answer is not narratives that regulate the body and control time, but the letting go of our tireless quest for self-knowledge and representation. We can't live time through keeping it or controlling it. Perhaps the only way to live our experiences and enter into the movement of the psychic body is to learn how to lose time and find it again unexpectedly – or, to really start giving it to other people.

I want to finish this book with a story of how my time of life was brought into question in the summer of 2005. Hamlet's dilemma, his inability to formulate an alternative to either being or doing, was brought home to me most forcibly one Thursday in July, the 21st to be exact. It was exactly two weeks after the 7th of July bombings on the London Underground and I was nervous about travelling to London. However, my therapy supervision was valuable and I was acutely aware that, had my last appointment on the 7th not been cancelled, I would have been travelling through Edgware Road station on the Circle Line, at about the same time as one of the bombs had exploded.

I decided to be cautious and took a round-about route on the tube, a route that took me out to Hammersmith from Victoria and then up to Westbourne Park. Instead of my usual and immediate daydreaming that I immerse myself in when travelling, I was hyper-aware of my fellow passengers and jumpy. I remember looking nervously at a small man, with grey untidy hair and a tiny rucksack, standing next to me in the crowded train. I laughed inwardly as I saw a bottle of water sticking out of one of its pockets, suddenly reminding me of the ludicrous fantasies I had just been entertaining.

Notting Hill is for me a place where I go regularly for therapy supervision. As I normally arrive slightly early, I go to the nearest place to have coffee, and observe all the rich and apparently idle women who seem to spend their days hanging out in dress shops or expensive cafés. I wander down the street and look in an estate agent's window, realising with a slight shock that the rental price of £1600 is for a week's not a month's rent. I am struck and disgusted by the extravagance of the women I am mingling with. Don't they have jobs? Even the mothers with young children seem to radiate a sense of complete inviolability to the world outside their haven of luxurious consumption.

I know these are all my stereotypes, I don't know these people, and yet it makes me think of my mother and her lifelong battle to help the so-called third world or developing countries. I was always fiercely resentful of her refusal to buy nice clothes or luxurious food because, as she said, 'Half the world is starving', but as I watch these women, her words come back and I wonder about the anger of the terrorist bombers. It is easier to understand the targeting of innocent people as symbols of western decadence, when I observe what I think is a quite obscene display of wealth and consumption. But, then, how are their lives so very different from mine? As everyone who knows me can bear witness, I buy clothes I don't need in Jigsaw. Where do you draw the line between your entitlement to love, money and respect and when you should forget about yourself, and start giving these things away, to other people? One thing is for certain, I decide: these women quite definitely do not travel on the tube; indeed, I wonder if they travel anywhere, outside their expensive houses and designer frock shops.

Supervision is over and I am feeling happy, pleased that I have conquered my neurotic fears and made the effort to come. I hurry down the steps to the tube and see the train pulling in. I get on, sit down, sit down next to you, and am immediately lost in my daydreams. How do I represent what happened in that carriage, not so much a face-to-face encounter as side by side? And it is not that I can't find a language or narrative for those images in my head – it's just that they don't move or lead anywhere else; they are stuck, not just in the public stories that surround this event, but in my inability to recreate them into an experience I can live and move with, in time.

Perhaps I can talk about the things that everyone knows, the detonator going off, like a cork popping, some people say, and yet to me it was an explosion, a big firework. I am writing this at the end of October and the fireworks have already started in the evenings. My dog reacts with fright and so do I. We are both paralysed with dread, my dog shivering and quaking, trying to get under the sofa; me full of rage for her, because I don't want to admit how those bangs send me into unspeakable panic.

I can talk about the bag, blown open, like the picture of the one on top of the bus, with smoke and white yellowy sick oozing out all over it. And yet, how to talk about such a near encounter with death, about you and me in the carriage? So near and yet, I was so far away. I climbed out of my body when the explosion happened and hovered somewhere above my head, looking on as the film unrolled. As I write, it is just over three months now and I am no nearer to working out what this has meant, or how I explain it, least of all what I think or feel about you.

Trauma is hard to speak about and it's even harder to write, especially, as I have discovered, because narrative and representation is so useful in giving us our identities, politics and history, but it also fixes us in our suffering and our states of injury; it becomes the hysterical story we cannot escape from. And I don't have one story to tell about you. I tell one story and maybe that seems right for a while and then it becomes undone and unrolls into something else. For example, sometimes I feel so angry with you and set you up in a story of the Grudge. This is the story of your deadly sense of injury and narcissism which allows you to slaughter yourself and others in the name of your particular super-ego or God. Your omnipotence is terrifying; killing other people is just a way to feed your self-esteem.

And yet, as this unknowable and revengeful figure, it feels there is nothing I can say that you will hear. I feel cemented to my seat alongside the crowd, bearing witness to your death drive as some kind of avant-garde, awe-inspiring act. And so I reject that narrative; I don't want you up there as some avenging angel. Who wants to live with that kind of fear or hate? Besides, I don't want to write about, or be read into, being your victim. But even as I say this, I realise that just as suddenly as my anger comes, so it has gone and I wonder about why you did this terrible thing, what feelings of dispossession and non-belonging made you want to murder people and how you managed to make them different or other enough to try.

However awful the events in Iraq, that can't be a reason, not for me anyway. Frankly, I don't want you as a representative of opposition to this terrible war. I think about my own anger against Blair and the invasion, and how powerless I feel watching television footage of Iraqi people being killed on a daily basis. The awful symmetry hits me, of those people as regrettable 'collateral damage' and the way I can be so casually eradicated to prove your ultimate cause. Newspapers carry stories and politics gives us narratives, but I can't quite make one up about you. If I'm not going to excuse you, or romanticise you, or hate you, then what narrative can I have? What does it mean not to have a story or claim to injury or to refuse to cast you as some powerful, enemy other?

The papers write about you as a teenager, playing baseball and drinking beer. Your nickname with the girls is Bambi and I think, how did you get from there to West London, last summer, and what has happened to you on the way? I can't put those images of you as this ordinary guy, not particularly hardened by a deprived existence, together with those other unforgettable pictures of you, the sick-covered rucksack and that bang ringing in my mind . . .

I watch you. The train is swaying, rocking from side to side, as I hover above my head, watching myself, watching myself watching you. You are beautiful and athletic, trained for the gym, and yet you look so bewildered, like anyone's lost son. Nevertheless, I know you are so dangerous. My dilemma is, I guess, a bit like Hamlet's 'To be or not be'. Am I alive or dead?

But as I stand on the swaying train and I watch your dazed face and I think 'To be or not to be': you are Hamlet too . . .

Suicide bomber doesn't do much for me. I mean, it conjures up an image, of a murderous fanatic, or a religious zealot, or a poor brainwashed victim, but it doesn't tell me about you: who You are. I wonder about that day, when you woke up. What were you feeling? Were you on your own or with your family? Did you feel nervous, heroic, or just – nothing but cool determination? I wonder, what was going through your mind, and how and when you said goodbye to the people you loved? Did your wife know? How did you part from your kids? I need to know really ordinary things about you. Who do you trust and what is your contingent self like, what does it bump into, when it's out and about in the world?

Do you like football and which team do you support? Do you read bedtime stories to your kids and what are you like to your wife when she is sick? Do you have fights with her, or get jealous? Which brother or sister do you most hate and which one do you most love? How is your religion a part of your life? How is praying or listening to Islamic teachings and discussing them with your friends woven into your everyday life? What kindnesses, cruelties and betrayals have you committed and what are the accidents that have happened to you, life's shapes that drew you to Westbourne Park tube station last July?

How long before the 21st did you agree and plan to do this? I have this fantasy about you on that morning; it was a beautiful day. Maybe you too, like me, had taken a stroll around the streets and shops full of decadent, western women wasting so much money, so oblivious to the needs and suffering of the women and children that you claim to have seen on video, being killed in Iraq.

Perhaps strolling through the shops in Notting Hill hardened you, gave you that extra edge to the certainty needed to carry through what you had set out to do. But I also have another fantasy that you wandered around and saw the sun glinting off the trees and that you left the posh shops and found yourself striding through Portobello Road market nearby. Market stalls are flanked by pubs, fast food outlets and the numerous global chains of fashion shops and coffee houses. Here you meet the bustle, irritation and friendliness of many different people: a diversity of race, religion and politics, buying and selling clothes or vegetables. Workers and consumers, real people like you who struggle and suffer, who feel disenfranchised and angry, envious and loving. People who are different and yet you can chat to, not just about politics or religion, but about everyday life and its objects; those obstacles you wander into, that receive or stop you, nudging, sometimes kicking you, into different experiences and directions. People who aren't pinned down into what they have or lose – unlike the frozen mannequins in and outside of the designer shop windows.

My fantasy is that you probably had to leave Portobello Road in a hurry, but that had you lingered, if the bombs had been planned to go off at teatime say, then you simply would not have done it. Perhaps you would have got chatting to someone in the market, a man whom you really felt a connection to, and when the time came you would have been too hungry, or too full of missing your family to have blown yourself up. Your perception of everyday life, going on all around you, would have met up with the imagination and memory of your ordinary life and in that moment your masculine doing and certainty would have deserted you. You would have dumped the rucksack in some park, or behind some bush, and gone home to your kids. My other fantasy is that your certain purpose deserted you walking on to that tube train – I still can't remember who sat, or stood, next to whom and that bothers me. I imagine that, as I sat in my daydream, you sat frozen with fear, so scared you couldn't feel anything – just like me, you were watching yourself on film.

I need to know ordinary things about you: not your fundamentalist beliefs, your hatred of Tony Blair, your identity as cold murderer or brainwashed idiot. I can get all that from the newspapers, but my dilemma is that I don't want to be left with that certainty, or that one truth of you as a suicide bomber. That for me is a continuation of the trauma. It leaves me with a pure and passive being as a victim, or a ruthless revenge to match yours, a sadistic certainty of doing.

As I think back to my dissociation on the train, being Hamlet and watching myself watching you, I realise that in that face to non-face moment, where I was torn between the dazed, bewildered look on your face and the wires hanging out of your T-shirt, that in that suspended moment, time stood still. The question of 'to be or not to be' for me in some ways remains unanswered, the bomb did not go off, and that has saved me from death and perhaps what might otherwise have been a certain narrative of sadomaso-chism – my wound to your murderous doing.

I know of so many people who were bereaved or severely injured on 7th July, remarkable people who don't seek blame or vengeance, but I know I'm not that strong and that if I had lost my daughter on one of those trains, I would never have forgiven you. I didn't lose my life, my legs, my lover or my child, and so I can still hold out on that question, for me – and for you. I am writing this because the alternatives of your pure doing and bombing and my pure being and death are simply unacceptable. There has to be another way out of this just pure doing or being, another way of answering Blair's mad foreign policy on Iraq or your certain hatred of the Notting Hill shop mannequins. I'm afraid I can't just label you 'a fringe fanatic' and lose myself in the god-given certainty or currency that modern politics and religion seem to thrive on.

Uncertainty isn't fashionable but it's the thread, I realise more and more, that my life, and my creative time of life, hangs on. Try as I might, I can't fix this event into some narrative that provides me or you with an identity, but surely that does not mean that I have to remain silent, that I can at least disrupt the surety of those grand scripts with the confusion of more multiple voices. This event was virtual; one that I need to bring into some kind of reality and yet to do that is to seemingly end with Hamlet's poor alternative and answer to being, namely my non-being or death. Maybe I need to keep weaving different stories precisely because of this need for, and impossibility of, reality. How, in actuality, can your casual indifference to my life, my likes and differences ever be really healed over by writing to you about my self – the things I think and feel? Sometimes I have a fantasy of going to Belmarsh prison and making you talk to me, because although I watch myself watching you, you, on the other hand, don't see me. Wresting myself out of that invisibility seems so impossible. In the evening I knit more stories and by morning they lie unravelled on the floor.

I can't get my head round what might have happened to me on that sunny day in July and the worst thing for me is imagining what dying like that would have done to my daughter. So, I wonder whether you also have the same problem, that your doing and masculine certainty is one thing, like Hamlet's tragedy, everyone dies but your false self keeps going; except there is another side – your being and suffering. So, I wonder and keep wondering, how maybe the thought you can't get your head round is: if the bomb had gone off what would it have done to my kids? Maybe, like Hamlet, you are too far gone, too mad with rage and certainty perhaps, to feel remorse for the people who were killed and injured on 7th July. But as autumn follows summer, to quote Tony Blair's 2005 conference speech, the suffering in Iraq and for the victims of 7th of July continues. Maybe remorse, not respect, is a way to undo some of that hideous certainty. Remorse brings you back over the edge from madness into something more ordinary. And so I wonder about your sadness and loneliness because I really want you to feel those things, it makes you more human, and I want to believe in the side of you that can choose life. I need to know really ordinary things about you.

Notes

1 Dora

1 I am not advocating a 'female symbolic' here as an alternative to the phallus, which can be cemented within language and culture. I am talking about the possibility of ideal, creative fantasies which can be transformed within lived time to something more embodied.

2 Time, affect and the unconscious

1 See 'The Ego and the Id' where Freud (1923) states that the unconscious has to pass into pre-consciousness before rising into the conscious mind.

3 Hysteria and hypnosis

1 According to Ernest Jones and Carl Jung, Freud had told both of them that Anna had not been cured. See H. F. Ellenberger (1970) 'Sigmund Freud and Psychoanalysis', in *The Discovery of the Unconscious: The History and Evolution of Dynamic Psychiatry*, p. 483.

References

Balint, M. (1968) *The Basic Fault: Therapeutic Aspects of Regression*, London: Tavistock.

Barber, T. (1969) *Hypnosis: A Scientific Approach*, New York: Van Nostrand.

Becker, E. (1973) *The Denial of Death*, New York: Free Press.

Benjamin, W. (1973) *Charles Baudelaire: A Lyric Poet in the Era of High Capitalism*, trans. H. Zohn, London: New Left Books.

Bergson, H. (1960 [1889]) *Time and Free Will*, trans. F. L. Pogson, New York: Harper & Row.

Bergson, H. (2002 [1908a]) 'Bergson–James Correspondence', in K. A. Pearson and J. Mullarkey (eds) *Henri Bergson: Key Writings*, New York and London: Continuum, 357–365.

Bergson, H. (2002 [1908b]) 'Memory of the Present and False Recognition', in K. A. Pearson and J. Mullarkey (eds) *Henri Bergson: Key Writings*, New York and London: Continuum, 141–157.

Bergson, H. (1911) *Creative Evolution*, London: Macmillan.

Bergson, H. (2004 [1912]) *Matter and Memory*, trans. N. M. Paul and W. S. Palmer, Mineola, NY: Dover.

Bergson, H. (1920) 'The Soul and the Body', in *Mind-Energy*, trans. H. W. Carr, London: Macmillan.

Bergson, H. (1968 [1946]) *The Creative Mind*, trans. M. L. Andison, New York: Greenwood.

Bernheim, H. (1957 [1897]) *Suggestive Therapeutics*, Alex M. Yudkin Associates.

Binswanger, L. (1963) *Being in the World*, introd. J. Needleman, London: Basic Books.

Bollas, C. (1987) *The Shadow of the Object: Psychoanalysis of the Unthought Known*, London: Free Association Books.

Bollas, C. (1993) *Being in Character*, London: Routledge.

Bollas, C. (2000) *Hysteria*, London and New York: Routledge.

Borch-Jacobsen, M. (1988) *The Freudian Subject*, trans C. Porter, Stanford, CA: Stanford University Press.

Borch-Jacobsen, M. (1992) *The Emotional Tie: Psychoanalysis, Mimesis and Affect*, trans. D. Brick and C. Porter, Stanford, CA: Stanford University Press.

Borch-Jacobsen, M. (1996) *Remembering Anna O: A Century of Mystification*, London and New York: Routledge.

Breuer, J. (1974 [1895a]) 'Fräulein Anna O', in *Studies in Hysteria*, Harmondsworth: Penguin, 73–103.

Breuer, J. (1974 [1895b]) 'Unconscious Ideas and Ideas Inadmissible to Consciousness: Splitting of the Mind', in *Studies in Hysteria*, Harmondsworth: Penguin, 300–320.

Breuer, J. (1974 [1895c]) 'Hypnoid States', in *Studies in Hysteria*, Harmondsworth: Penguin, 292–300.

Breuer, J. and Freud, S. (1974 [1895]) *Studies in Hysteria*, trans. J. and A. Strachey, Pelican Freud Library, Vol. 3, Harmondsworth: Penguin.

Bromberg, P. M. (1998) *Standing in the Spaces: Essays on Clinical Process, Trauma and Dissociation*, Hillsdale, NJ and London: Analytic Press.

Bromberg, P. M. (2001) 'Hysteria, Disassociation and Cure: Emmy Von N. Revisited', in M. Dimen and A. Harris (eds) *Storms in her Head: Freud and the Constructions of Hysteria*, New York: Other Press, 121–143.

Brown, W. (1920) 'The Revival of Emotional Memories and its Therapeutic Value I', in T. W. Mitchell (ed.) *The British Journal of Medical Psychology*, Vol. 1, Cambridge: Cambridge University Press, 16–20.

Campbell, J. (2005) *Film and Cinema Spectatorship: Melodrama and Mimesis*, Cambridge: Polity.

Caruth, C. (ed.) (1995) *Trauma: Explorations in Memory*, Baltimore, MD and London: Johns Hopkins University Press.

Caruth, C. (1996) *Unclaimed Experience: Trauma, Narrative and History*, Baltimore, MD and London: Johns Hopkins University Press.

Charcot, J-M. (1991) *Clinical Lectures on Diseases of the Nervous System*, ed. R. Harris, London: Routledge/Tavistock.

Chertok, L. and Stengers, I. (1992) *A Critique of Psychoanalytic Reason: Hypnosis as a Scientific Problem from Lavoisier to Lacan*, trans. M. N. Evans, Stanford, CA: Stanford University Press.

Claparède, E. (1911) 'La Question de la "mémoire affective"', *Archives de Psychologie* 10: 367–369.

Damasio, A. R. (1994) *Descartes' Error: Emotion, Reason and the Human Brain*, New York: Grosset/Putnam.

Damasio, A. R. (2000) *The Feeling of What Happens: Body, Emotion and the Making of Consciousness*, London: Vintage.

Damasio, A. R. (2004) *Looking for Spinoza: Joy, Sorrow and the Feeling Brain*, London: Vintage.

Deleuze, G. (1988a) 'Memory as Virtual Coexistence', in *Bergsonism*, New York: Zone.

Deleuze, G. (1988b) *Bergsonism*, New York: Zone.

Deleuze, G. and Guattari, F. (1984) *Anti-Oedipus: Capitalism and Schizophrenia*, trans. R. Hurley, M. Seem and H. R. Lane, preface by M. Foucault, London: Athlone.

Derrida, J. (1984) *Margins of Philosophy*, trans A. Bass, Chicago, IL: University of Chicago Press.

Deutsch, F. (1957) 'A Footnote to Freud's "Fragment of an Analysis of a Case of Hysteria"', *Psychoanalytic Quarterly* 26: 159–167.

Diderot, D. (1957) *The Paradox of Acting*, New York: Hill and Wang.

Ellenberger, H. F. (1970) *The Discovery of the Unconscious: The History and Evolution of Dynamic Psychiatry*, London: Allen Lane, Penguin Press.

Erickson, Milton H. (1980) *Hypnotic Investigations of Psychodynamism Processes: The Collected Papers of Milton H. Erickson on Hypnosis*, ed. E. L. Rossi, New York: Irvington.

Fairbairn, W. R. (1952) 'A Revised Psychopathology of the Psychoses and Psychoneuroses', in *Psychoanalytic Studies of the Personality*, London: Tavistock.

Fanon, F. (1986) *Black Skins, White Masks*, London: Pluto.

Ferenczi, S. (1912) 'Suggestion and Psychoanalysis', in *Further Contributions*, 55–68.

Ferenczi, S. (1919) 'On the Technique of Psychoanalysis', in *Further Contributions*, 177–189.

Ferenczi, S. (1920) 'The Further Development of Active Therapy in Psychoanalysis', in *Further Contributions*, 198–217.

Ferenczi, S. (1921) 'Psychoanalytic Observations on Tic', in *Further Contributions*, 142–174.

Ferenczi, S. (1923) 'The Dream of the Clever Baby', in *Further Contributions*, 349–350.

Ferenczi, S. (1930) 'The Principle of Relaxation and Neocatharsis', in *Final Contributions*, 108–125.

Ferenczi, S. (1931) 'Child Analysis in the Analysis of Adults', in *Final Contributions*, 126–142.

Ferenczi, S. (1933) 'Confusion of Tongues between Adults and the Child', in *Final Contributions*, 156–167.

Ferenczi, S. (1951) *Further Contributions to the Theory and Technique of Psychoanalysis*, compiled J. Rickman, trans. J. I. Suttie, London: Hogarth Press.

Ferenczi, S. (1952) 'Introjection and Transference', in *First Contributions to Psychoanalysis*, London: Hogarth Press, 35–94.

Ferenczi, S. (1955) *Final Contributions to the Problems and Methods of Psychoanalysis*, ed. M. Balint, London: Hogarth Press.

Ferenczi, S. (1988) *The Clinical Diary of Sandor Ferenczi*, ed. J. Dupont, Cambridge, MA: Harvard University Press.

Ferenczi, S. and Rank, O. (1925) *The Development of Psychoanalysis*, trans. C. Newton, New York: Mental and Nervous Disease Publishing.

Foucault, M. (1976) *The History of Sexuality, Volume 1, An Introduction*, trans. R. Hurley, Harmondsworth: Penguin.

Freud, S. (1893a) 'Some Points for a Comparative Study of Organic and Hysterical Motor Paralyses', SE 1: 160–172.

Freud, S. (1893b) 'Charcot', SE 3: 9–11. Also in *Collected Papers*, Vol. 1, trans. J. Riviere, London: Hogarth Press, 9–24.

Freud, S. (1895a) 'The Psychotherapy of Hysteria', in *Studies in Hysteria*, Harmondsworth: Penguin, 337–397.

Freud, S. (1895b) 'Frau Emmy Von N', in *Studies in Hysteria*, Harmondsworth: Penguin, 103–169.

Freud, S. (1895c) 'Katharina', in *Studies in Hysteria*, Harmondsworth: Penguin, 190–201.

Freud, S. (1900–1901) 'The Interpretation of Dreams', SE 4 and 5.

Freud, S. (1905) 'A Fragment of an Analysis of a Case of Hysteria', SE 7: 7–122.

Freud, S. (1914) 'On Narcissism: An Introduction', SE 14: 73–102.

Freud, S. (1915a) 'Repression', in *Collected Papers*, Vol. 4, trans. J. Riviere, London: Hogarth Press, 84–97.

Freud, S. (1915b) 'The Unconscious', in *Collected Papers*, Vol. 4, trans. J. Riviere, London: Hogarth Press, 98–136.

Freud, S. (1995 [1915c]) 'Observations on Transference Love', in *The Freud Reader*, ed. P. Gay, London: Vintage, 381.

Freud, S. (1917) 'Mourning and Melancholia', SE 14: 243–258.

Freud, S. (1918) 'From the History of an Infantile Neurosis', SE 17: 7–122.

Freud, S. (1920) 'Beyond the Pleasure Principle', SE 19: 6–65.

Freud, S. (1921) 'Group Psychology and the Analysis of the Ego', SE 18: 67–143.

Freud, S. (1923) 'The Ego and the Id', in *On Metapsychology: The Theory of Psychoanalysis*, Vol. 2, ed. J. Strachey, Harmondsworth: Penguin, 357–365.

Freud, S. (1924) 'Dissolution of the Oedipal Complex', SE 19: 173–179.

Freud, S. (1925a) 'A Note upon the "Mystic Writing Pad"', in *Collected Papers*, Vol. V, ed. J. Strachey, London: Hogarth Press, 175–181.

Freud, S. (1925b) 'An Autobiographical Study', SE 20: 7–71.

Freud, S. (1926) 'Inhibitions, Symptoms and Anxiety', SE 20: 114–163.

Freud, S. (1927) 'The Future of an Illusion', SE 21: 5–59.

Freud, S. (1930) 'Civilisation and its Discontents', SE 21: 59–145.

Freud, S. (1933) *New Introductory Lectures*, London: Hogarth Press.

Freud, S. (1937) 'Moses and Monotheism', SE 23: 80–92.

Freud, S. (1953–1974) *The Standard Edition of the Complete Psychological Works of Sigmund Freud*, trans. and ed. J. Strachey, London: Hogarth Press (SE).

Freud, S. (1977) 'Five Lectures on Psychoanalysis', in *Two Short Accounts of Psychoanalysis*, trans. and ed. J. Strachey, London: Penguin, 40.

Giddens, A. (1990) *The Consequences of Modernity*, Cambridge: Polity.

Giddens, A. (1991) *Modernity and Self-Identity*, Cambridge: Polity.

Gill, M. and Brenman, M. (1961) *Hypnosis and Related States: Psychoanalytic Studies in Regression*, New York: International Universities Press.

Green, V. (2003) 'Introduction', in V. Green (ed.) *Emotional Development in Psychoanalysis, Attachment Theory and Neuroscience*, Hove and New York: Brunner-Routledge.

Hacking, I. (1995) *Rewriting the Soul: Multiple Personality and the Sciences of Memory*, Princeton, NJ: Princeton University Press.

Hardt, M. and Negri, A. (2000) *Empire*, London and Cambridge, MA: Harvard University Press.

Heidegger, M. (1967) *Being and Time*, Oxford: Basil Blackwell.

Henry, M. (1993) *The Genealogy of Psychoanalysis*, trans. D. Brick, Stanford, CA: Stanford University Press.

Herman, J. L. (1992) *Trauma and Recovery: From Domestic Abuse to Political Terror*, New York: Basic Books.

Hilgard, E. (1968) *The Experience of Hypnosis*, New York: Harcourt, Brace and World.

Husserl, E. (1964) *The Phenomenology of Internal Time Consciousness*, The Hague: Nijhoff.

Irigaray, L. (1985) *This Sex Which is Not One*, trans. C. Porter and C. Burke, Ithaca, NY: Cornell University Press.

Irigaray, L. (1991a) 'The Bodily Encounter with the Mother', in *The Irigaray Reader*, ed. M. Whitford, Oxford: Basil Blackwell, 34–46.

Irigaray, L. (1991b) *The Irigaray Reader*, ed. M. Whitford, Oxford: Basil Blackwell.

Irigaray, L. (1993) 'Fleshcolours', in *Female Genealogies*, trans. G. C. Gill, New York: Columbia University Press, 153–165.

Isaacs, S. (1952) 'The Nature and Function of Phantasy', in *Developments in Psychoanalysis*, ed. J. Riviere, London: Hogarth Press, 67–121.

James, W. (1901) 'The Relation of Minds to Other Things', in *The Principles of Psychology*, Chicago, IL and London: William Benton.

Jameson, F. (2000) 'Globalization and Political Strategy', *New Left Review* 4 (July–August): 49–68.

Janet, P. (1976 [1919]) *Psychological Healing: A Historical and Clinical Study*, New York: Arnold.

Janet, P. (1965 [1920]) *The Major Symptoms of Hysteria*, 2nd edn, New York: Macmillan.

Jung, C. G. (1954 [1913]) *The Theory of Psychoanalysis, Collected Works of C. G. Jung, Vol. 4*, ed. H. Read, M. Fordham and G. Adler, ed. and trans. R. F. C. Hull, London: Routledge.

Jung, C. G. (1921) 'The Question of the Therapeutic Value of "Abreaction"', in T. W. Mitchell (ed.) *The British Journal of Medical Psychology*, Vol. 2, Cambridge: Cambridge University Press, 13–22.

Jung, C. G. (1989 [1934–1939]) 'Nietzsche's Zarathustra': Notes of the Seminar Given in 1934–1939 by C. G. Jung, 2 vols, ed. J. L. Jarrett, London: Routledge.

Kaplan-Solms, K. and Solms, M. (2000) *Clinical Studies in Neuro-Psychoanalysis*, London and New York: Karnac.

Klein, M. (1986) *The Selected Melanie Klein*, ed. J. Mitchell, Harmondsworth: Penguin.

Kracauer, S. (1995) 'The Mass Ornament', in *The Mass Ornament: Weimar Essays*, trans. T. Y. Levin, London and Cambridge, MA: Harvard University Press, 75–89.

Kubie, L. (1975) *Practical and Theoretical Aspects of Psychoanalysis*, New York: International Universities Press.

Lacan, J. (1980 [1932]) *De la psychose paranoïaque dans ses rapports avec la personnalité*, Paris: Editions du Seuil.

Lacan, J. (1977) 'The Function and Field of Speech and Language in Psycho-analysis', in *Ecrits: A Selection*, trans. A. Sheridan, New York: Norton, 30–113.

Lacan, J. (1985) 'Intervention on Transference', in C. Bernheimer and C. Kahane (eds) *In Dora's Case: Freud, Hysteria, Feminism*, London: Virago, 92–105.

Laing, R. D. (1960) *The Divided Self: A Study of Sanity and Madness*, London: Tavistock.

Laing, R. D. (1961) *The Self and Others*, London: Penguin.

Leys, R. (2000) *Trauma: A Genealogy*, Chicago, IL and London: University of Chicago Press.

McDougall, W. (1920) 'The Revival of Emotional Memories and its Therapeutic Value III', in T. W. Mitchell (ed.) *The British Journal of Medical Psychology*, Vol. 1, Cambridge: Cambridge University Press, 23–29.

Merleau Ponty, M. (1962) *Phenomenology of Perception*, London: Routledge & Kegan Paul.

Mitchell, J. (2000) *Mad Men and Medusas: Reclaiming Hysteria*, New York: Basic Books.

Morrison, T. (1987) *Beloved*, London: Chatto and Windus.

Nietzsche, F. (1966) *Beyond Good and Evil*, ed. W. Kaufmann, New York: Random House.

Nietzsche, F. (1967a) *The Genealogy of Morals*, ed. W. Kaufmann, New York: Random House.

Nietzsche, F. (1967b) *The Will to Power*, ed. W. Kaufmann, London: Vintage.

Pally, R. (2000) *The Mind–Brain Relationship*, London and New York: Karnac.

Phillips, A. (1994) *On Success, on Flirtation*, London: Faber & Faber, 42–58.

Phillips, A. (1995) *Terrors and Experts*, London: Faber & Faber.

Phillips, A. (1998) *The Beast in the Nursery*, London: Faber & Faber.

Phillips, A. (2000) 'Winnicott's Hamlet', in *Promises, Promises: Essays on Literature and Psychoanalysis*, London: Faber & Faber, 72–91.

Phillips, A. (2005) *Going Sane*, London: Penguin.

Plath, S. (2001) *The Bell Jar*, London: Faber & Faber.

Rank, O. (1993 [1924]) *The Trauma of Birth*, New York: Dover.

Rank, O. (1958) 'Two Kinds of Love', in *Beyond Psychology*, New York: Dover.

Rank, O. (1989) *The Double: A Psychoanalytical Study*, ed., trans. and with an introduction by H. Tucker, London: Karnac.

Roustang, F. (1993) 'A Philosophy for Psychoanalysis?', introduction to M. Henry, *The Genealogy of Psychoanalysis*, trans. D. Brick, Stanford, CA: Stanford University Press, ix–xxviii.

Roustang, F. (1996) *How to Make a Paranoid Laugh: Or, What is Psychoanalysis?*, trans. A. C. Vila Penn, Philadelphia, PA: University of Pennsylvania.

Rudnytsky, P. L. (2002) *Reading Psychoanalysis: Freud, Rank, Ferenczi, Groddeck*, Ithaca, NY and London: Cornell University Press.

Rustin, M. (2001) *Reason and Unreason: Psychoanalysis, Science and Politics*, London and New York: Continuum.

Samuels, A. (1993) *The Political Psyche*, London: Routledge.

Sartre, J-P. (2003 [1958]) *Being and Nothingness: An Essay on Phenomenological Ontology*, trans. H. E. Barnes, London and New York: Routledge.

Sass, L. A. (1994) *The Paradoxes of Delusion: Wittgenstein, Schreber and the Schizophrenic Mind*, Ithaca, NY and London: Cornell University Press.

Searles, H. F. (1977) *Borderline Personality Disorders*, ed. P. Hartocollis, New York: International Universities Press.

Showalter, E. (1997) *Hystories: Hysterical Epidemics and Modern Culture*, London: Picador Macmillan.

Spanos, N. (1989) *Hypnosis: The Cognitive-Behavioral Perspective*, ed. N. P. Spanos and J. F. Chaves, Buffalo, NY: Prometheus Books.

Stern, D. N. (1985) *The Interpersonal World of the Infant*, New York: Basic Books.

Stern, D. N. (2004) *The Present Moment: Psychotherapy and Everyday Life*, New York and London: W. W. Norton.

Stewart, H. (1992) *Psychic Experience and Problems of Technique*, New Library of Psychoanalysis, general editor E. Bott Spillius, London and New York: Tavistock and Routledge.

Sullivan, H. (1953) *The Interpersonal Theory of Psychiatry*, New York: Norton.

Turnball, O. and Solms, M. (2003) 'Memory, Amnesia and Intuition: A Neuropsychoanalytic Perspective', in V. Green (ed.) *Emotional Development in Psycho-analysis, Attachment Theory and Neuroscience*, Hove and New York: Brunner-Routledge, 55–85.

van der Kolk, B. and van der Hart, O. (1995) 'The Intrusive Past: The Flexibility of Memory and the Engraving of Trauma', in C. Caruth (ed.) *Trauma: Explorations in Memory*, Baltimore, MD and London: Johns Hopkins University Press.

van der Kolk, B., McFarlane, A. C. and Weisaeth, L. (eds) (1996) *Traumatic Stress: The Effects of Overwhelming Experience on Mind, Body and Society*, New York and London: Guilford.

Wilde, O. (2000 [1890]) *The Picture of Dorian Gray*, Letchworth: Broadview Literary Press.

Winnicott, D. W. (1958 [1949]) 'Mind and its Relation to the Psyche-Soma', in *Through Paediatrics to Psychoanalysis*, New York: Basic Books.

Winnicott, D. W. (1971a) 'Dreaming, Fantasying and Living', in *Playing and Reality*, London: Tavistock, 30–43.

Winnicott, D. W. (1971b) 'Creativity and its Origins', in *Playing and Reality*, London: Tavistock, 76–100.

Winnicott, D. W. (1971c) 'The Use of an Object and Relating through Identi-fications', in *Playing and Reality*, London: Tavistock, 101–111.

Winnicott, D. W. (1971d) *Playing and Reality*, London: Tavistock.

Index